Windows Live Essentials for Seniors

Studio Visual Steps

Windows Live Essentials for Seniors

Get Acquainted with Free Windows Live Essentials Applications

www.visualsteps.com

This book has been written using the Visual Steps™ method.
Cover design by Studio Willemien Haagsma bNO

© 2010 Visual Steps
Edited by Jolanda Ligthart, Rilana Groot and Mara Kok
Translated by Chris Hollingsworth, *1st Resources* and Irene Venditti, *i-write* translation services.
Editor in chief: Ria Beentjes

First printing: November 2010
ISBN 978 90 5905 356 4

Resources used: Some of the computer terms and definitions seen here in this book have been taken from descriptions found online at the Windows Help and Support website.

Do you have questions or suggestions?
E-mail: info@visualsteps.com

Would you like more information?
www.visualsteps.com

Website for this book:
www.visualsteps.com/windowslive
Here you can register your book.

Register your book
We will keep you aware of any important changes that are necessary to you as a user of the book. You can also take advantage of our periodic newsletter informing you of our product releases, company news, tips & tricks, special offers, free guides, etcetera.

Table of Contents

Appendices

Foreword

Dear readers,

Surely you must have heard about *Windows Live Hotmail* and *Windows Live Messenger*. Both these programs are part of the *Windows Live Essentials* package. This package includes useful software, part of which will be installed to your computer, while other programs are accessible on the Internet. For example, from any place in the world you can use the Internet to access your personal blog, your e-mail messages, your calendar, and your address book.

The *Windows Live Essentials* products are especially designed for keeping in touch with other people and managing files on your computer or on the Internet. Like exchanging e-mail messages, chatting, and sharing photos and all sorts of other files.

In this book you will learn how to efficiently use all elements for various purposes, step by step.

Have lots of fun with this hands-on book!

Emma Schipper

P.S.
Feel free to send us your questions and suggestions.
The e-mail address is: info@visualsteps.com

Register Your Book

You can register your book. We will keep you informed of any important changes that you need to know of, as a user of the book. You can also take advantage of our periodic Newsletter informing you of our product releases, company news, tips & tricks, special offers, etcetera.

Introduction to Visual Steps™

The Visual Steps handbooks and manuals are the best instructional materials available for learning how to work with computers and computer programs. Nowhere else will you find better support for getting to know the computer, the Internet, *Windows* or related software.

Properties of the Visual Steps books:
- **Comprehensible contents**
  Addresses the needs of the beginner or intermediate computer user for a manual written in simple, straight-forward English.
- **Clear structure**
  Precise, easy to follow instructions. The material is broken down into small enough segments to allow for easy absorption.
- **Screen shots of every step**
  Quickly compare what you see on your own computer screen with the screen shots in the book. Pointers and tips guide you when new windows are opened so you always know what to do next.
- **Get started right away**
  All you have to do is switch on your computer, place the book next to your keyboard, and begin at once.

In short, I believe these manuals will be excellent guides for you.

dr. H. van der Meij
Faculty of Applied Education, Department of Instruction Technology, University of Twente, the Netherlands

What You Will Need

In order to work through this book, you will need a number of things on your computer:

Your computer should run the English version of **Windows 7** or **Windows Vista**.
The screen shots in this book have been made on a *Windows 7* computer. For using the exercises in this book it does not make any difference whether your computer runs *Windows 7* or *Windows Vista*. Any possible differences between the *Windows* editions will be clearly indicated in the text.

Network and Internet	In order to download and use the programs you will need an active Internet connection.
Windows Live	Make sure you have the English *Windows Live Essentials* edition. In *Chapter 1 Starting with Windows Live* you can read how to install the *Windows Live* products. **Please note:** *Windows Live Essentials* is undergoing development. Most likely, various updates will be issued from time to time containing new editions of the programs that are currently available. *Windows Live* can also decide to retire *Windows Live* programs. If necessary, on the website that goes with this book, you will find information on all major changes to *Windows Live*.

Visual Steps Newsletter

All Visual Steps books follow the same methodology: clear and concise step-by-step instructions with screen shots to demonstrate each task.
A complete list of all our books can be found on our website **www.visualsteps.com**
You can also sign up to receive our **free Visual Steps Newsletter**.
In this Newsletter you will receive periodic information by e-mail regarding:
- the latest titles and previously released books;
- special offers, supplemental chapters, tips and free informative booklets.
Also, our Newsletter subscribers may download any of the documents listed on the web pages **www.visualsteps.com/info_downloads** and
www.visualsteps.com/tips
When you subscribe to our Newsletter you can be assured that we will never use your e-mail address for any purpose other than sending you the information as previously described. We will not share this address with any third-party. Each Newsletter also contains a one-click link to unsubscribe.

How to Use This Book

This book has been written using the Visual Steps™ method. You can work through this book independently at your own pace.

In this Visual Steps™ book, you will see various icons. This is what they mean:

Techniques
These icons indicate an action to be carried out:

  The mouse icon means you should do something with the mouse.

The keyboard icon means you should type something on the keyboard.

 The hand icon means you should do something else, for example insert a CD-ROM in the computer. It is also used to remind you of something you have learned before.

In addition to these icons, in some areas of this book *extra assistance* is provided to help you successfully work through each chapter.

Help
These icons indicate that extra help is available:

 The arrow icon warns you about something.

 The bandage icon will help you if something has gone wrong.

 Have you forgotten how to do something? The number next to the footsteps tells you where to look it up at the end of the book in the appendix *How Do I Do That Again?*

In separate boxes you will find tips or additional, background information.

Extra information
Information boxes are denoted by these icons:

 The book icon gives you extra background information that you can read at your convenience. This extra information is not necessary for working through the book.

The light bulb icon indicates an extra tip for using the program.

Prior Computer Experience

If you want to use this book, you will need some basic computer skills. If you do not have these skills, it is a good idea to read one of the following books first:

 **Windows 7 for SENIORS**
Studio Visual Steps
ISBN 978 90 5905 126 3

 **Windows Vista for SENIORS**
Studio Visual Steps
ISBN 978 90 5905 274 1

Website

On the website that accompanies this book, **www.visualsteps.com/windowslive**, you will find practice files and more information about the book. This website will also keep you informed of any errata, recent updates or other changes you need to be aware of, as a user of the book.
Please, also take a look at our website **www.visualsteps.com** from time to time to read about new books and other handy information such as informative tips and booklets.

Test Your Knowledge

Have you finished reading this book? Then test your knowledge with the *Windows Live* test. Visit the website: **www.ccforseniors.com**

This multiple-choice test will tell you how good your knowledge is of the *Windows Live* applications covered in this book. If you pass the test, you will receive your free *Computer Certificate* by e-mail.

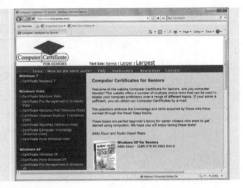

For Teachers

This book is designed as a self-study guide. It is also well suited for use in a group or a classroom setting. For this purpose, we offer a free teacher's manual containing information about how to prepare for the course (including didactic teaching methods) and testing materials. You can download this teacher's manual (PDF file) from the website which accompanies this book: **www.visualsteps.com/windowslive**

The Screen Shots

The screen shots in this book were made on a computer running *Windows 7 Ultimate*. The screen shots used in this book indicate which button, folder, file or hyperlink you need to click on your computer screen. In the instruction text (in **bold** letters) you will see a small image of the item you need to click. The black line will point you to the right place on your screen.
The small screen shots that are printed in this book are not meant to be completely legible all the time. This is not necessary, as you will see these images on your own computer screen in real size and fully legible.

Here you see an example of an instruction text and a screen shot. The black line indicates where to find this item on your own computer screen:

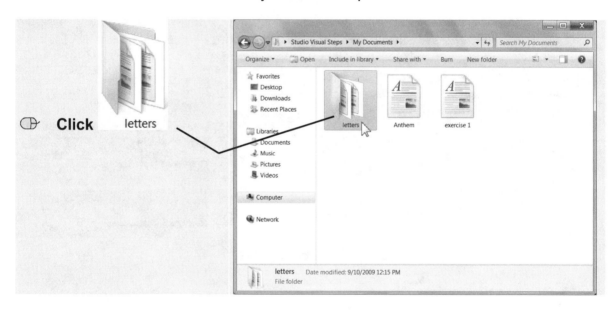

Sometimes the screen shot shows only a portion of a window. Here is an example:

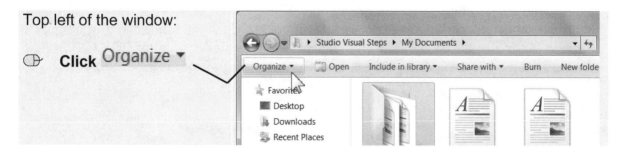

It really will **not be necessary** for you to read all the information in the screen shots in this book. Always use the screen shots in combination with the image you see on your own computer screen.

1. Starting With Windows Live Essentials

You probably already know a little about *Windows Live Hotmail* and you may also be familiar with the *Windows Live Messenger* program. This program used to be called *MSN Messenger*. Many people these days say they are going '*to msn*' when what they mean is that they are going to chat with *Windows Live Messenger*.

Apart from these well-known programs, *Windows Live Essentials* contains many other free online services and software. These products focus mainly on communicating with other people and managing the files on your computer as well as the Internet. You can easily send e-mails, chat, or share your photos or other files with your family and friends. *Windows Live Essentials* offers additional products, such as *Family Safety,* which allows you to limit your children's use of the Internet. The *Windows Live Calendar* lets you maintain your own diary, or a joint agenda.

With the vast array of products available and the numerous ways in which these products work together, it is difficult to sum up all of the features in *Windows Live Essentials* in one quick overview. Some of these products can also be started up in several different ways, which can make you feel even more confused. Don't be dismayed! This book will guide you step by step and help you to make sense of the many options and features available in *Windows Live Essentials*.

In the beginning of this chapter, we will introduce you to a variety of *Windows Live Essentials* products that are currently available. Next, you will learn how to create a *Windows Live ID*. To work with *Windows Live Essentials*, you will need to have a *Windows Live ID*. After that, you will learn how to download several products from the *Windows Live Essentials Home Page*. Finally, you will learn how to edit your profile, add contacts, and change the privacy settings.

In this chapter you will learn:

- which products are included in *Windows Live Essentials*;
- how to create a *Windows Live ID*;
- how to use the *Windows Live Essentials Home Page*;
- how to download various *Windows Live Essentials* products;
- how to edit your profile;
- how to add contacts;
- how to change the privacy options.

Please note:

The latest version of *Windows Live Essentials* is still undergoing development. Most likely, various updates will be issued from time to time containing new editions of the programs that are currently available. It is also possible that some products may no longer be available. On the news page by the website that goes with this book, you will find information on all major changes to *Windows Live Essentials*.

1.1 An Overview of Windows Live Essentials

Windows Live Essentials consists of a large number of different products. Some of these products require that you *download* and *install* them to your computer first, while others can be used directly online.

Below you will see an overview and a brief description of the *Windows Live Essentials* products.

For your computer
Products you need to download and install.

Mail

With *Mail* you can manage your e-mail messages from one single, central location.

Messenger

With *Messenger* you can communicate by means of written text, sound and vision.

Photo Gallery

With *Photo Gallery* you can organize, edit, and share photos.

Movie Maker

With *Movie Maker* you can create videos, edit them and publish them online.

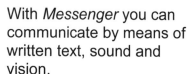
Writer

With *Writer* you can create and publish blog messages.

Family Safety

With *Family Safety* you will be able to monitor the Internet behavior of your children. Also for online use.

For online use
Products which do not require download and installation.

Hotmail

With *Hotmail* you can access your e-mail messages any time, wherever you are.

Photos

With *Photos* you can save photos and share them with others.

Calendar

With *Calendar* you can maintain a diary and share it with others.

Groups

With *Groups* you can communicate with a specific group and share a calendar with group members.

SkyDrive

With *SkyDrive* you get 25 GB of online storage space, either for yourself or to share.

Bing Toolbar

With the *Bing Toolbar* you can search the Internet and open various websites.

Mobile

Finally, *Mobile* allows you to use *Windows Live* on your cell phone.

The products work together in different ways. For instance, *Messenger* will let you check your *Hotmail* e-mail messages, and in *Photos* you can add pictures to *Groups*. In the following chapters you will find more information about this subject.

1.2 Create a Windows Live ID

If you want to work with *Windows Live Essentials* you must first have your own *Windows Live ID*. A *Windows Live ID* consists of an e-mail address and a password. You will also be asked for a small amount of personal information when you sign up. This will help you to reset your password or edit your information later on, if you ever need to.

☞ **Open *Internet Explorer*** 🐾¹

☞ **Open the home.live.com website** 🐾³

➥ **Please note:**

If you already have an e-mail address that ends in *hotmail.com* or *live.com* you do not need to create a *Windows Live ID*.

⌨ **By** Windows Live ID: **type your e-mail address and password**

⊕ **Click** Sign in

You can continue reading the next section.

⊕ **Click** Sign up

If your window looks a little different, just go ahead and click Sign up .
The *Windows Live Essentials* sign up page may change over time.

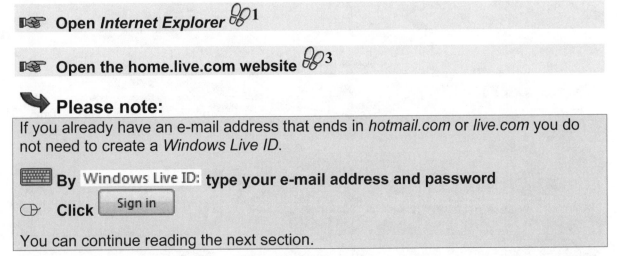

By Windows Live ID: **type the e-mail address** ————

Click

Check availability

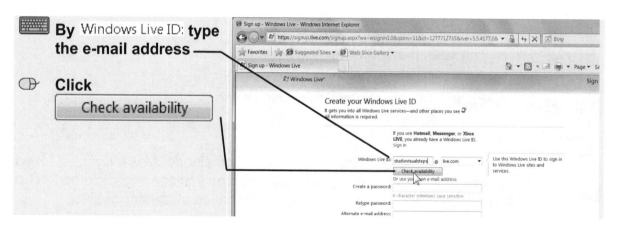

HELP! Not available

If the e-mail address you have chosen is not available, you will see this message:
⊗ yourname@live.com isn't available.

Type a different e-mail address ————

Click X

Or:

Click one of the suggested IDs

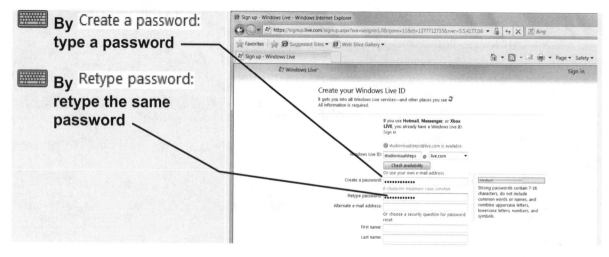

By Create a password: **type a password** ————

By Retype password: **retype the same password**

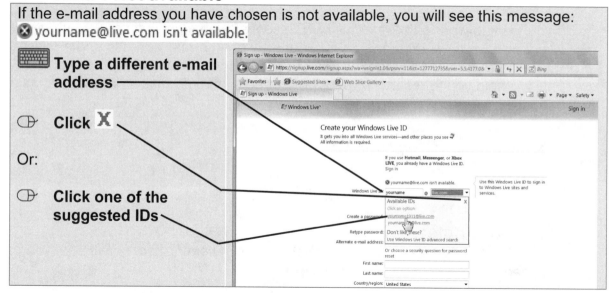

In case you forget your password, you can enter an alternate e-mail address. You can also select a security question which will help you reset your password later on.

Click
Or choose a security que
reset

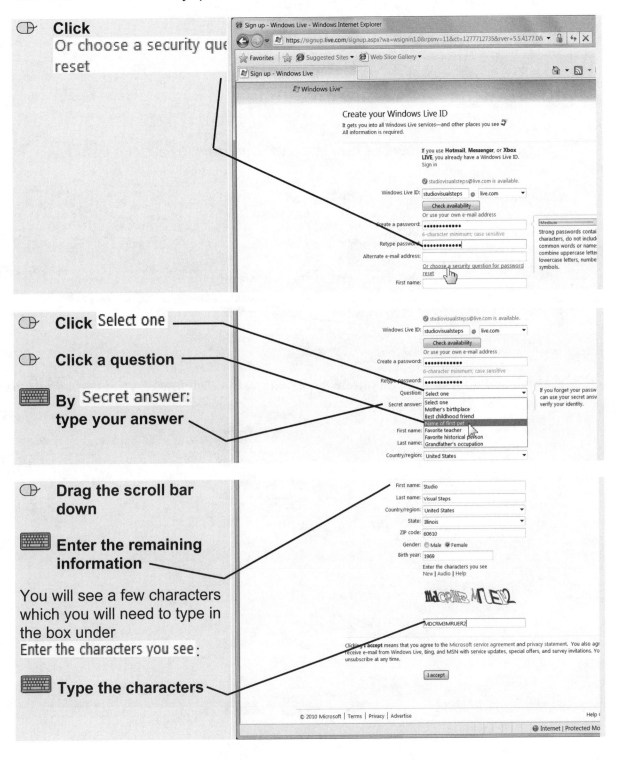

Click Select one

Click a question

By Secret answer:
type your answer

Drag the scroll bar down

Enter the remaining information

You will see a few characters which you will need to type in the box under
Enter the characters you see :

Type the characters

HELP! I cannot read the characters properly

If you have difficulty reading the characters, you can listen to them as an audio file:

☞ **Click** Audio

☞ **Click** 🔊 ▶

You can also easily request a new string of characters, by clicking 🔄.

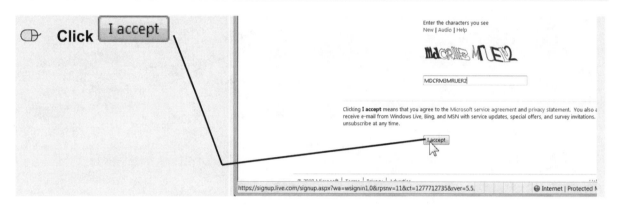

☞ **Click** I accept

You will see your Inbox straight away. To show the *Windows Live Essentials Home Page*:

☞ **Click** Home

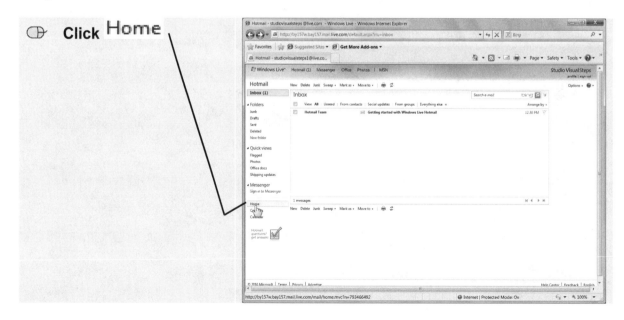

1.3 Windows Live Essentials Home Page

The *Home Page* is the central web page for working with *Windows Live Essentials*. You can use the menu to navigate through the various *Windows Live Essentials* components.

Here you see the *Home Page* menu:

Please note: the web page may look different now. The internet changes all the time.

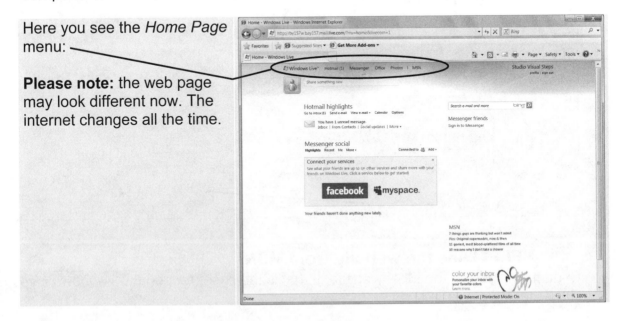

To practice signing in, you have to sign out first:

In the top right-hand corner of the window you can see that you are still signed in:

☞ Click `sign out`

Now you can sign in again:

☞ **Click your e-mail address**

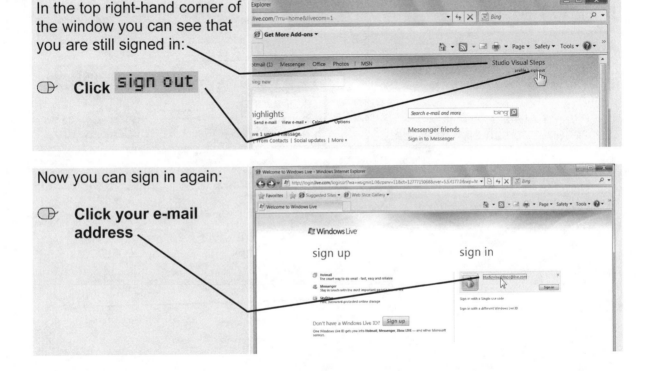

HELP! I see a different window

In case you see a different window, here is how you sign in:

 Type your new e-mail address and your password ———

If you wish, you can allow the computer to remember this information for you:

Click [**Sign in**]

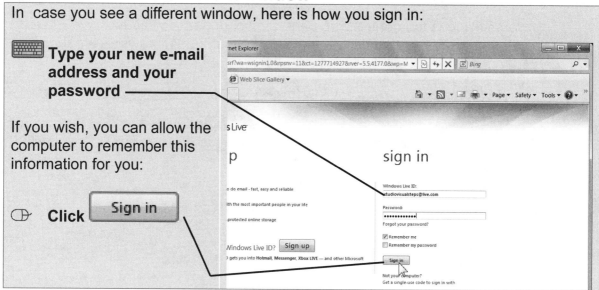

 HELP! I see the website from MSN

You may now see the MSN website. If that is the case, reopen the *Windows Live* website. Here is how to do that:

Click the address bar

Type: home.live.com

Press [Enter ⏎]

Now you will see the website where you can sign in again.

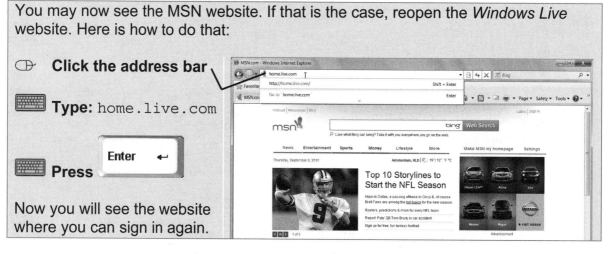

Type your password

Click [**Sign in**]

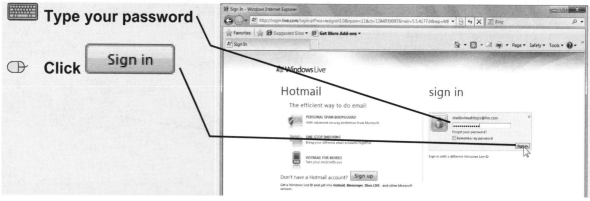

Now you will once again see the *Windows Live Essentials Home Page*:

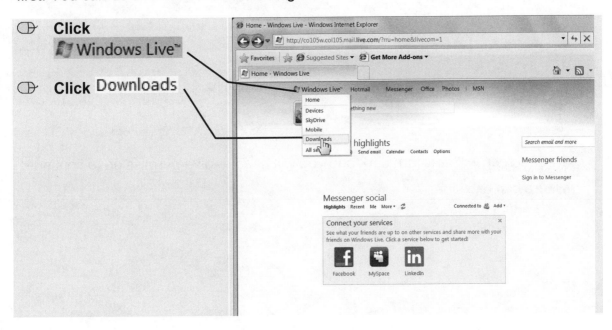

1.4 Download Windows Live Essentials Products

You will need to download and install some of the *Windows Live Essentials* products first. You can do this from the *Home Page*:

☞ **Click** 🚩 **Windows Live™**

☞ **Click** Downloads

Now you will see the web
page where you can
download the *Windows Live
Essentials* programs:

⊕ **Click** `Download now`

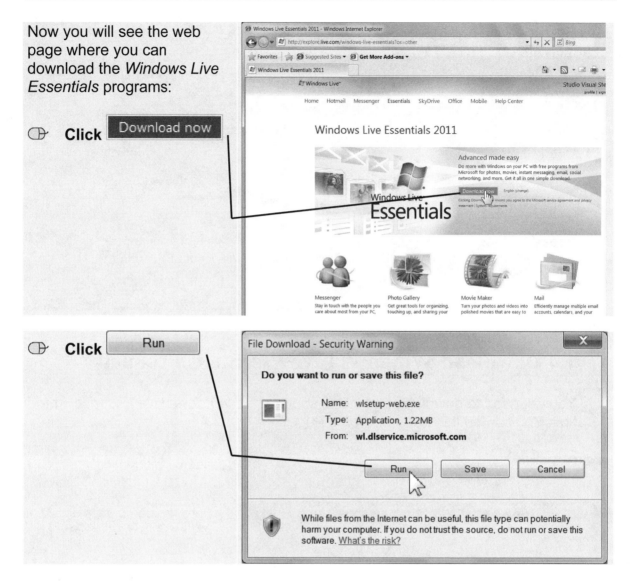

⊕ **Click** `Run`

Your screen will now turn dark and you will need to give permission to continue:

⊕ **Click** `Yes`

You will see the installation window of *Windows Live Essentials*.

☞ **Click**
→ Choose the progr

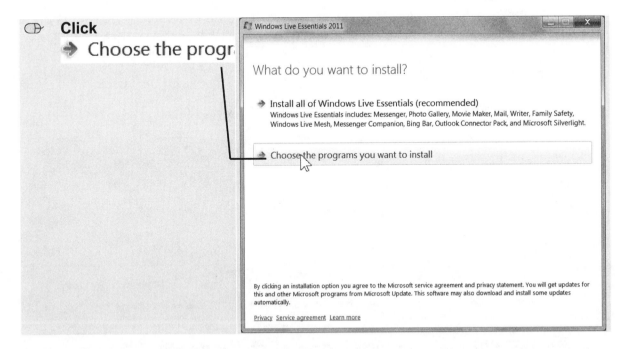

Here you can select the programs you want to install.

☞ **If you wish, uncheck the box ☑ next to**
Messenger Companion
and Windows Live Mesh

☞ **Click** Install

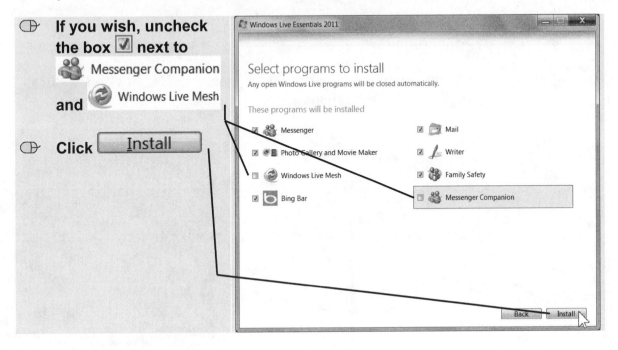

Please note:

Windows Live Essentials is still in the developing stage. Most likely, various updates will be issued from time to time containing new editions of the programs that are currently available. Check the website that goes with this book for major changes in the *Windows Live Essentials* programs.

When the installation is done, you need to restart your pc:

⬤ **Click** Restart Now

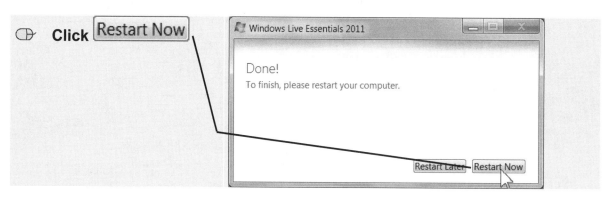

 ### HELP! I see another window or no window

If you see another window or no window:

☞ **Close all windows** 𝒪𝒪⁶

☞ **Restart your computer**

After *Internet Explorer* starts up, you can take a look at the list of *Windows Live Essentials* products that have been installed:

⬤ **Click**

⬤ **Click ▶ All Programs**

⬤ **Drag the scrollbar down**

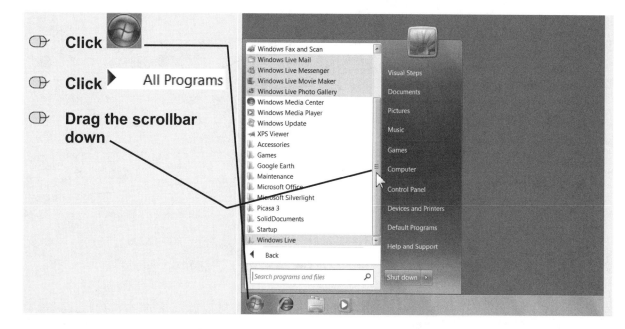

You can find the programs *Windows Live Family Safety* and *Windows Live Writer* in the folder Windows Live .

You will not see the *Bing Toolbar* in the list. This program is an *Internet Explorer* add-on and that is why it is not included in the program list.

1.5 Edit Your Profile

If you want to edit your profile:

☞ **If necessary, open** *Internet Explorer* 👣¹

Note that *Internet Explorer* now contains an additional menu bar: ‒

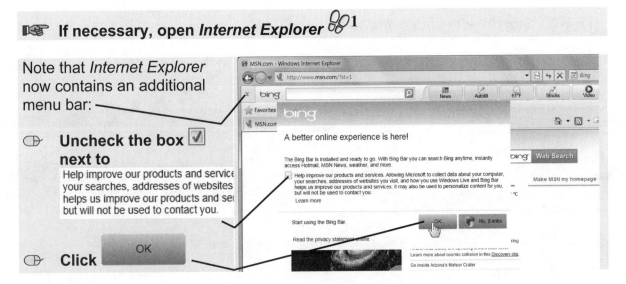

☞ **Uncheck the box ☑ next to**
Help improve our products and service your searches, addresses of websites helps us improve our products and sel but will not be used to contact you.

☞ **Click** OK

🔖 **Please note:**
You will learn more about the *Bing Toolbar* in *Chapter 13 The Bing Toolbar*.

❌ **HELP! I do not see the Bing Toolbar**
This is how to add the *Bing Toolbar*:

☞ **Right-click the menu bar**

☞ **Click** Bing Bar

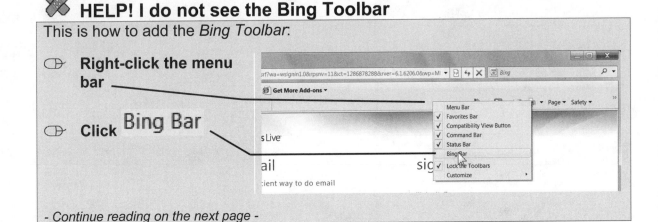

- Continue reading on the next page -

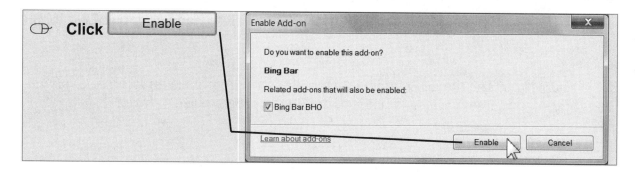

☞ Open the home.live.com website 👣3

☞ Sign in with your *Windows Live ID* 👣4

You can change your profile information by going to the *Windows Live Essentials Home Page*:

In this window you can enter information about yourself, such as your favorite music, your educational background or your work:

You can also add a photo:

👉 **Click** Edit

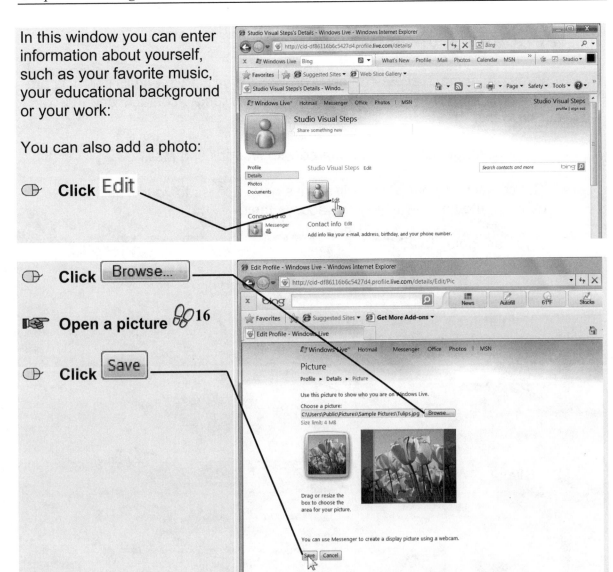

👉 **Click** Browse...

👉 **Open a picture** 🦶16

👉 **Click** Save

Now the photo has been added to your profile:

1.6 Adding Contacts

Now you are going to add a contact. The *Windows Live Essentials* contacts are divided according to two network groups: the *Messenger* contacts and the contacts in your *profile*:

- The *Messenger* contacts are shared with *Hotmail* and *Mail*.

- The contacts in your profile will always have access to your profile and your updates, the same way you can access theirs.

First, you are going to add a contact to your profile:

☞ **Place the mouse pointer on** Messenger

☞ **Click** Contacts

☞ **Click** New

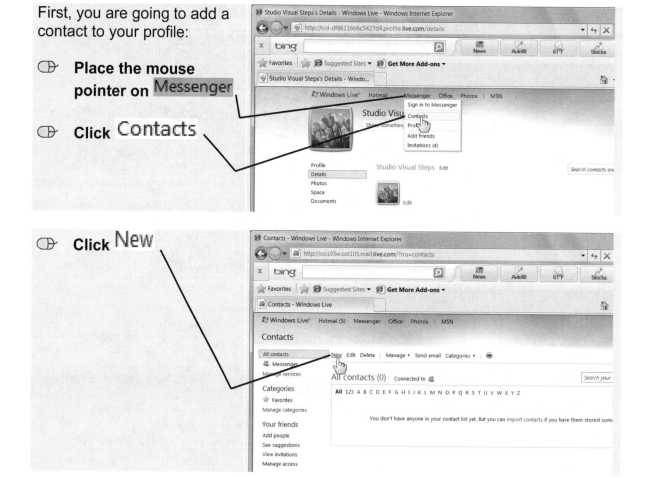

In the next window you can enter the information regarding this contact. You will need to enter at least one e-mail address or *Windows Live ID*.

Type a first name and a last name ——

Type an e-mail address or a *Windows Live ID* ——

If you want, type the information in the other fields

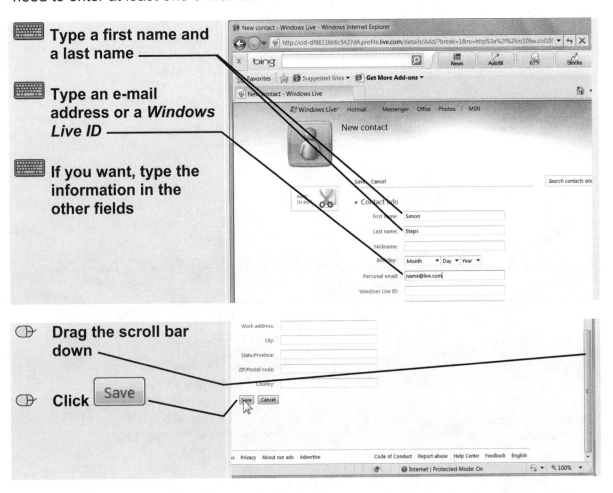

Drag the scroll bar down ——

Click Save

This contact has now been added to your contact list. Now you can add the contact to your *Messenger* contact list:

Click Messenger

Click Add friends

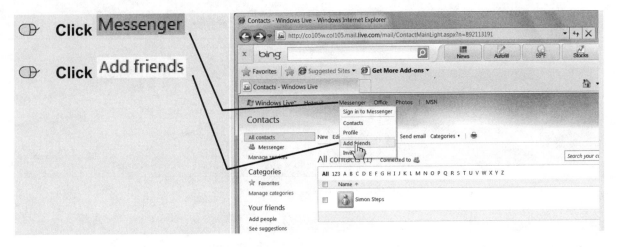

Before you can accept the invitation, you will see a message about privacy settings. By default, the *Limited* setting is selected.

 Click Save

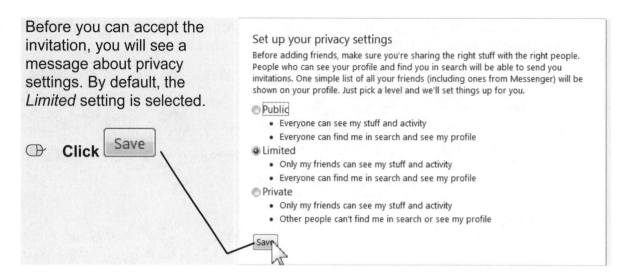

Set up your privacy settings

Before adding friends, make sure you're sharing the right stuff with the right people. People who can see your profile and find you in search will be able to send you invitations. One simple list of all your friends (including ones from Messenger) will be shown on your profile. Just pick a level and we'll set things up for you.

○ Public
  • Everyone can see my stuff and activity
  • Everyone can find me in search and see my profile

◉ Limited
  • Only my friends can see my stuff and activity
  • Everyone can find me in search and see my profile

○ Private
  • Only my friends can see my stuff and activity
  • Other people can't find me in search or see my profile

Save

➥ Please note:

In the *Set up your privacy settings* window you can select one of three different options, that is to say: *Public*, *Limited*, and *Private*.

Public   Everybody will be able to see the changes in your profile and will be able to find and view your profile.

Limited   Only your friends will be able to see the changes in your profile and everybody will be able to find and view your profile.

Private   Only your friends will be able to see the changes in your profile, others will not be able to find and view your profile.

🩹 HELP! I see another window

When you see this window:

 Click add people to Messenger

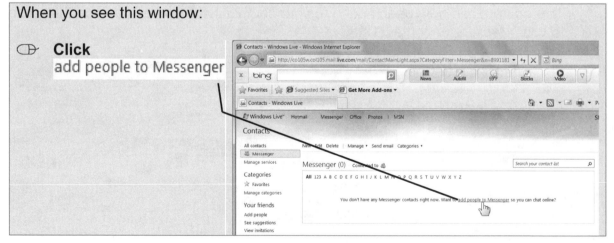

Click
Select from your contact list

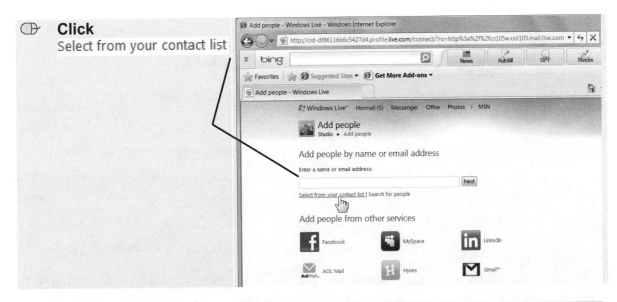

If necessary, check the box ☑ next to the contact

Click Invite

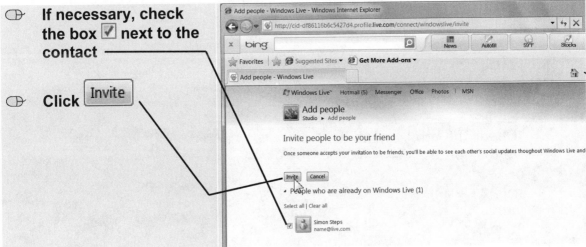

The invitation has been sent:

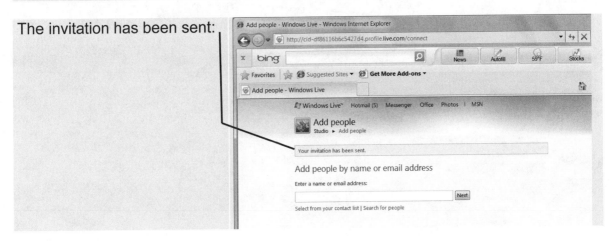

The contact will receive an invitation to be part of your social network, by e-mail or in *Messenger*. He or she can accept or ignore this invitation. You can also receive an invitation yourself, to be added to someone else's network.

Your contact can decide for yourself if you want to accept the invitation or not:

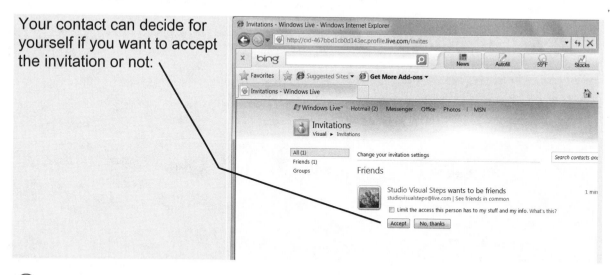

💡 Tip

Delete a contact
This is how you delete a contact:

☞ **Check the box ☑ next to the contact**

☞ **Click Delete**

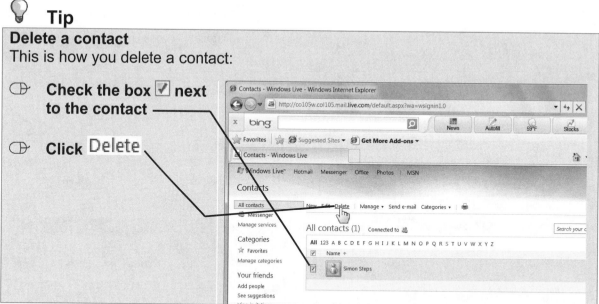

💡 Tip

Contacts from different networks
You can also add contacts from different networks:

👆 **Click** Add people

These are the networks you can choose from:

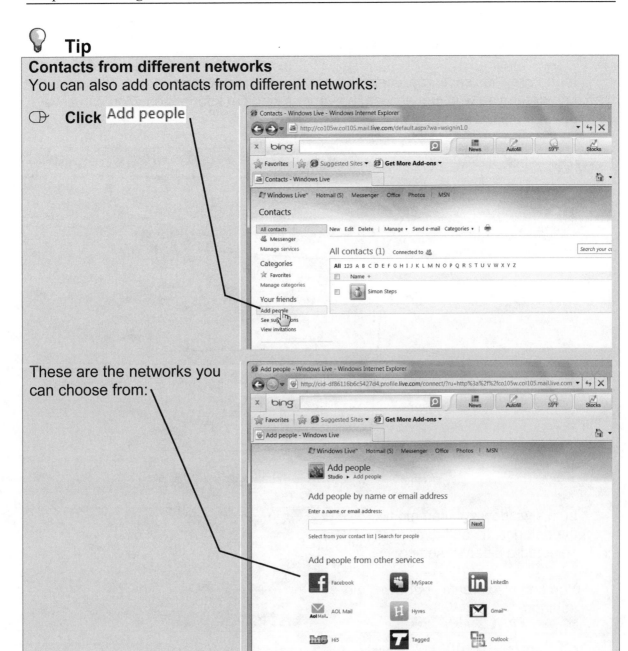

1.7 Edit Privacy settings

In the previous section you learned how to set the privacy settings. In this way, you can determine who can access the various kinds of information. You can always change these settings later on:

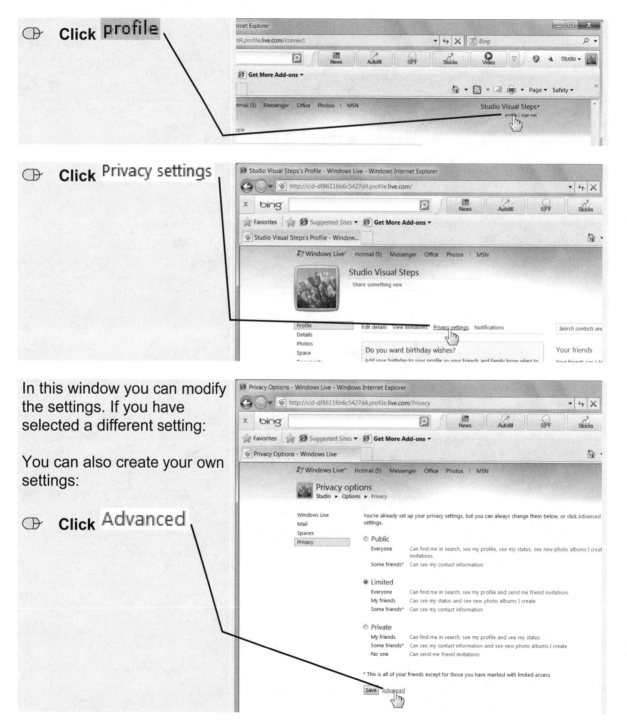

☞ **Click** profile

☞ **Click** Privacy settings

In this window you can modify the settings. If you have selected a different setting:

You can also create your own settings:

☞ **Click** Advanced

In this window you can select your own customized privacy settings:

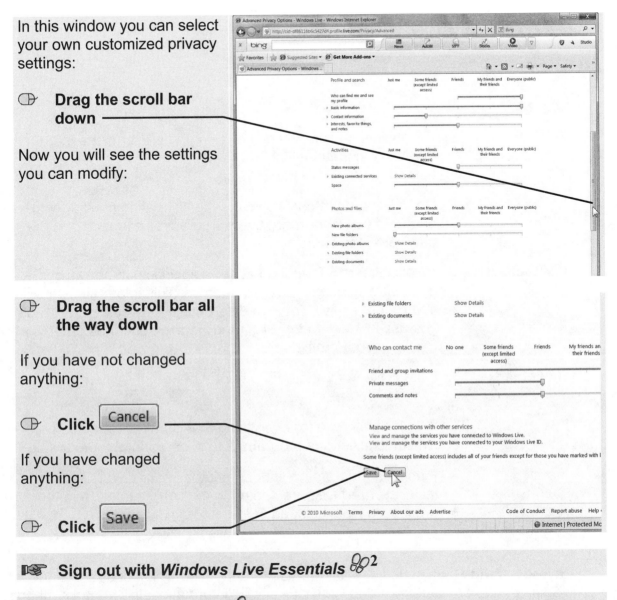

☞ **Drag the scroll bar down** ————

Now you will see the settings you can modify:

☞ **Drag the scroll bar all the way down**

If you have not changed anything:

☞ **Click** Cancel ————

If you have changed anything:

☞ **Click** Save ————

🖝 **Sign out with *Windows Live Essentials* 𝄞2**

🖝 **Close *Internet Explorer* 𝄞6**

In this chapter you have read about the products that make up *Windows Live Essentials*, and their use for various tasks. You have created a *Windows Live ID* and you have become acquainted with the *Windows Live Essentials Home Page*. You have also downloaded a number of products from the *Home Page*.
Furthermore, you have learned how to edit your profile, how to add contacts and how to change privacy settings. In short, you have started working with *Windows Live Essentials*.

In the next chapter, you will learn more about the various products or programs and what you can do with them and you will be able to explore some of their features.

1.8 Background Information

Dictionary	
Blog	A website that is regularly updated and presents the information in reverse chronological order (the most recent message will appear at the top of the list).
Chat	Conducting an Internet conversation by typing messages back and forth by two or more users who are all connected to the Internet at the same time.
Contact	A collection of information about a specific person, which contains at least their e-mail address. This information is stored in the Contact list. You can differentiate between the contacts you use in *Messenger*, *Mail,* and *Hotmail*, and the contacts who can view your profile.
Download	Copy a file from another computer or from the Internet to your own computer.
File	A collective name for everything that is stored on a computer. A file can consist of a program, a text, or a photo, for example.
Install	Placing a program on your computer's hard drive. During the installation, all files are copied to the correct folder and the program will be included in the program list.
Online	Connected to the Internet.
Privacy setting	A setting that allows you to determine which people are authorized to view your profile information, the remarks others make on your profile, your files, your diary, or a photo album. You can decide for yourself who is allowed to view your contact information in *Windows Live Essentials*.
Profile	The details about yourself, your interests, activities and contact information. You can decide for yourself how to share these details with others.
Windows Live ID	An account that gives you access to all the *Windows Live Essentials* products. If you already have an e-mail address that ends in *hotmail.com* or *live.com*, you will automatically have a *Windows Live ID*.

Source: Windows Live Essentials Help, Windows Help and Support, Wikipedia

1.9 Tips

 Tip

Categorize your contacts
By categorizing your contacts you can keep your contact list well organized.
Moreover, you can also set authorizations for an entire category.

☞ **Click**
Manage categories

To add a new category:

☞ **Click New**

⌨ **Type the category name**

⌨ **Type the names of the contacts**

Enter ⏎

By pressing the
key you can fill in the full
name.

☞ **Click Save**

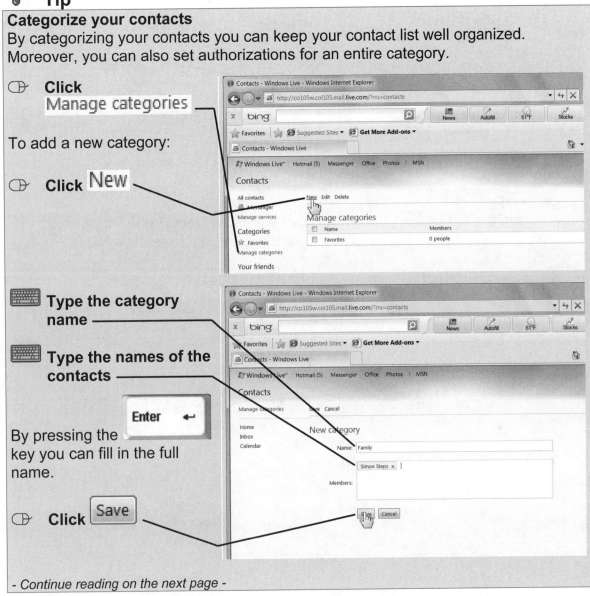

- Continue reading on the next page -

You can also select a category from the contact list:

⊕ **Check the box 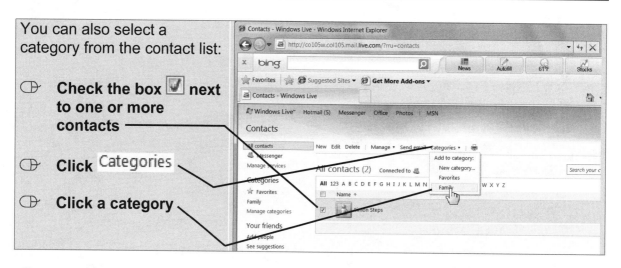 next to one or more contacts** ————

⊕ **Click Categories**

⊕ **Click a category**

💡 **Tip**

Change the lay out of your Windows Live Essentials Home Page
You can personalize the lay out of your *Windows Live Essentials Home Page*:

⊕ **Click Options**

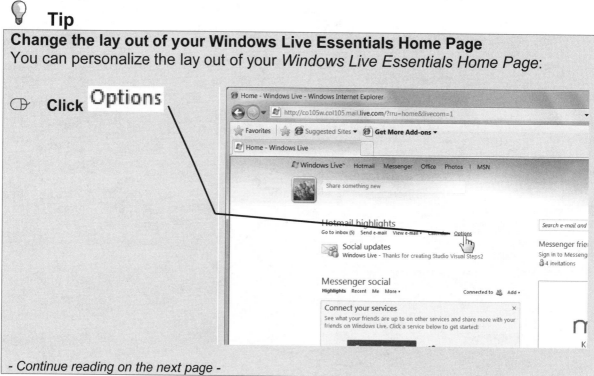

- Continue reading on the next page -

At the left-hand side of the window:

☞ **Click** Hotmail

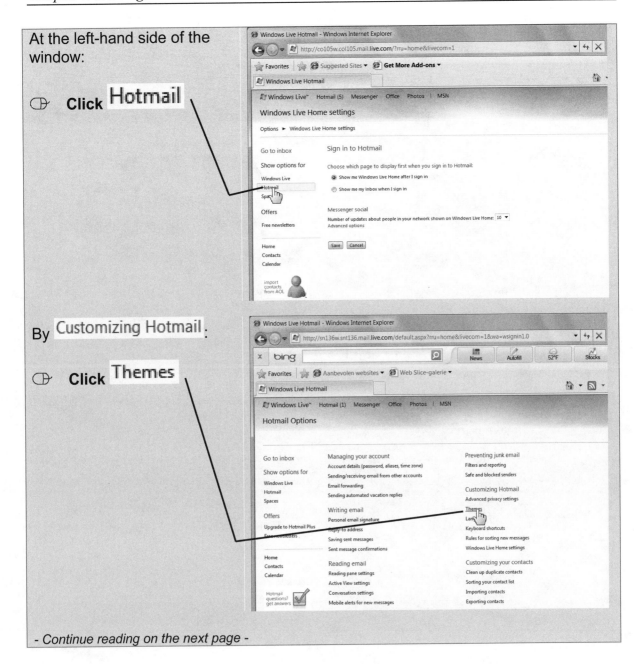

By Customizing Hotmail.

☞ **Click** Themes

- Continue reading on the next page -

Click a theme

Click Save

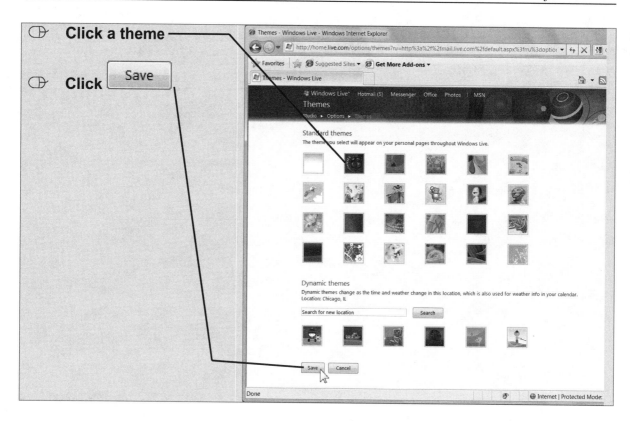

2. Windows Live Hotmail

Windows Live Hotmail is the world's most frequently used e-mail service. Its popularity is probably due to the fact that *Hotmail* is a free Internet application. All you need is access to the Internet and a browser, such as *Internet Explorer*, to access your mail wherever you are. You don't even have to use the webmail service to read your *Hotmail* messages. Nowadays, *Hotmail* offers a feature that allows you to retrieve your *Hotmail* messages in the e-mail program of your choice. See the tip in *section 2.7 Tips* to learn more about the settings you need to make in order to do this.

Many new options and extra features have been added to *Hotmail* in recent years. For instance, *Hotmail* messages that include attachments are checked for viruses when they are retrieved. Also, you can use a separate window to directly read your messages instead of in the main window. This means you do not need to reload the page each time you read a message. And the use of themes helps you personalize your *Hotmail* page.

There are several ways in which *Hotmail* communicates with other *Windows Live Essentials* products. For example, the contact list is shared with *Mail* and *Messenger*, and in *Messenger* you just need to click once to check your e-mail messages. The *Calendar* program lets you send reminders for appointments, the *Photos* product allows you to send an e-mail link to your photo album, and in *Groups* you can send e-mails to other group members. You can also open *Hotmail* from the *Bing Toolbar* and the *Mobile* application lets you access your e-mail messages from your cell phone.

In this chapter we will explain how to send and read an e-mail message with an attachment in *Hotmail*. We will show you how to handle unwanted e-mail messages and how to best organize your messages in folders. Finally, we will discuss a number of the extra options available, such as inserting a personal e-mail signature and activating the automatic response service.

In this chapter you will learn how to:

- send an e-mail message with an attachment;
- read an e-mail message with an attachment;
- handle unwanted e-mail messages;
- manage folders;
- use various options.

Please note:

To work through this chapter properly you will need to have a *Windows Live ID*. If you do not yet have a *Windows Live ID,* in *section 1.2 Create a Windows Live ID* you can read how to obtain one.

2.1 Sending an E-mail Message With an Attachment

You will learn how to send an e-mail message that contains an attachment by sending one addressed to yourself. In the next section you will then open and read this message.

If you want to use a free *Hotmail* account to send e-mail messages, you will be somewhat limited in the number of options that you can use. For instance, you can only send messages that do not exceed 10 MB (per message). Also, there are a maximum number of recipients to whom you can send messages. This number will increase further as long as you do not send unwanted messages (spam). Furthermore, *Hotmail* does not support all file formats. You can solve this problem by compressing the file, changing the file type, or uploading the file to *SkyDrive*. But *Hotmail* does support the most frequently used file formats.

☞ **Open** *Internet Explorer* ¹

☞ **Open the home.live.com website** ℬℬ³

☞ **Sign in with your** *Windows Live ID* ℬℬ⁴

⊕ **Place the mouse**
pointer on Hotmail

⊕ **Click** Inbox

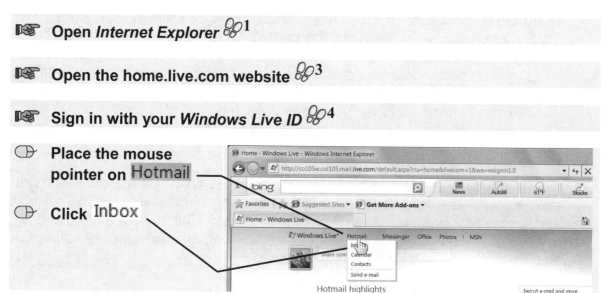

 Please note:

In this book we will open all *Windows Live Essentials* products from the *Home Page*. If you want, you can also access *Hotmail* directly by typing http://mail.live.com in the address bar of your Internet browser.

👆 **Click** New

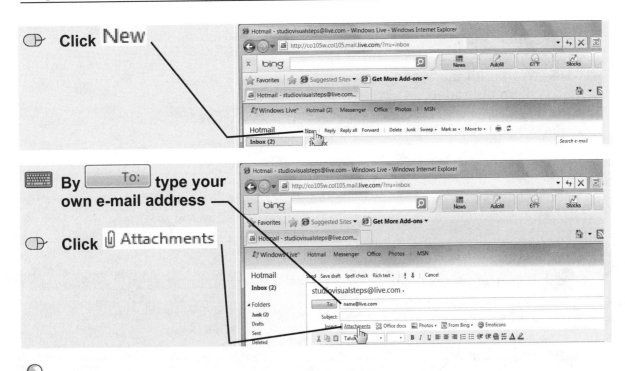

⌨️ **By** To: **type your own e-mail address**

👆 **Click** 📎 Attachments

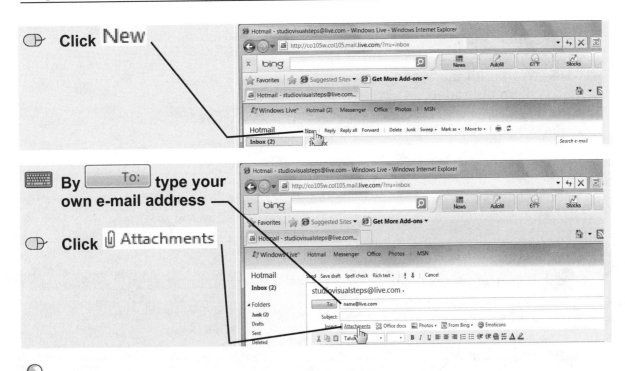

💡 **Tip**

Select a contact from the contact list
If you want to select one (or more) contact(s) from your contact list:

👆 **Click** To:

💡 **Tip**

CC and BCC
If you want, you can enter an address by CC: and BCC: as well:

At the right-hand side of the window:

👆 **Click** Show Cc & Bcc

⌨️ **By** CC: **or** BCC: **, type an e-mail address**

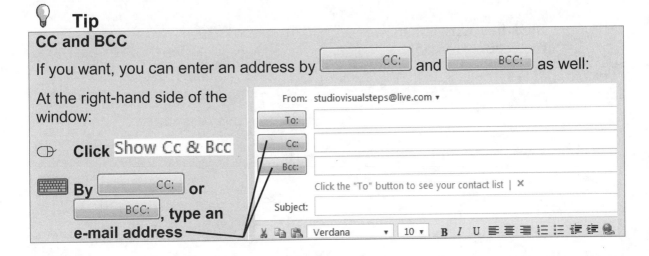

☞ **Open a file** 𝒽𝒽⁵

☞ **Wait until the file has been uploaded**

Here you can see if *Hotmail* is still busy uploading the file:

⌨ **If you want, you can type a subject and a message** ——

⊕ **Click Send**

You might see a safety warning:

⊕ **Click the hyperlink in the yellow area on the page** ——

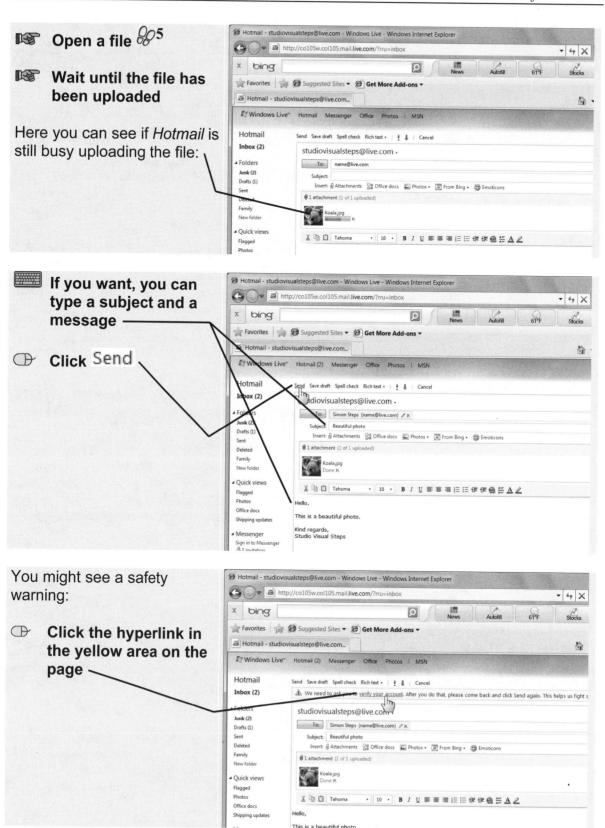

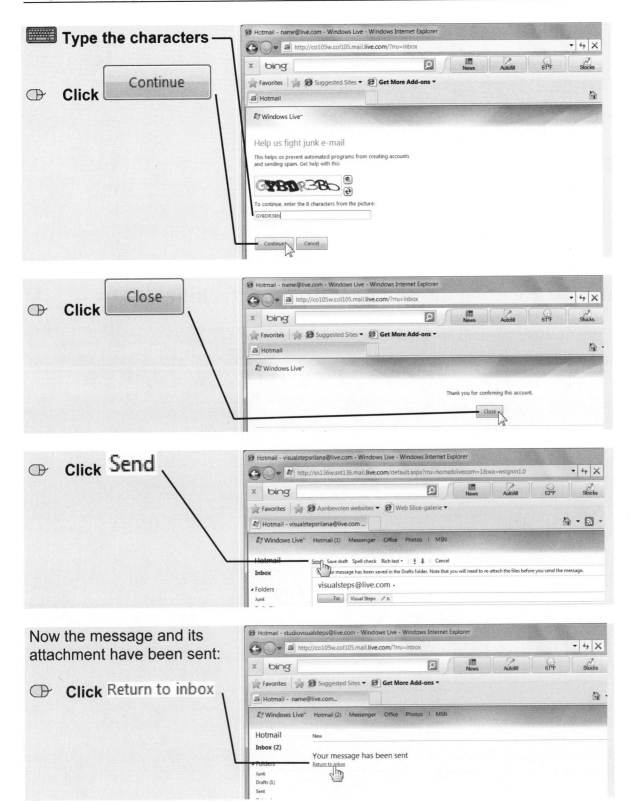

⌨ **Type the characters**

🖱 **Click** `Continue`

🖱 **Click** `Close`

🖱 **Click** **Send**

Now the message and its attachment have been sent:

🖱 **Click** Return to inbox

The message will be
displayed in your *Inbox*:

If you don't see the message
right away, just wait a few
more moments.

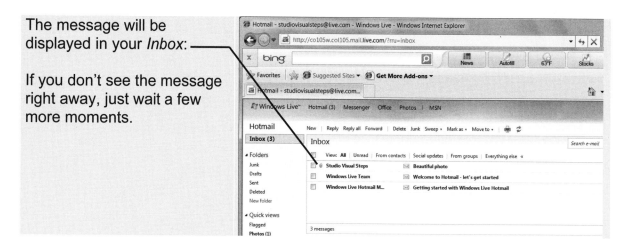

2.2 Reading an E-mail With an Attachment

An attachment to an e-mail
message is indicated by a
paperclip:

 Click the message

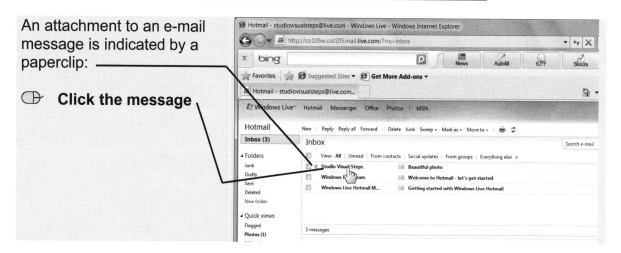

 HELP! I cannot see the message

If *Windows Live Essentials* does not identify the sender as a safe sender, you will
see this warning appear above the message:

> 🛡 Attachments, pictures, and links in this message have been blocked for your safety. .

If you trust the sender, click Show content .

☞ **Click the attachment**

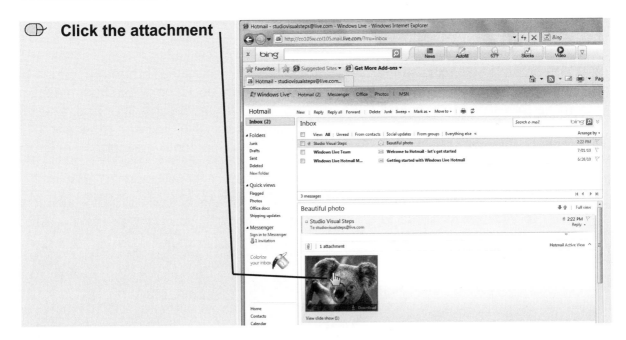

🖐 **Please note:**

When you try to open an attachment, the file will be scanned for viruses first. If the attachment contains a virus you will not be able to open it.

The attachment will be opened *in Hotmail Active View*:

☞ **Click**

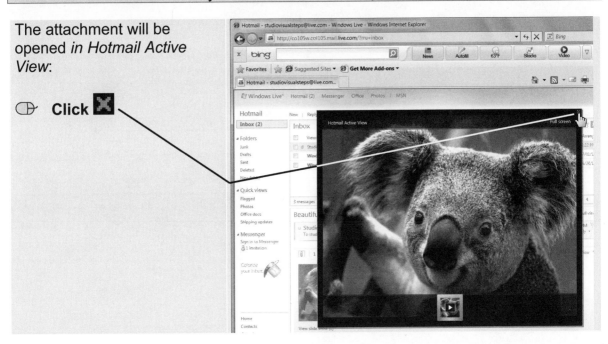

☞ **Open your *Inbox*** 🦶7

2.3 Junk E-mail

You can mark specific senders as 'unsafe', which means that future messages from these senders will be moved directly to the *Junk* folder. *Hotmail* itself uses a filter to move messages to this *Junk* folder as well. You can modify this filter and determine when you want to delete these unwanted messages. Also, you can mark each individual sender as safe or unsafe, which will result in some messages being blocked.

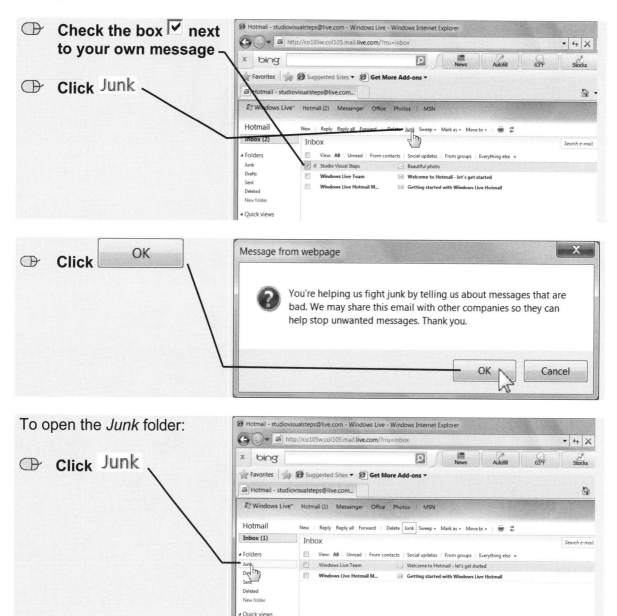

The message has been moved to the *Junk* folder:

Now you are going to mark this sender as safe again:

- Check the box ☑ next to your own message

- Click Move to ▾

- Click Inbox

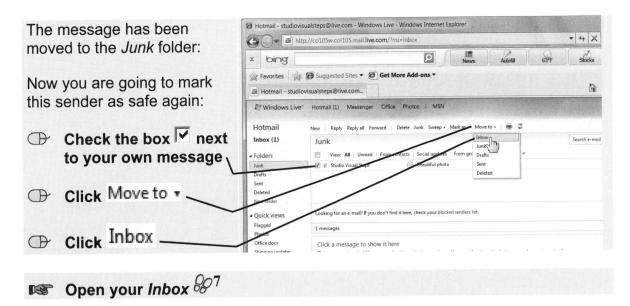

☞ **Open your *Inbox*** 🐾⁷

The message has been returned to your *Inbox*:

Hotmail can also mark messages as *Junk* all on its own. For this purpose, the program uses a filter which you can modify yourself.

- Click Options ▾

- Click More options

- Click Filters and reporting

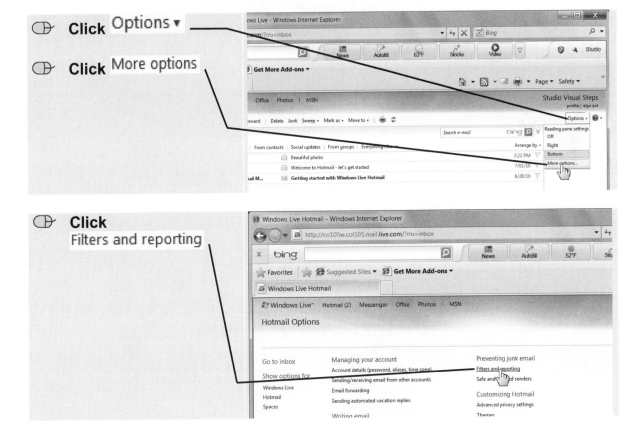

The filter level has been set to *Standard*: ————

☞ **If you wish, select a different filter level**

If you select *Low,* fewer messages will be marked as junk.

If you select *Exclusive*, you will only receive messages from contacts and safe senders.

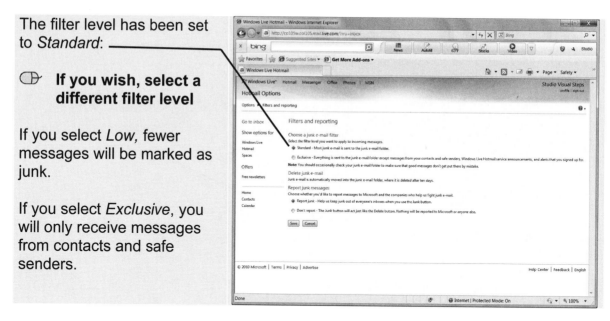

☞ **If necessary, drag the scroll bar down**

Junk e-mail is automatically moved into the junk e-mail folder: ————

You can also determine whether you want to report junk messages: ————

☞ **Click** Save

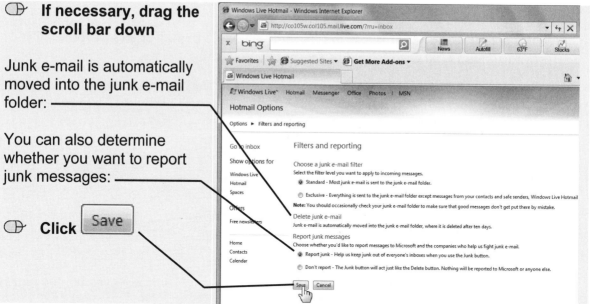

 Tip

Check the Junk folder

It is recommended to check the *Junk* folder regularly, to make sure that no important messages have accidentally been moved to this folder.

You can also mark individual senders as safe or decide to block them.

Click Safe and blocked senders

Click Safe senders

Now you can enter an e-mail address that you want to mark as safe:

Type the desired e-mail address

Click Add to list >>

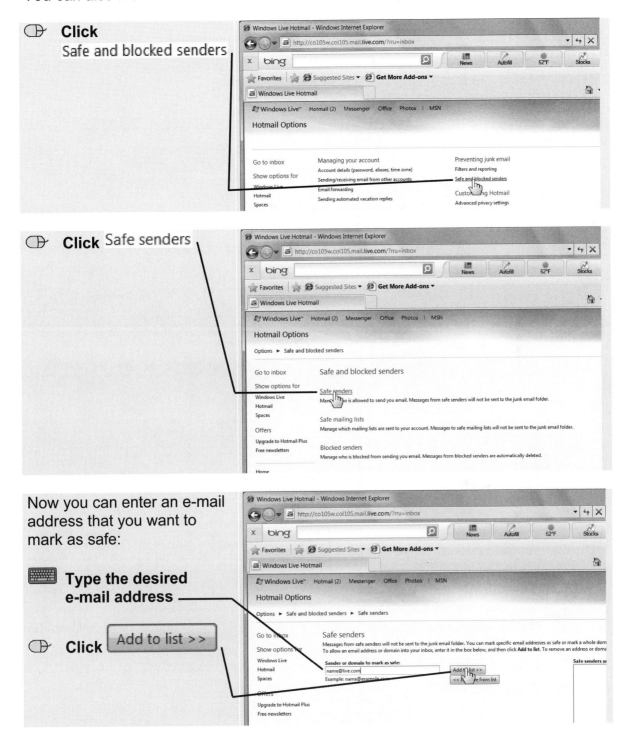

The e-mail address has been added to the safe senders list:

⊕ **Click**
 Safe and blocked senders

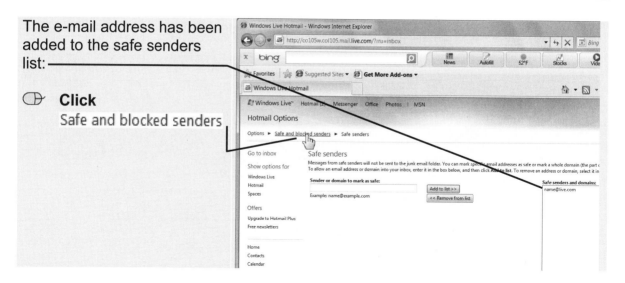

In the same way, you can also block senders:

⊕ **Click** Blocked senders

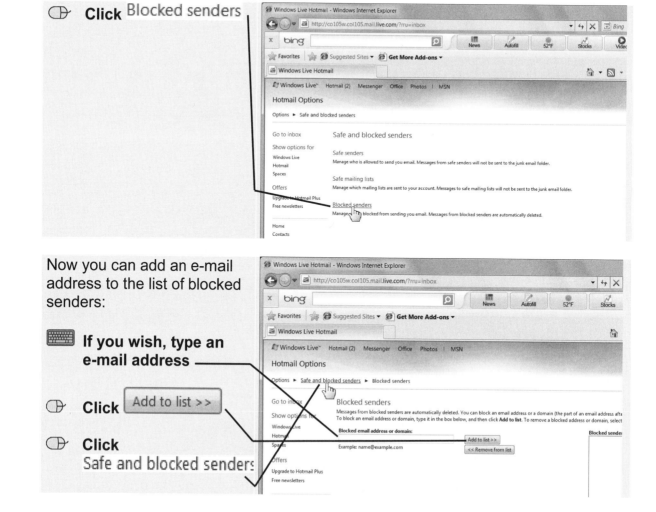

Now you can add an e-mail address to the list of blocked senders:

⌨ **If you wish, type an e-mail address**

⊕ **Click** Add to list >>

⊕ **Click**
 Safe and blocked senders

You can add safe mailing lists as well: ───

☞ **Open your *Inbox*** 👣7

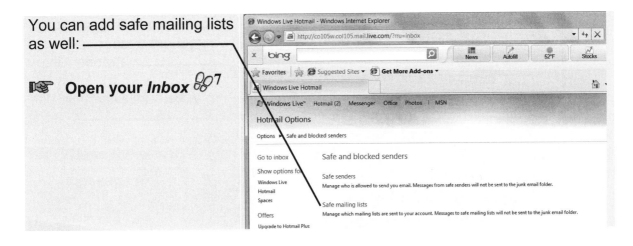

2.4 Managing Folders

Hotmail uses a number of default folders. You can add folders yourself and save your e-mail messages in an organized way. You can manually add messages to the desired folder, but you can also enable the program to do that automatically.

👆 **Click** New folder

👆 **Type a name for this folder. In this illustration, we have used 'Family'** ───

👆 **Click** Save

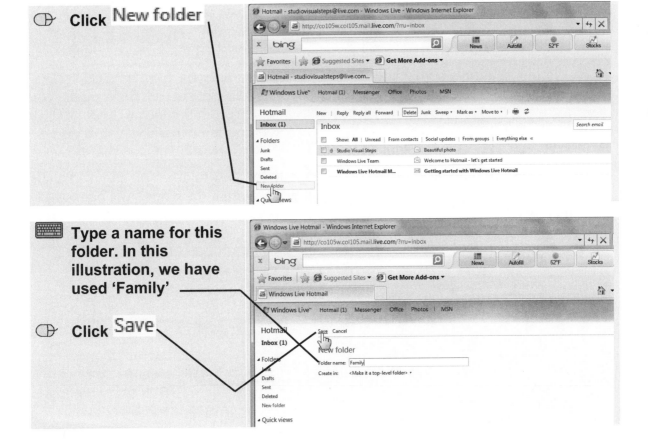

The new folder has been
added to the folder list: ―

⊕ **Click Inbox (1)**

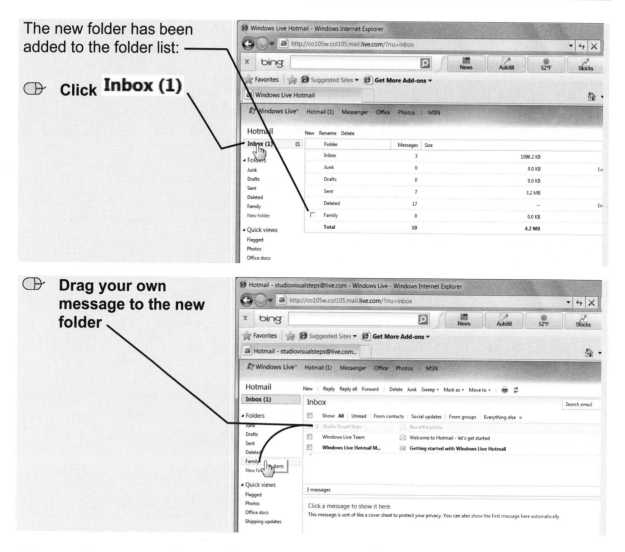

⊕ **Drag your own
message to the new
folder**

Now you have manually moved a message to the new folder. You can also adjust a
setting for this new folder, so that from now on, certain messages will be moved to it
automatically:

⊕ **Click Options ▾**

⊕ **Click More options**

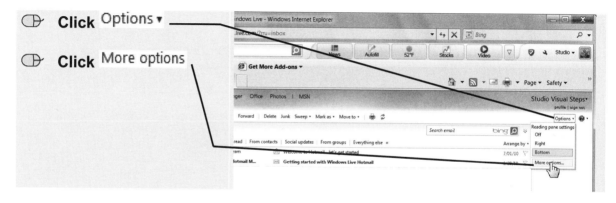

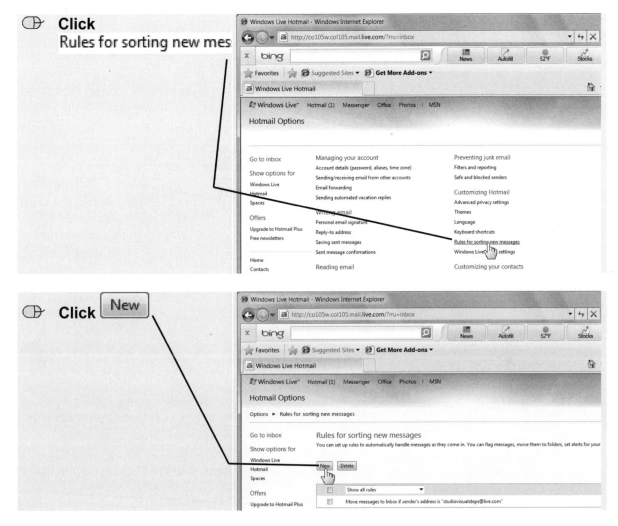

You can select various options to determine which messages should be moved to the new folder.

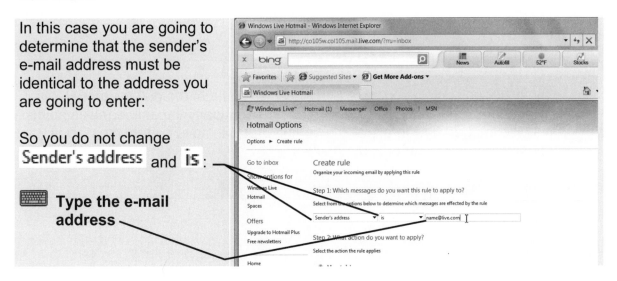

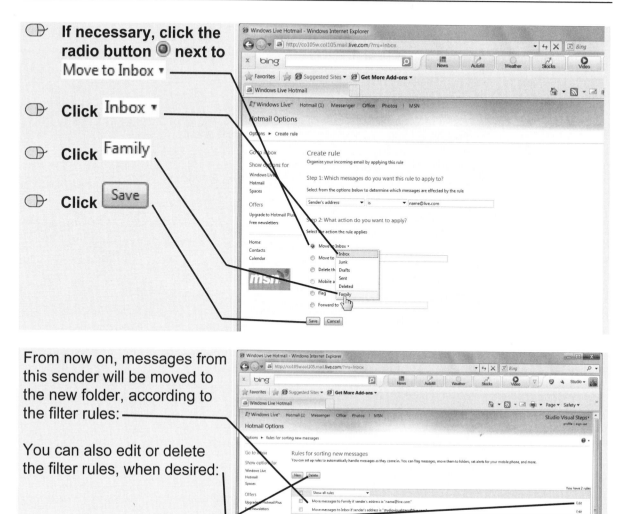

- If necessary, click the radio button ◉ next to *Move to Inbox ▾*
- Click *Inbox ▾*
- Click *Family*
- Click *Save*

From now on, messages from this sender will be moved to the new folder, according to the filter rules: ─────

You can also edit or delete the filter rules, when desired: ─────

☞ **Open your *Inbox*** 📖⁷

2.5 More Hotmail Options

In the previous section you were introduced to some of the options that *Hotmail* provides. For instance, you have learned how to modify the junk e-mail settings. You have also learned how to adjust the setting that will move certain messages automatically to a folder of your choice.

There are several other interesting options available in *Hotmail*. In this section we will discuss some of the personalization options. First, you will learn how to modify the settings for the message viewing window and make it more to your liking:

Click Options ▾

Click Right

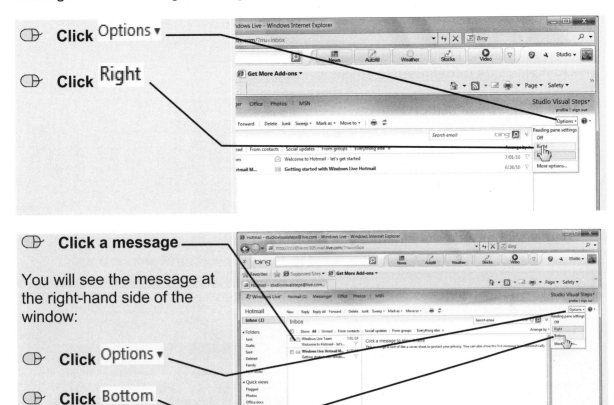

Click a message

You will see the message at the right-hand side of the window:

Click Options ▾

Click Bottom

Another option is the *Personal E-mail Signature*. This option allows you to enter a text which will be inserted at the bottom of all your e-mail messages.

Click Options ▾

Click More options

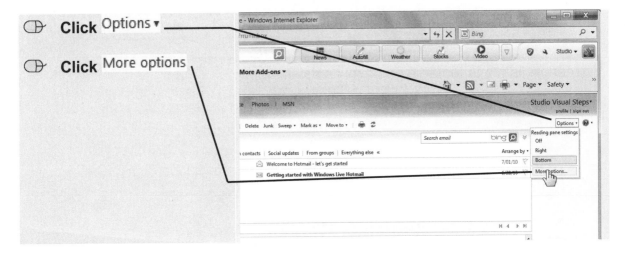

If necessary, drag the scroll bar down

Click Personal email signature

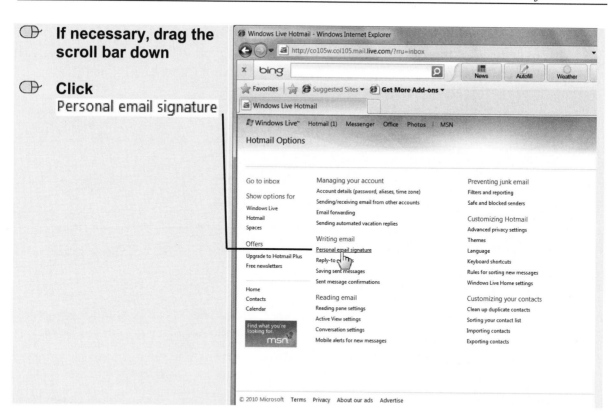

Type a text

If necessary, drag the scroll bar down

Click Save

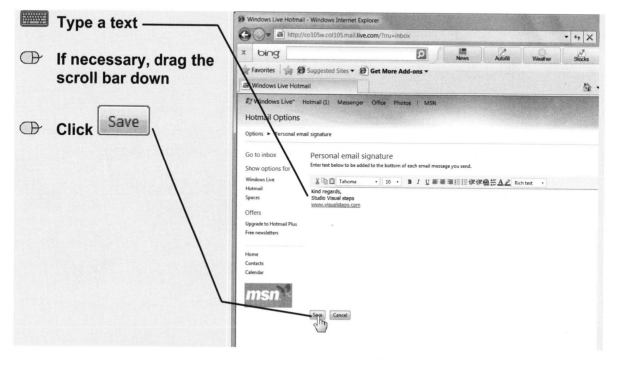

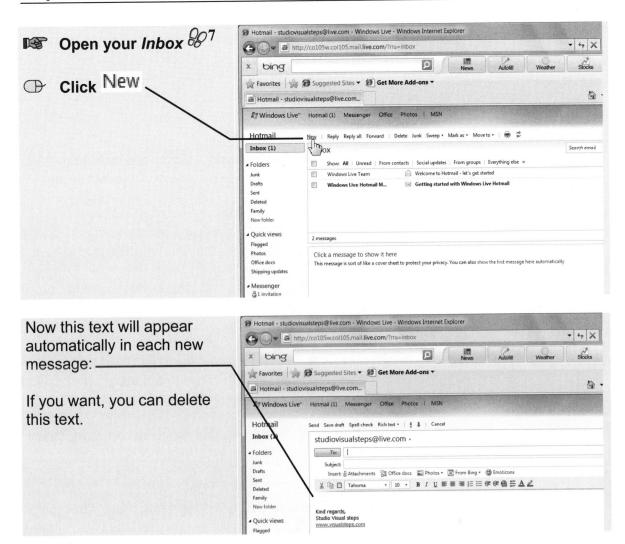

☞ **Open your** *Inbox* 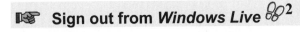7

👆 **Click** New

Now this text will appear
automatically in each new
message: ───

If you want, you can delete
this text.

☞ **Sign out from** *Windows Live* 🐾2

☞ **Close** *Internet Explorer* 🐾6

In this chapter you have learned how to send an e-mail message with an attachment
in *Windows Live Hotmail*. You have also learned how to modify various settings to
deal with unwanted (junk) mail.

 Tip

Additional information
This chapter is an introduction to some of the features in *Windows Live Hotmail*. In
the program's help pages you can find additional information about *Hotmail*. You can
open these help pages by clicking 🔵 and Help Center.

2.6 Background Information

Dictionary	
BCC	BCC stands for *Blind Carbon Copy*. If you use BCC, the various recipients of an e-mail message will not be able to see each other's e-mail address.
CC	CC stands for *Carbon Copy*. This is a copy of an e-mail message that will be sent to somebody else along with the addressee.
Compress	Reducing the size of a file, so it will take up less space and can be sent by e-mail more easily. Compressed files often use the .ZIP extension.
Contact	Information about a specific person, which contains at least the person's e-mail address. This information is stored in the *Contact* folder.
File	A collective name for everything that is stored on a computer. A file can consist of a program, a text, a photo, or music, for example.
File type	The way a file is formatted. The file type indicates what program was used to create the file and what program should be used to open the file.
POP3	POP stands for *Post Office Protocol*. POP is the most frequently used protocol for retrieving e-mail messages from a mail server. The 3 stands for version 3.
Upload	Copying a file from your own computer to another computer or to the Internet.
Webmail	This is the general name for a web application that enables the user to send and receive e-mail messages via a user interface that operates on the world wide web.
- Continue reading on the next page -	

Windows Live Hotmail	An e-mail service that uses the world wide web. As long as you have access to the Internet, you can use an Internet browser, such as *Internet Explorer,* to access your *Hotmail* account wherever you are.
Windows Live ID	An account that lets you use all *Windows Live Essentials* products. If you have a webmail address that ends in *hotmail.com* or *live.com*, this will automatically become your *Windows Live ID*.

Source: Windows Live Essentials Help, Windows Help and Support, Wikipedia

2.7 Tips

 Tip

POP3-settings

If you want to receive messages from your *Hotmail* account in a different e-mail program other than *Windows Live Hotmail*, you will need to have some additional information at hand. These so-called pop3 settings are required if you want to add a *Hotmail* account to another e-mail program. This is the information you will need:

Incoming e-mail (POP3)	pop3.live.com
Port for incoming e-mail (POP3)	995
POP with SSL required	Yes
User name	Your *Windows Live ID*
Password	Password for your *Windows Live ID*
Outgoing e-mail (SMTP)	smtp.live.com
Port for outgoing e-mail (SMTP)	25 or 587
Validation required	Yes (your *Windows Live ID* and password)
TLS/SSL required	Yes (select TLS if available, or else select SSL)

3. Windows Live Mail

The free *Windows Live Mail* program gives you access to multiple e-mail accounts. *Windows Live Mail* is comparable to *Outlook Express* and *Windows Mail*, except that *Windows Live Mail* stores its messages online. Furthermore, *Windows Live Mail* offers support for the POP3, IMAP, and HTTP protocols, which means that you can retrieve and read your e-mail messages from *Hotmail, Gmail or Yahoo!Mail* all in one place. You can also subscribe to various newsgroups and RSS feeds directly from the *Inbox* in the *Windows Live Mail* program.

Another very useful feature in *Mail* is the ability to send photo messages. You can send an e-mail with a single image or with a photo album of high resolution photos. The person receiving the e-mail can view the slide show of the photo album or download all photos.

There are various ways in which *Mail* communicates with other *Windows Live Essentials* products. For instance, the contact list is shared with *Hotmail* and *Messenger*. You can use *Mail* to check and see if a contact is already signed in to *Messenger*, and you can send chat messages directly from the *Mail* program. Finally, the diaries you have created in *Mail* are synchronized with the diaries in *Windows Live Calendar*.

In this chapter we will first explain how to add an e-mail account to *Mail*. Next, we will show you how to sign in to *Windows Live Essentials* from within *Mail* and why this can be very handy. After that, you will learn how to send a photo message. Finally, we will briefly discuss junk e-mail, how to handle unwanted messages and how to manage your folders.

In this chapter you will learn how to:

- add an e-mail account;
- sign in to *Windows Live Essentials*;
- send a photo message;
- handle junk mail;
- manage folders.

 Please note:

To work through this chapter properly you will need to have a *Windows Live ID*. If you do not yet have a *Windows Live ID,* in *section 1.2 Create a Windows Live ID* you can read how to obtain one.

3.1 Adding an E-mail Account

In this section you are going to add your *Hotmail* account to *Mail*.

☞ **Open** *Windows Live Mail* 🐾8

Now you will see the *Windows Live Mail* window:

When you open *Windows Live Mail* for the first time, you will also see the *Add your e-mail accounts* window:

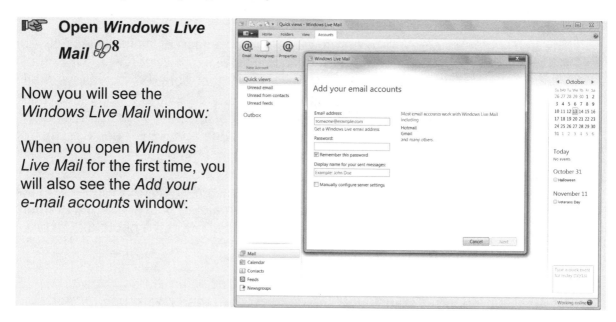

🩹 **HELP! I do not see the Add your e-mail accounts window.**

If you do not see the *Add your e-mail accounts* window:

☞ **Click the** Accounts **tab**

☞ **Click** Email

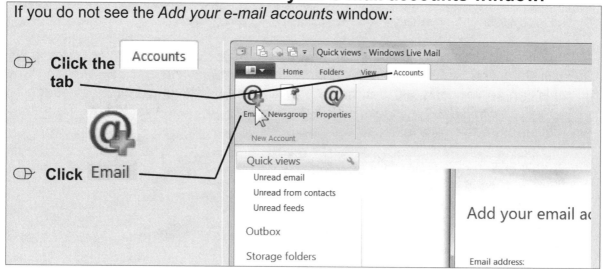

HELP! I see another window

If you are using a different e-mail program, for example *Windows Mail*, then you will first see the following window:

Do you want to set *Windows Live Mail* as your default e-mail program?

👈 **Click** Yes

If you do not want to do this?

👈 **Click** No

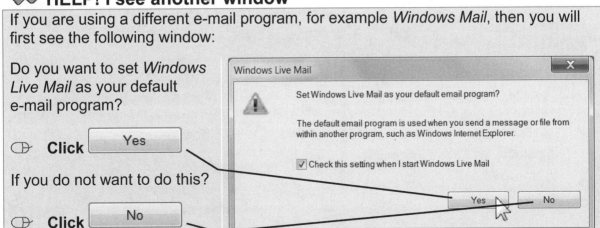

⌨ **By** E-mail address: **type your *Windows Live ID***

⌨ **By** Password: **type your password**

⌨ **By** Display Name: **type your name**

👈 **Click** Next

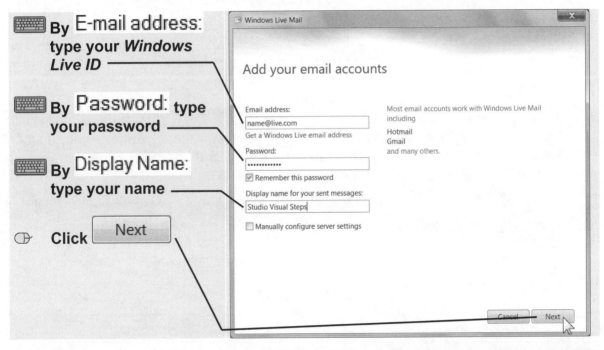

You will see this message:

👈 **Click** Yes

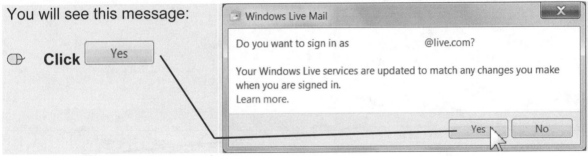

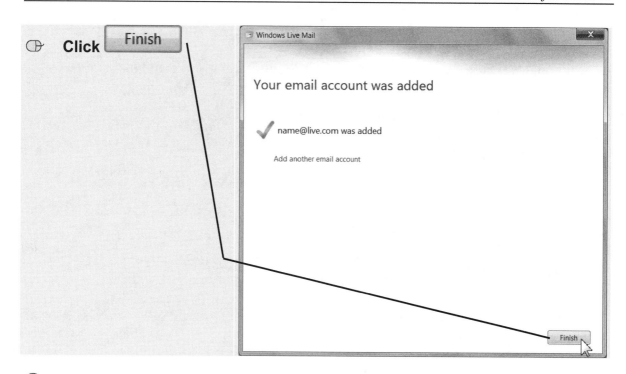

Click Finish

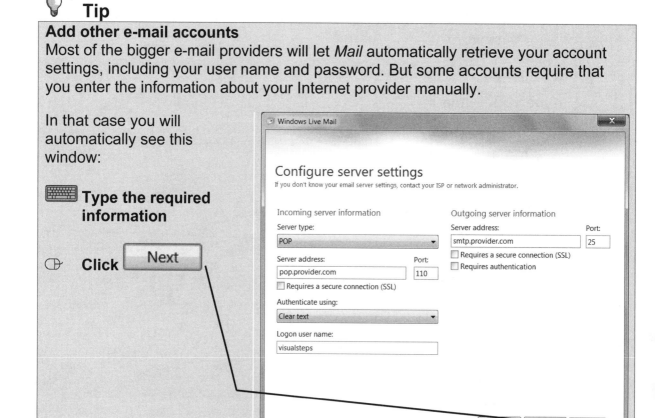

🔆 Tip

Add other e-mail accounts

Most of the bigger e-mail providers will let *Mail* automatically retrieve your account settings, including your user name and password. But some accounts require that you enter the information about your Internet provider manually.

In that case you will automatically see this window:

⌨ **Type the required information**

Click Next

Now you will be automatically signed in for *Windows Live Essentials*.

You see the folders of
Hotmail:

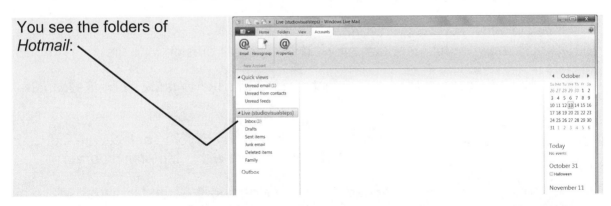

⊕ **Click the** View **tab**

Click Reading pane ▾

⊕ **Click** ▦ Off

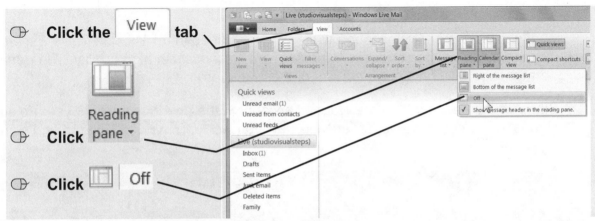

In the folder window you will
see a separate folder for all
your *Hotmail* messages:

⊕ **Click** Inbox

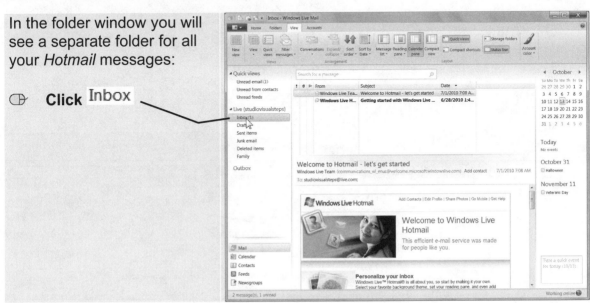

3.2 Sign In To Windows Live Essentials

If you want to use the *Mail* program, it is not actually necessary to sign in to *Windows Live Essentials*. But there are a few advantages if you sign in to first:

• Your *Mail* contact list will be synchronized with the *Windows Live Essentials* contact list.

• In your contact list, you will be able to see if any of your contacts are logged on to *Messenger.* You can start a chat session from within the *Mail* program.

• Your *Mail* diary will be added to Calendar and your *Calendar* diaries will be added to *Mail*.

• If you send a photo message while you are signed in for *Windows Live Essentials*, the photos will be stored by *Windows Live Essentials* in high quality. The e-mail message will contain thumbnails of these photos.

Since you already added your *Hotmail* account in the previous section, you are still signed in to *Windows Live Essentials*. Now you will learn how to sign out and sign in again.

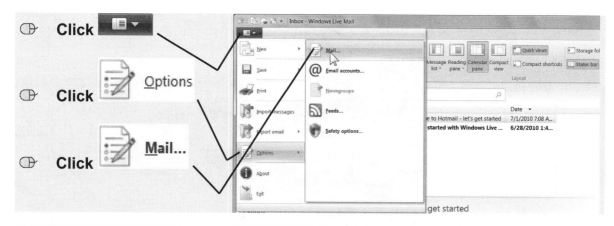

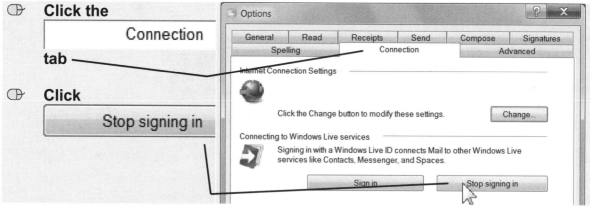

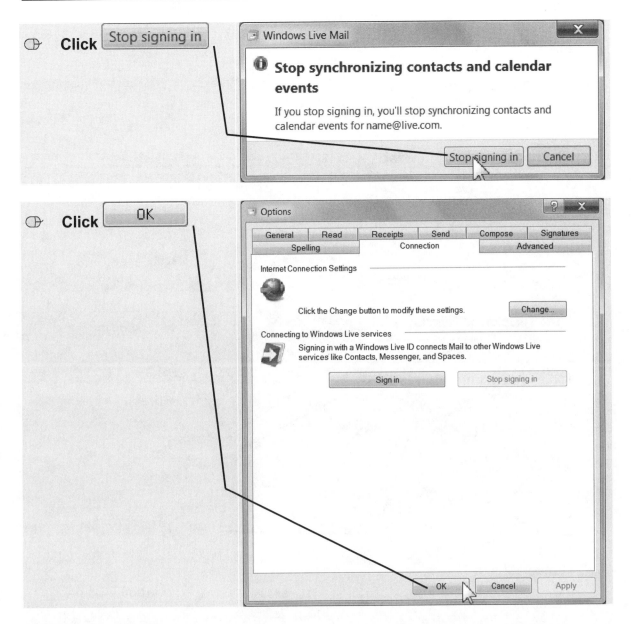

⊕ **Click** Stop signing in

⊕ **Click** OK

🠖 Please note:

If you have signed out from *Windows Live Essentials*, this does not mean that others who use the same *Windows*-account will not be able to access your e-mail. After you have opened *Mail* all e-mail accounts are displayed. If you want to secure the e-mail messages of other individuals who use your computer, you will need to create separate *Windows* user accounts for these people.

Now you have signed out from *Windows Live Essentials*. You can sign in again like this:

In the top right-hand corner of the window:

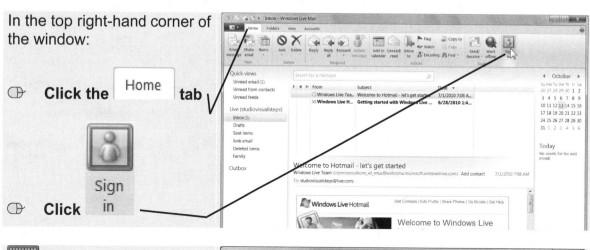

☞ **Click the** Home **tab**

☞ **Click** Sign in

⌨ **Type your *Windows Live ID***

⌨ **Type your password**

☞ **Click** Sign in

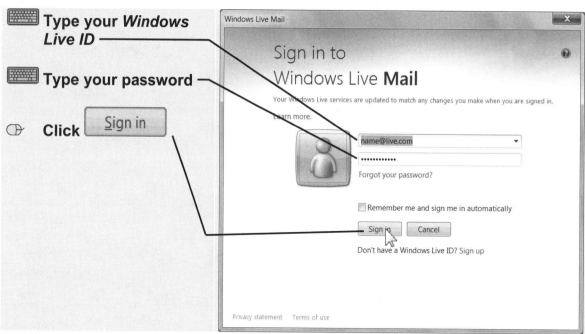

Now you are once again signed in to *Windows Live Essentials*:

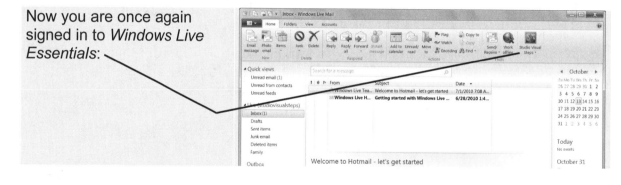

3.3 Sending a Photo E-mail

If you use *Mail* to send a photo e-mail, the photos will be stored on a separate, secure web location and the e-mail will contain thumbnails of these photos. The recipients can surf to this web location from within the e-mail message, view the photos and download them, if they want to. The recipients can also view a slide show.

In this way you are able to send large numbers of high quality photos. You have the possibility to change the display of the photos.

Please note:

If you want to use the options described above and store your photos on a separate web location with the thumbnails included in your e-mail message, you will need to be signed in to *Windows Live Essentials*.

In the top left-hand corner of the window:

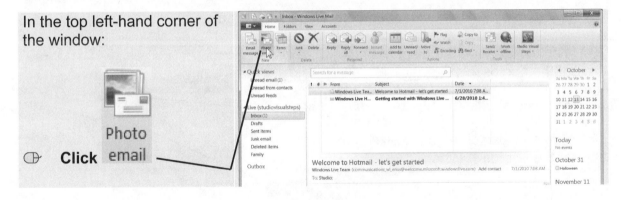

Click Photo email

Tip

Alternative way to send a photo e-mail

Email message

You can create a new e-mail message by clicking message . You can also send a photo message from a regular e-mail message like this:

Click the Insert tab

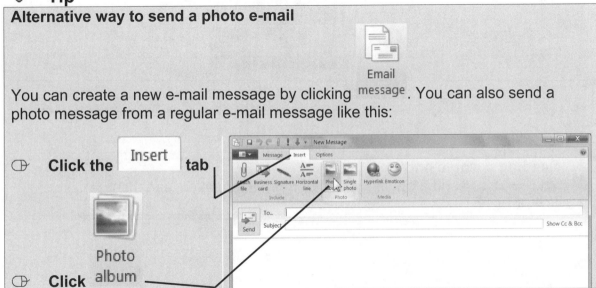

Click Photo album

Click a few photos —

If you want to select multiple

photos at once, use Ctrl

⇧ Shift

or   .

Click Open ▼

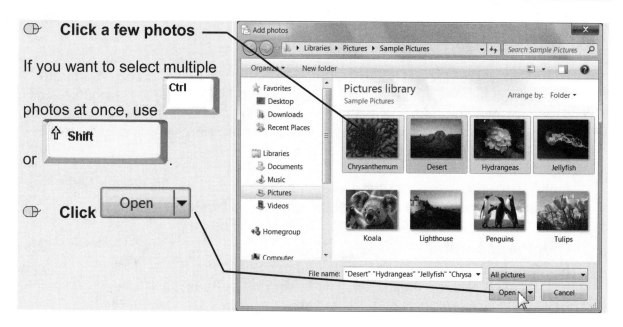

You can make some changes before you send them:

You can change the display
of the photos: —

You can shuffle the photos: —

You can also change the size
of the photos —

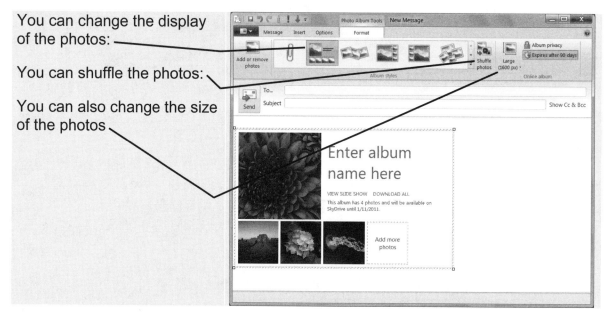

 Tip

Sending a single photo
You can also send a single photo. For more information, see the tip in *section
3.7 Tips*.

⌨ By ᵀᵒ⁻⁻ type your e-mail address

⌨ Type a subject and a text message, if you wish

⊕ Click Send

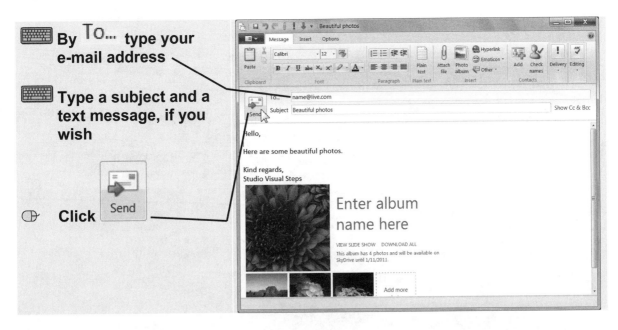

💡 Tip

Multiple e-mail accounts
If you have added multiple e-mail accounts to *Mail*, you can select the account from which you want to send this message:

⊕ By ᶠʳᵒᵐ: click your e-mail account

⊕ Click the e-mail account you want to use

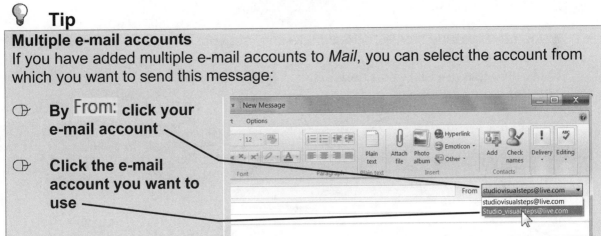

💡 Tip

Select contacts from the contact list
If you want to select a contact or multiple contacts from your contact list:

⊕ Click ᵀᵒ⁻⁻

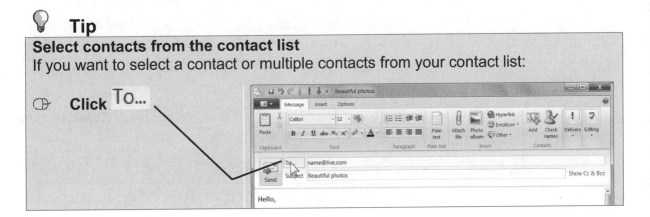

♀ **Tip**

CC and BCC

If you want to enter an address by Cc... or Bcc...:

⊕ **Click**
Show Cc & Bcc

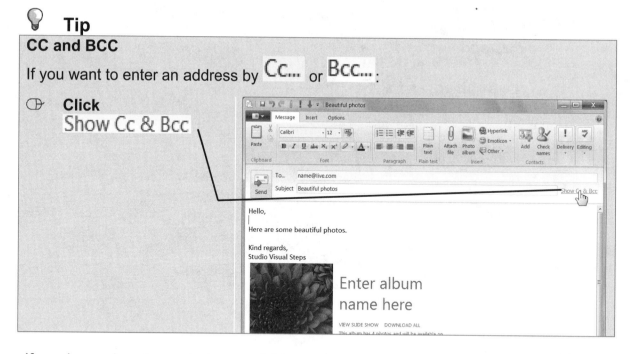

If you have already created a new folder and set your e-mail program to automatically move the e-mail messages to it as described in the previous chapter, you will be able to retrieve this e-mail in that new folder. You will also find this e-mail message in the *Unread e-mail* folder.

⊕ **Click** Unread e-mail (1)

⊕ **Double-click the e-mail message**

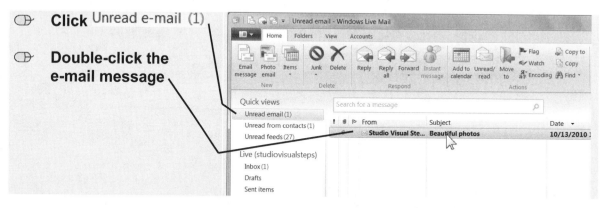

🩹 **HELP! I do not have any new e-mail.**

Is there no new message in your *Inbox*? Perhaps it has not yet been received. Try again later to receive the message:

⊕ **Click**

By clicking a thumbnail, you can open or save the high quality photo:

You can also play a slide show:

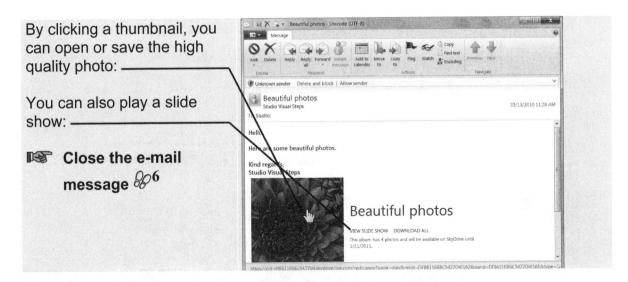

☞ **Close the e-mail message** 6

➥ Please note:

Photos that have been stored on the *Windows Live Essentials* server will be available for a period of ninety days. You can store up to 25 gigabytes (GB) of photos ans files to the *Windows Live Essentials* servers.

3.4 Junk e-mail

In *Mail* you can mark specific senders as unsafe, which means that all future messages from the sender will be moved to the *Junk e-mail* folder. *Mail* itself uses a filter to move unwanted messages to this folder as well. You can change the filter level and determine at what point the unwanted messages are to be deleted. Also, you can mark each individual sender as safe or as junk.

☞ **If necessary, click an e-mail message**

☞ **Click**

You can add the sender to the blocked senders list:

Or you can add the sender to the safe senders list:

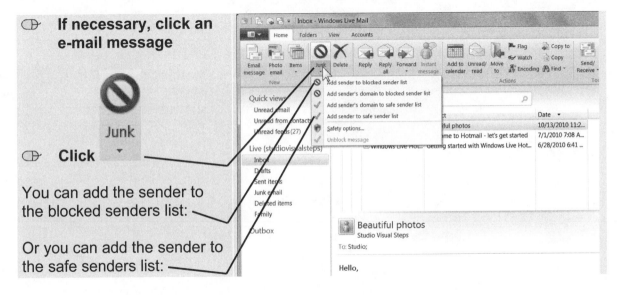

Now you are going to take a look at a number of safety options in *Mail*.

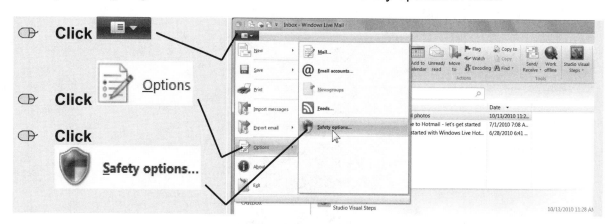

Click

Click **Options**

Click **Safety options...**

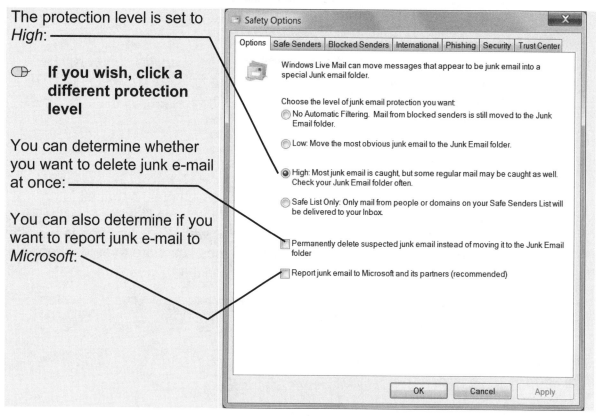

The protection level is set to *High*:

☞ **If you wish, click a different protection level**

You can determine whether you want to delete junk e-mail at once:

You can also determine if you want to report junk e-mail to *Microsoft*:

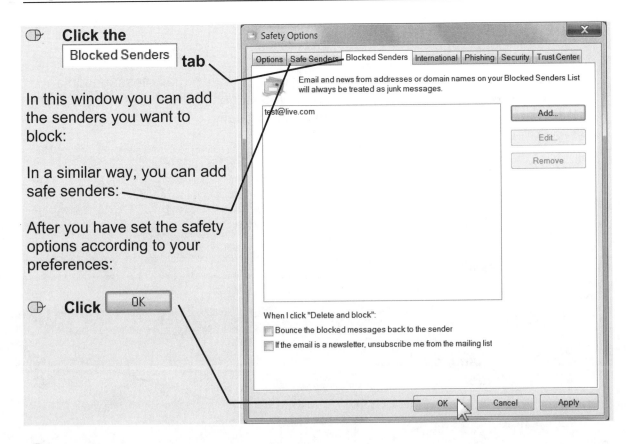

☞ **Click the**

Blocked Senders **tab**

In this window you can add the senders you want to block:

In a similar way, you can add safe senders:

After you have set the safety options according to your preferences:

☞ **Click** OK

💡 **Tip**

Check the Junk e-mail folder
It is recommended that you check the *Junk e-mail* folder regularly, to make sure it does not contain any possible important messages that have inadvertently been assigned as junk.

3.5 Managing Folders

In *Mail* you can add folders that will help you sort your e-mail messages in an organized way. You can manually add the messages to the desired folder, but you can also let the program do this for you automatically.

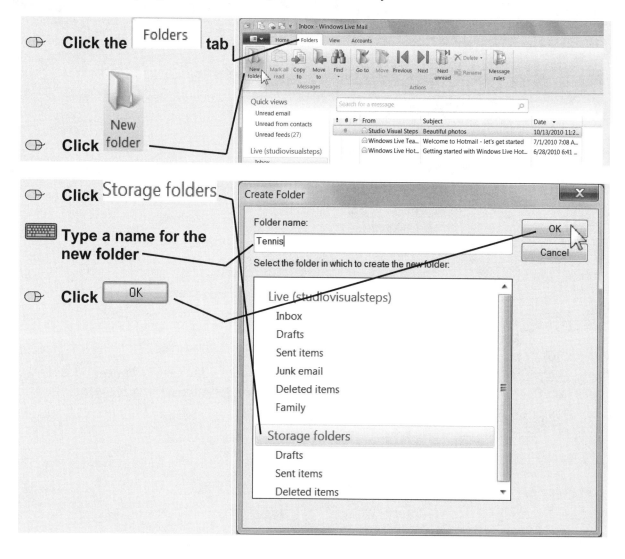

HELP! I do not see the Storage folders

You can add the *Storage folders* folder to your window. You do that like this:

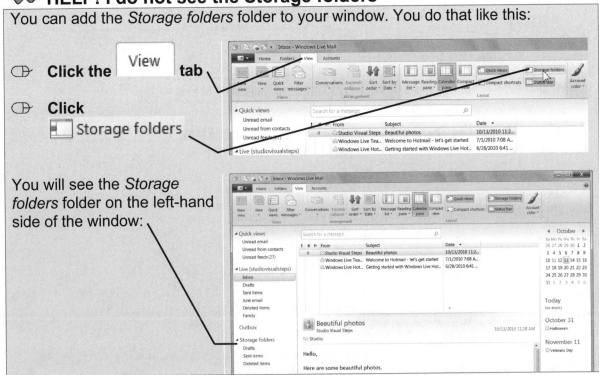

⟜ **Click the** | View | **tab**

⟜ **Click**
🗔 Storage folders

You will see the *Storage folders* folder on the left-hand side of the window:

From now on, you can make sure that messages from specific senders are automatically moved to specific folders.

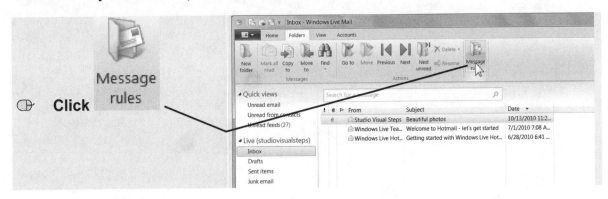

⟜ **Click** Message rules

In this window you can create rules for your e-mail accounts:

- Check the box ☑ next to
  Where the From line contains

- Check the box ☑ next to
  Move it to the specified

- Click contains people

Type a name or an e-mail address

You can also select a name from your contact list:

- Click Add

- Click OK

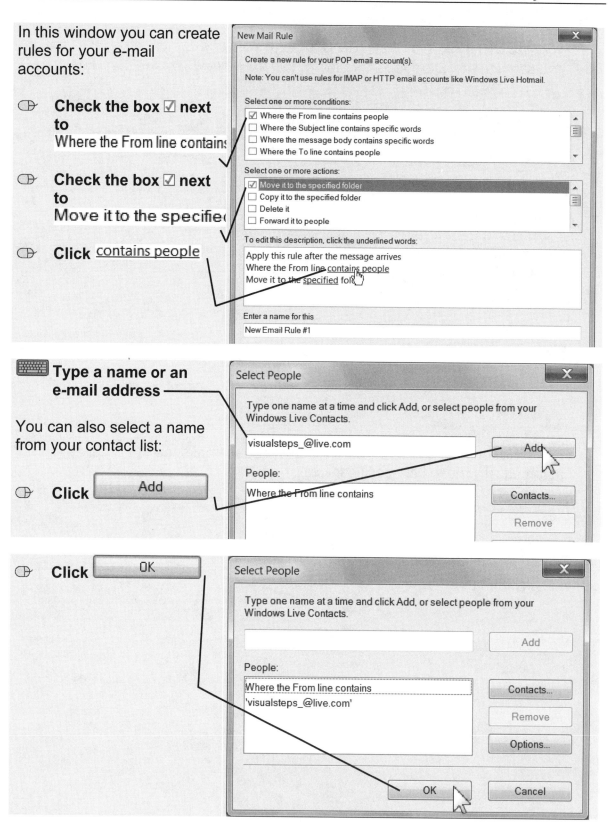

Click <u>specified</u>

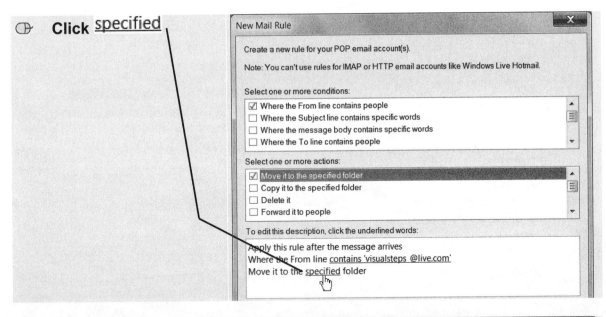

Click **the new folder**

Click [OK]

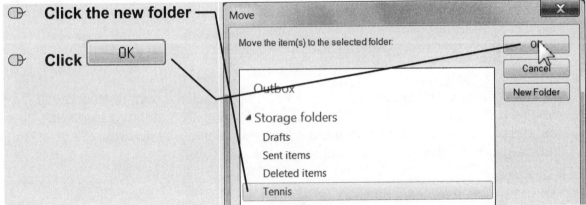

At the bottom of the window:

Click [Save rule]

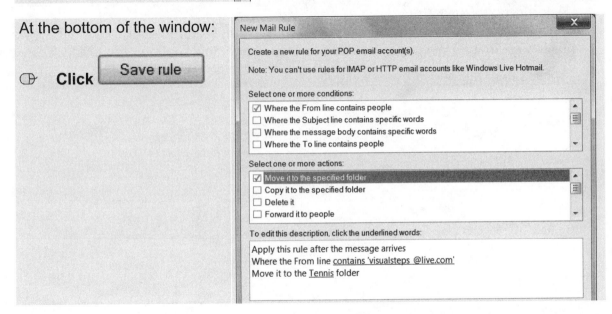

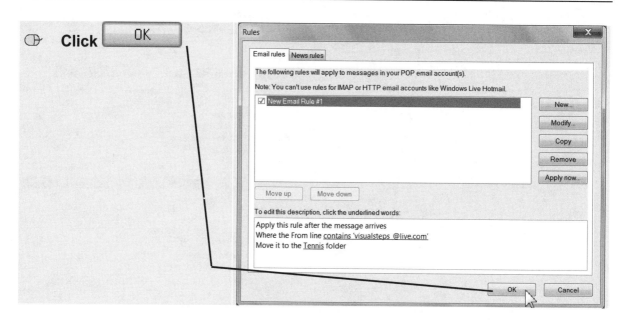

Click [OK]

📩 **Sign out from** *Windows Live Mail* 👣¹²

📩 **Close** *Windows Live Mail* 👣⁶

In this chapter you have learned how to add an e-mail account to *Windows Live Mail*, and how to sign in and out of *Windows Live Essentials*. You have also seen how to send a photo message, how to handle junk e-mail and how to organize your e-mail messages into folders.

💡 Tip

Additional information
This chapter is an introduction to some of the main features available in *Windows Live Mail*. In the help pages you can find additional information about *Mail*. You can access the help pages by clicking .

3.6 Background Information

Dictionary

BCC	BCC stands for *Blind Carbon Copy*. If you use BCC, the various recipients of an e-mail message will not be able to see each other's e-mail address.
CC	CC stands for *Carbon Copy*. This is a copy of an e-mail message that will be sent to somebody else along with the addressee.
Chat	Conducting a conversation by typing messages back and forth between two users who are both connected to the Internet.
Contact	Information about a specific person, which contains at least the person's e-mail address. This information is stored in the *Contact* folder. There are different types of contacts: the contact you can use in *Messenger*, *Mail* and *Hotmail* and the contacts who can view your profile.
Download	Copying a file from the Internet to your own computer.
E-mail account	An account consists of a server name, a user name, a password and an e-mail address. This information will allow you to connect to an e-mail service.
HTTP	HTTP stands for *Hypertext Transfer Protocol*. This is a standard set of rules, used by computers to transfer data via the Internet.
IMAP	IMAP stands for *Internet Message Access Protocol*. This is a method used by computers to send and receive e-mail messages. This method provides access to your e-mail messages without you having to download them to your computer.
Online	Connected to the Internet.

- Continue reading on the next page -

Outlook Express	*Outlook Express* is a *Microsoft* e-mail program and news reader. The program was included in the *Windows XP* operating system. In *Windows Vista* this program has been replaced by *Windows Mail*, in *Windows 7* by *Windows Live Mail*.
POP3	POP stands for *Post Office Protocol*. POP is the most frequently used protocol for retrieving e-mail messages from a mail server. The 3 stands for version 3.
RSS feeds	RSS feeds, also called *feeds*, contain content that is continually updated by a website. RSS feeds are often used by news sites and blogs. They are also used to distribute other types of digital content, such as images and audio or video files. *Internet Explorer* can recognize and display RSS feeds while you are visiting a website. You can subscribe to RSS feeds, and then the program will automatically check for updates and download these updates, so you can view them later on.
Upload	Copying a file from your own computer to another computer or to the Internet.
Webmail	This is the general name for a web application that enables the user to send and receive e-mail messages via a user interface that operates on the world wide web.
Windows account	The information that *Windows* uses to set user privileges and access privileges to a specific computer. The user account contains the user name, the password, and a unique account ID.
Windows Live ID	An account that lets you use all *Windows Live Essentials* products. If you already have a webmail address that ends in *hotmail.com* or *live.com*, this will automatically become your *Windows Live ID*.
Windows Live Mail	*Windows Live Mail* is an e-mail program that can be downloaded from the *Windows Live Essentials* website. *Windows Live Mail* is comparable to *Outlook Express* and *Windows Mail*, except that the *Windows Live Mail* messages are stored online.
Windows Mail	*Windows Mail* is an e-mail program and news reader that is exclusively included in the *Windows Vista* operating system. It is the successor of *Outlook Express*. In *Windows 7* it is replaced by *Windows Live Mail*.

Source: Help for Windows Live Essentials, Windows Help and Support, Wikipedia

3.7 Tips

💡 **Tip**

Add default text to an e-mail message
You can type a text which will be included in all your new e-mail messages. In *Mail* this is called a *signature*.

👉 **Open the *Options* window** ℘⁹

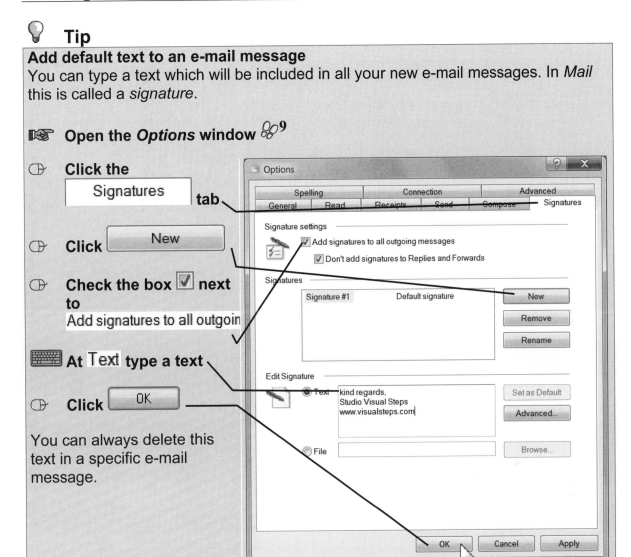

⊕ **Click the** Signatures **tab**

⊕ **Click** New

⊕ **Check the box** ☑ **next to** Add signatures to all outgoin

⌨ **At** Text **type a text**

⊕ **Click** OK

You can always delete this text in a specific e-mail message.

Tip

Change the layout of your window

You can change the layout of your *Mail* window. For example, you can activate the reading pane:

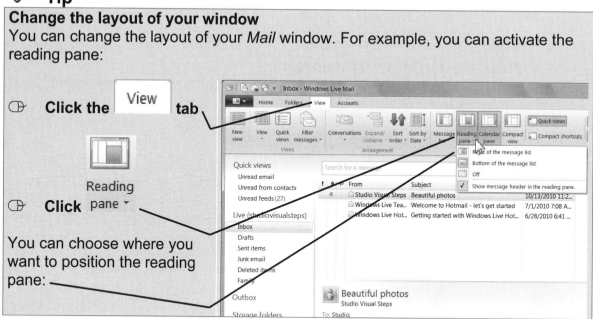

⏵ **Click the** View **tab**

⏵ **Click** Reading pane ▾

You can choose where you want to position the reading pane:

 Tip

Manage your diary

Mail allows you to maintain more than one diary. If you have signed in with *Windows Live Essentials*, the *Calendar* diaries will be added to *Mail* and the *Mail* diaries will be added to *Calendar*.

⏵ **Click** 📅 Calendar

Now you can add and delete appointments.

You can add and delete diaries and determine which diaries you want to display.

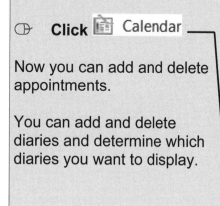

Tip

Read RSS feeds
In *Mail* you can read the *RSS feeds* you have subscribed to in *Internet Explorer*.

At the bottom left of the
window:

⊕ **Click** 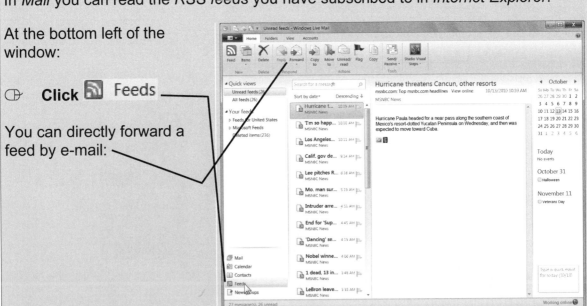 Feeds

You can directly forward a
feed by e-mail:

Do you want to find out more about RSS feeds? Read the free PDF file *Subscribing
to RSS* feeds: you can download this file from the
www.visualsteps.com/info_downloads web page.

 Tip

Sending a single Photo
If you use the option *Single photo* you can edit the photo before you send it.

☞ **Make a new e-mail
message** ℘13

⊕ **Click the** Insert **tab**

⊕ **Click** Single photo

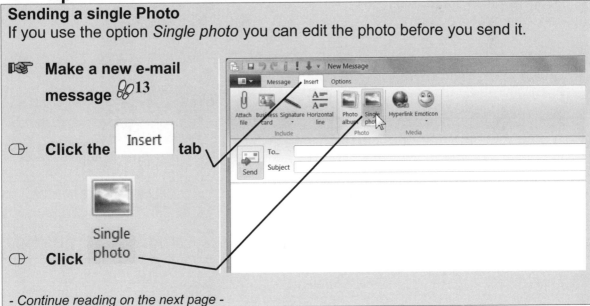

- Continue reading on the next page -

☞ **Open a photo** ✇16

⊕ **Click the photo**

The mouse pointer will turn

into ✛:

You can crop the photo:

You can determine the photo quality:

You can rotate the photo:

You can add a border to the photo, and choose a border color:

You can add effects to the photo:

You can also change the alignment of the photo:

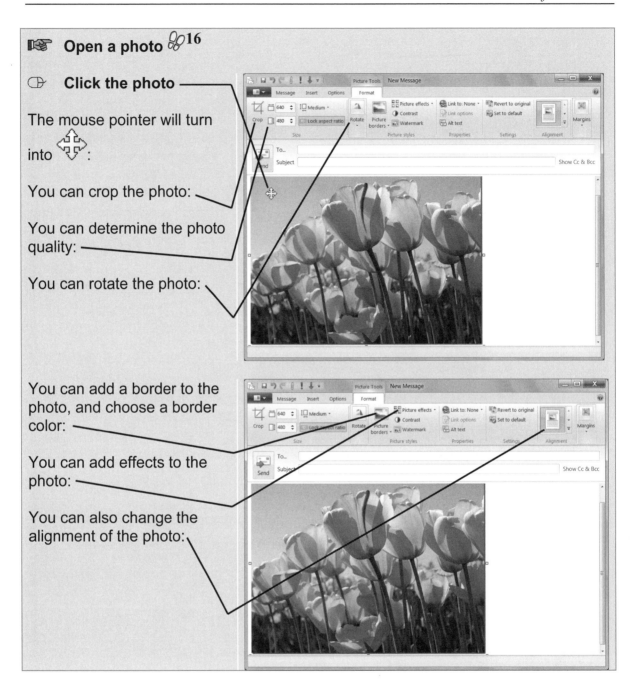

4. Windows Live Messenger

The *Windows Live Messenger* program allows you to chat with other users who have a *Windows Live ID* and who also already have *Messenger* installed. *Messenger* lets you communicate with others by text, sound, and vision.
You can also use *Messenger* to communicate with users of the popular social networks, *Facebook* and *LinkedIn*.

Windows Live Messenger used to be called *MSN Messenger*. There is still some confusion regarding the use of this name. *Messenger* used to be a *MSN* product, but now it has become a *Windows Live Essentials* product. Whenever you see a link to *MSN*, this will refer to the msn.com home page.
In *Messenger* you can change your online status whenever you want. For instance, you can select the 'appear offline' or 'busy' setting even when you are actually signed in. With *Messenger* you can also conduct a video conversation, exchange files, and send *emoticons*, *winks* and *nudges*. *Emoticons* are little pictures that reflect your mood, *winks* are short flash video clips that are played automatically, and a *nudge* is a vibration of the window. Other *Messenger* features include options for conducting a group conversation and playing online games. Finally, you can personalize *Messenger* by selecting a personal background or inserting a personal message under your name.

Messenger communicates with other *Windows Live Essentials* products in various ways. For example, the contact list is shared with both *Hotmail* and *Mail*. In *Messenger* you only need to click once to check your *Hotmail* messages. You can send an e-mail message in *Messenger* and likewise use *Mail* to send chat messages to *Messenger*. You can also use *Messenger* to conduct group conversations with the groups you have created in *Groups*.

This chapter begins with the sign in procedure for *Messenger*. Next, we will explain how you manage your contact list. Afterwards, we will discuss how to chat with *Messenger*, along with several other useful features. Finally, we will show you to modify some of the various settings in *Messenger*.

In this chapter you will learn how to:

- sign in with *Messenger*;
- manage contacts;
- chat;
- use additional options in *Messenger*;
- modify settings.

Please note:

To work through this chapter effectively you will need to have a *Windows Live ID.* If you do not yet have a *Windows Live ID,* go to *section 1.2 Create a Windows Live ID* and you can read how to get one.

4.1 Sign In With Messenger

With *Messenger*, you always need to sign in separately:

 Open *Windows Live Messenger*

⌨ **Type your e-mail address and your password**

You can decide to let the computer remember your e-mail address and password:

You can also determine whether you want to sign in automatically, after you have opened *Messenger*:

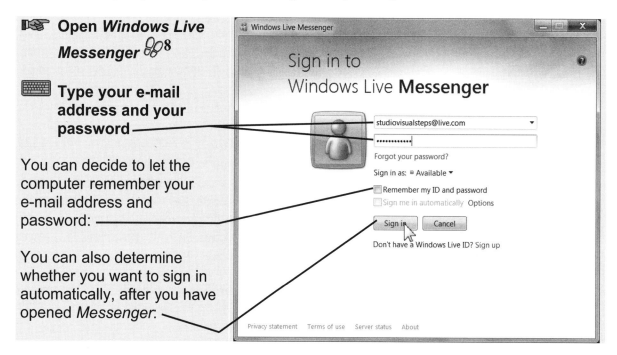

 Please note:

If you let the computer remember your password, other people who use this same computer and the same *Windows* account, will also have access to your *Windows Messenger* and *Hotmail* accounts.

You can change the status that is displayed to your contacts while you are signed in:

⊕ **Click**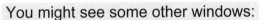

⊕ **If you wish, select a different status**

⊕ **Click**

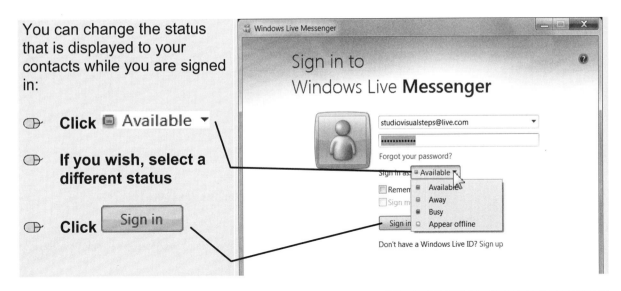

You might see some other windows:

⊕ **Click** Skip

You want to start working with *Messenger* right away:

⊕ **Click**

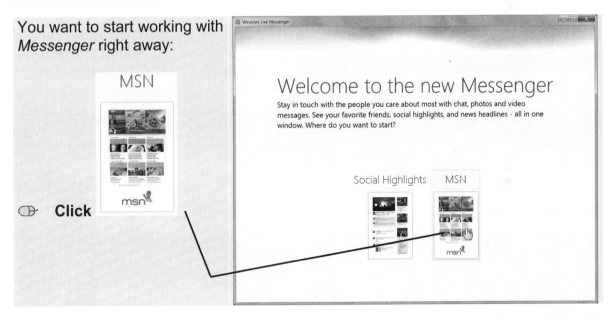

To reduce the size of the window so that the MSN videos do not appear:

⊕ **Click**

Now you have signed in with *Messenger*.

By clicking Inbox you can access your *Hotmail Inbox*:

You can immediately see if your contacts are online or offline:

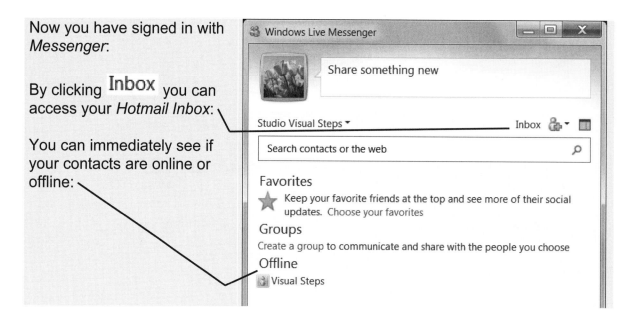

4.2 Contacts

In *Messenger* you can find the contacts you have already added to your *Messenger* network in *Windows Live Contacts* (see *section 1.6 Adding Contacts*). The contacts you have added in *Hotmail* and *Mail* will also be displayed in *Messenger*. But you can also use *Messenger* itself to add additional contacts.

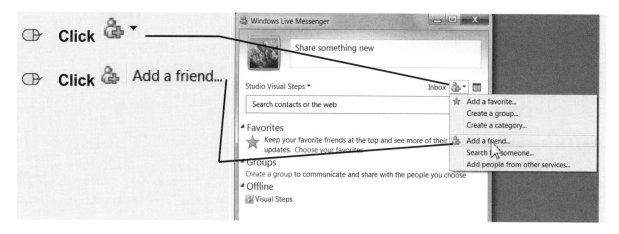

⊕ **Click**

⊕ **Click   Add a friend...**

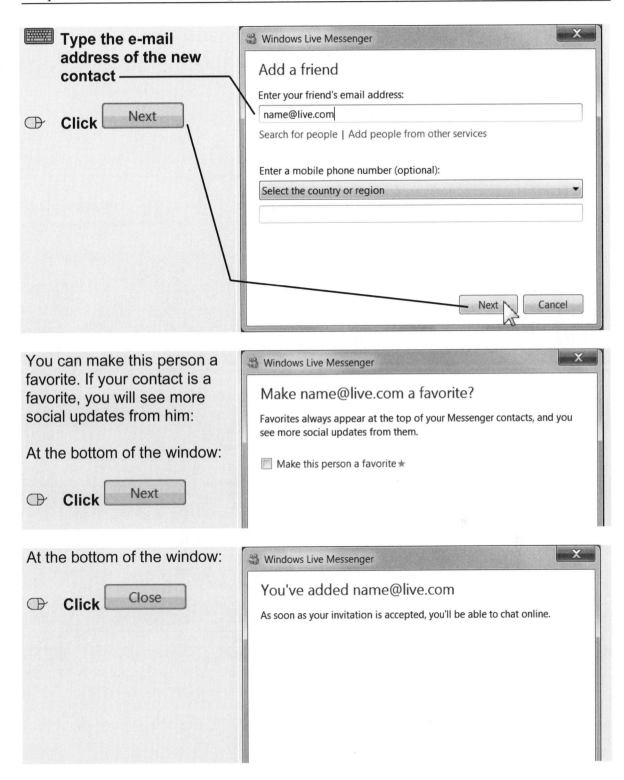

The contact will receive an invitation to be included in your network. He or she can accept or refuse this invitation. If the contact accepts the invitation, you can start chatting with him or her.

You can also receive an invitation yourself, for other people's networks.

Here is an example of such an invitation:

You can decide for yourself if you want to accept or refuse this invitation:

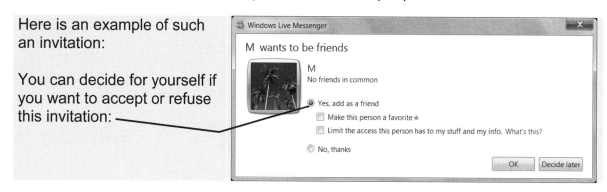

💡 Tip

Delete a contact
You can delete a *Messenger* contact:

☞ **Right-click the contact**

☞ **Click**
   Delete contact

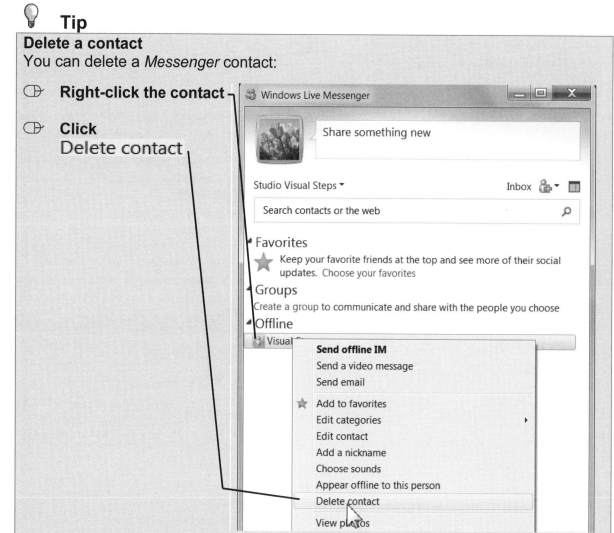

- Continue reading on the next page -

Click Delete

Windows Live Messenger

Delete Visual Steps from your contact list?

You'll delete this person from your contact list and from your list of friends.

Delete   Cancel

4.3 Chatting

If a contact has accepted your invitation, or if you have accepted somebody else's invitation, you can start chatting with this person.

Please note:

The following operation can only be performed if one of your contacts is actually online. However, if your contact is not online, you can still send an offline message. The contact will be able to read this message next time, as soon as he or she is signed in.

If a contact has signed in with *Messenger*, you will see this window at the bottom right of your desktop:

Windows Live Messenger

Visual Steps has just signed in

In *Messenger* itself you will also see that this contact is now online:

☞ **Double-click the contact**

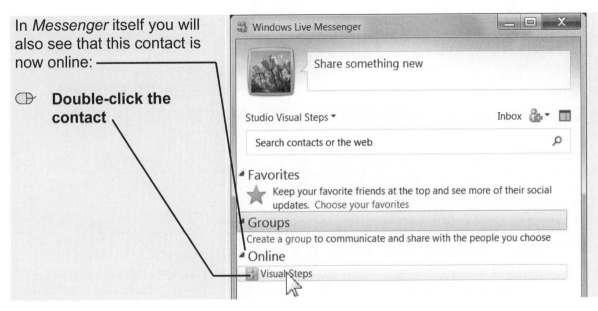

Windows Live Messenger

Share something new

Studio Visual Steps ▾   Inbox

Search contacts or the web

▲ Favorites
⭐ Keep your favorite friends at the top and see more of their social updates. Choose your favorites

Groups
Create a group to communicate and share with the people you choose

▲ Online
Visual Steps

Type a chat message

Press Enter ↵

Now the message will be sent.

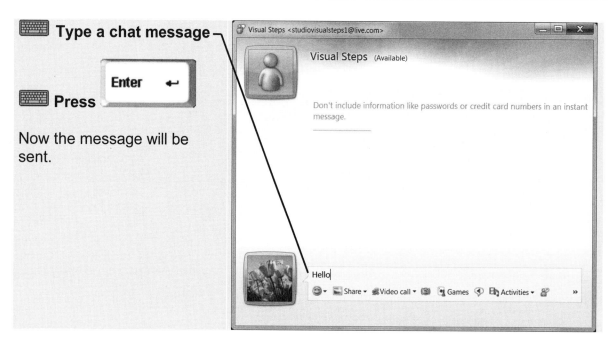

⮡ Please note:

The message you have just typed will be sent right away, when you press Enter ↵.

Do you want to start a new line in your text message? Then press simultaneously ⇧ Shift and Enter ↵. This is also known as a soft return.

You can tell when your contact is typing a message:

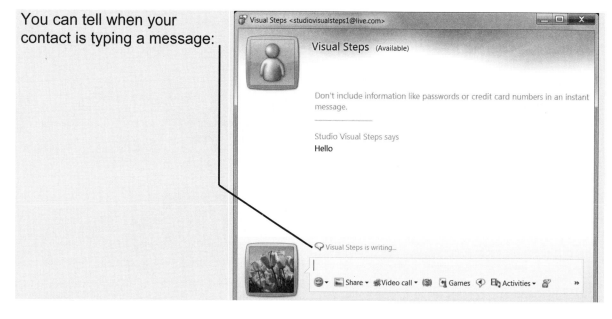

A little bit later you will see the message appear:

⊙→ **Click** ≫

You can change the font and the text color of your messages:

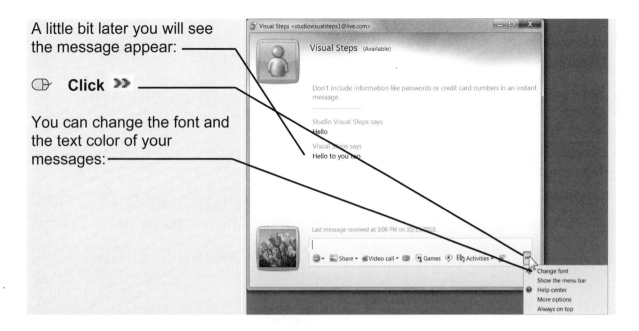

4.4 More Messenger Options

Apart from sending chat messages, *Messenger* contains a number of other interesting options. For instance, you can easily exchange photos, and conduct a video conversation. In this paragraph we will discuss some of these options.

⊙→ **Click** ☺ ▾

Besides text you can also send emoticons ☺ ▾, nudges 🌀 and winks:

Emoticons are little images that reflect your mood, winks are short flash clips that will automatically be played, and a nudge is a vibration of the window.

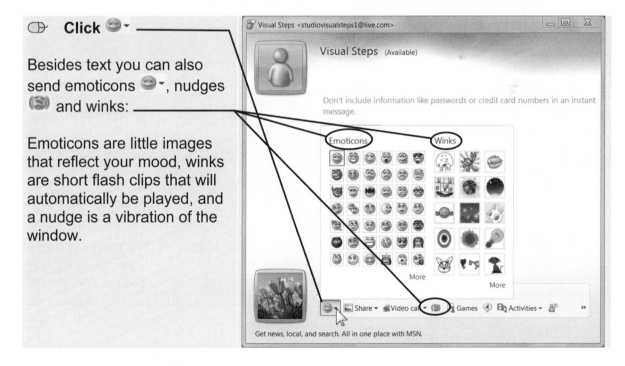

You can play games together:

You can record a *voiceclip*

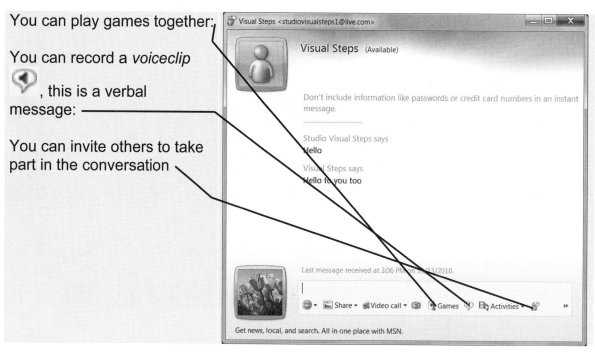, this is a verbal message: ─────────

You can invite others to take part in the conversation

It is very easy to exchange photos:

👆 **Click** 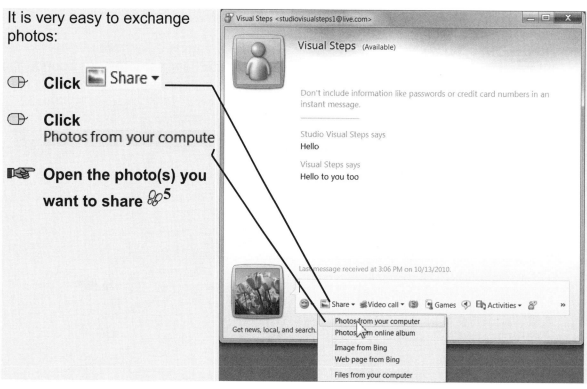 **Share ▼**

👆 **Click** Photos from your compute

👉 **Open the photo(s) you want to share** ✂️5

To add more photos:

⊕ **Click** Share ▾

To close the sharing option:

⊕ **Click** ✖

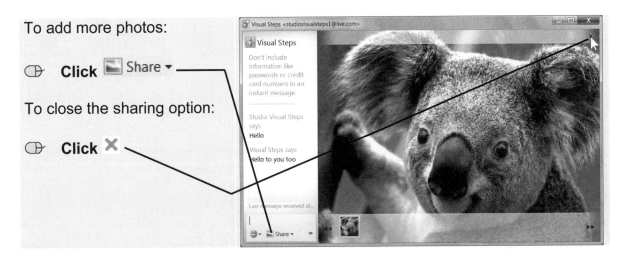

🔈 Please note:
With *Messenger* you can only send photos of the following file types: JPEG, GIF, BMP, and PNG.

You can also exchange files:

⊕ **Click** Share ▾

⊕ **Click**
Files from your computer

☞ **Open the files** 𝒪ₒ5

This may also be photo files.

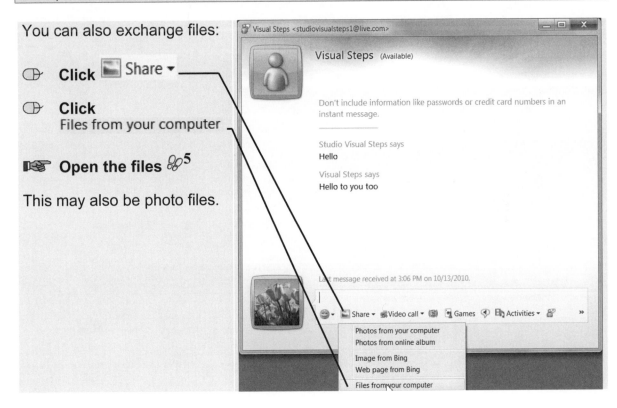

Now you will need to wait until your contact has accepted the file:

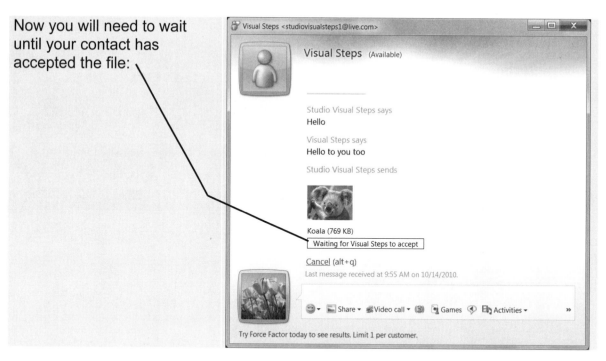

The contact has received the file:

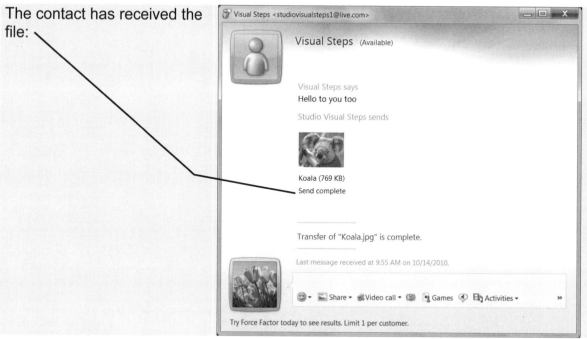

If you and your contact have a webcam, you can conduct a video conversation:

👆 **Click** 📹Video call ▼

👆 **Click** Video call

You can also start a regular call, where you will only be able to hear each other:

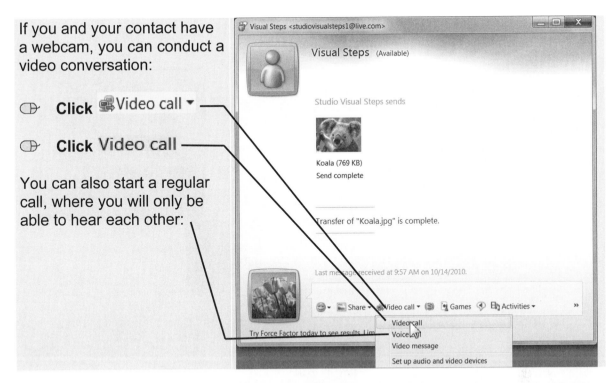

If you both have a working webcam, you will see yourself and your contact:

👆 **Click** Open IM

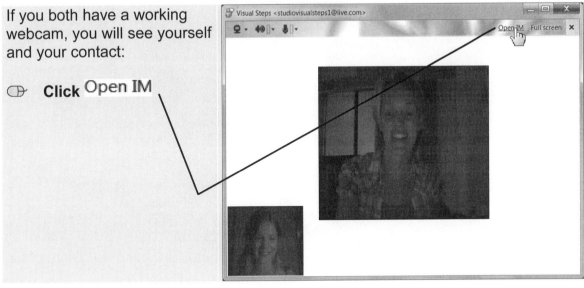

To end the video call:

Click <u>End call</u>

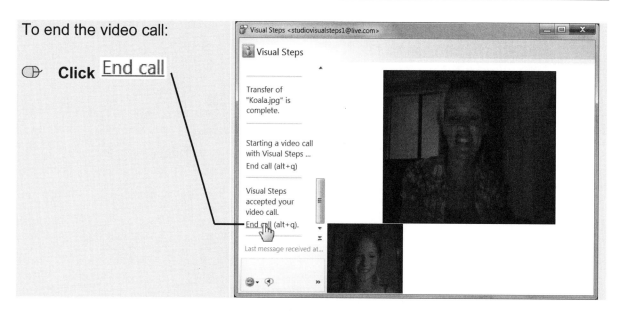

To end the conversation:

Click ▨

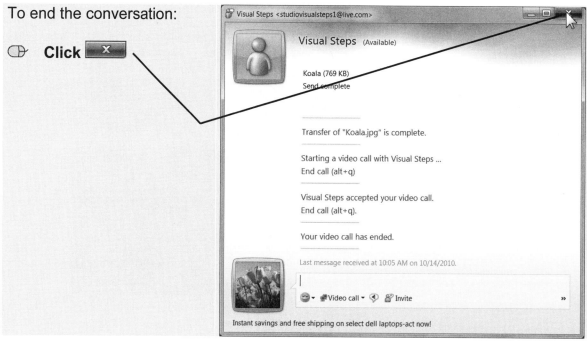

You can save this text conversation by clicking Yes, and ⌈ OK ⌉ :
If you don't want to save the conversation:

☞ **Click the radio button**
◉ **next to**
No, do not save my messac

☞ **Click** ⌈ OK ⌉

Please note: anyone who has access to this computer will have access to your saved conversations.

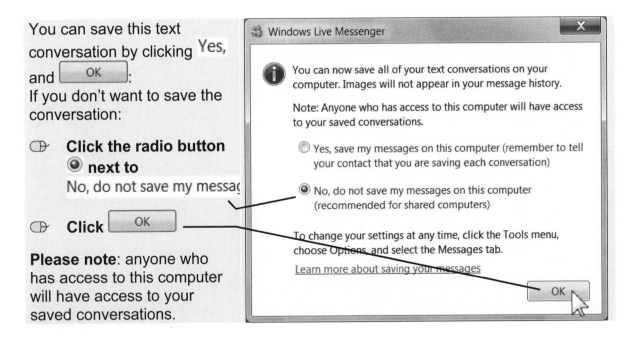

4.5 Modifying the Messenger Settings

You can modify a number of the *Messenger* settings. Use the *Options* window to do this:

☞ **Click**
Studio Visual Steps ▾

Please note: you will see your own account name.

☞ **Click** More options

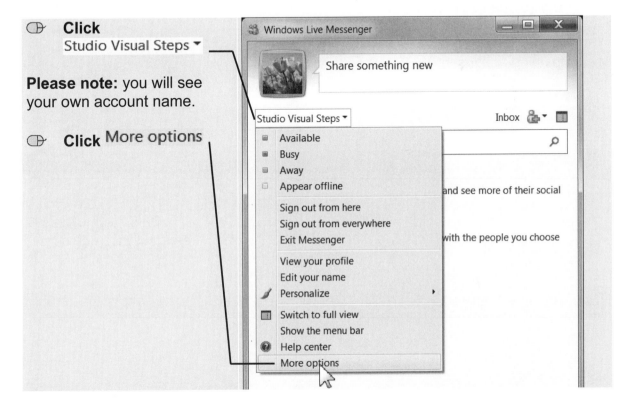

For example, you can change the display name that is displayed to your contacts:

You can change the information in your profile:

You can determine the period of time, before you are shown as 'Away':

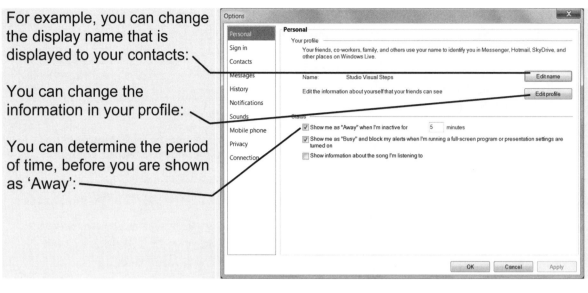

Click Sign In

Here you can determine if you want to automatically run *Messenger* when you log on to *Windows*, for instance:

Here you can also determine whether you want the main window to be opened when *Messenger* signs in:

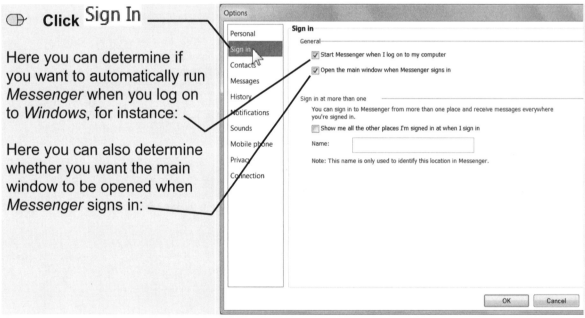

⊕ **Click** History

In this window you can choose to save your conversations, among other things:

You can also determine where the conversations will be stored:

☞ **View the other settings**

To save your settings and close the *Options* window:

⊕ **Click** OK

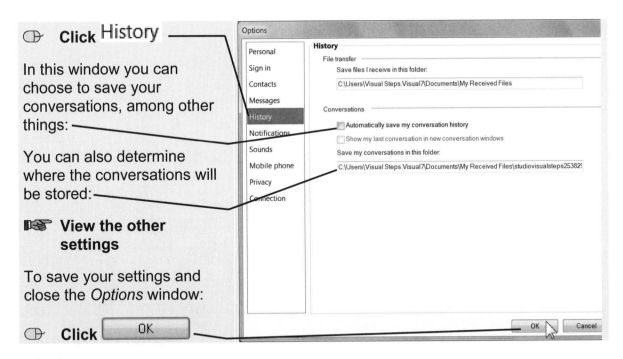

🠶 **Please note:**

Anyone who has access to this computer will have access to your saved conversations.

To sign out with *Messenger*:

⊕ **Click your name**

⊕ **Click** Sign out from here

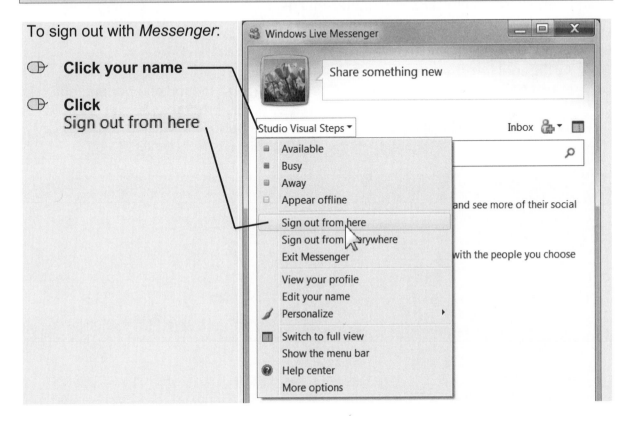

You will see the *Sign in* window of *Messenger*:

 Click X

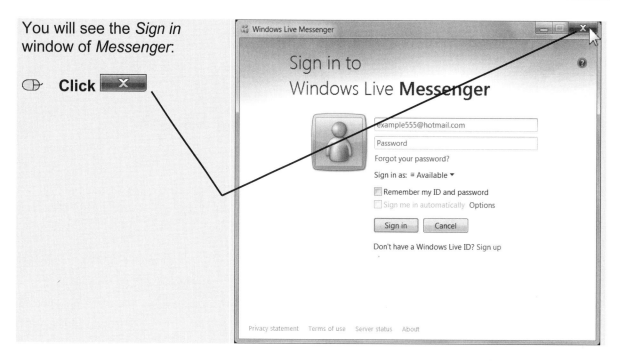

In this chapter you have learned how to sign in with *Messenger* and how to add contacts. Next, we discussed how to chat, and how to use some of the additional features that *Messenger* provides such as video conversations. And lastly, you have learned how to modify some of the settings.

Tip

Additional information
In this chapter you have been introduced to some of the most important features in *Windows Live Messenger*. In the help pages of this program you can find additional information on *Messenger*. You can open these pages by clicking your account name at the top left-hand side of the window and ❓ Help center .

4.6 Background Information

Dictionary	
Chat	Conducting a conversation by typing messages back and forth between two users who are both connected to the Internet.
Contact	A collection of data about a specific person, which contains at least the person's e-mail address. This data will be stored in the *Contact* folder. There are different types of contacts: the contacts you use to communicate with in *Messenger*, *Mail* and *Hotmail*, and the contacts who can view your profile.
Emoticon	Tiny pictures that reflect your mood. You can use these pictures in *Messenger* while chatting.
File	A collective name for everything that is stored on a computer. A file can consist of a program, a text, or a photo, for example.
File type	The way a file is formatted. The file type indicates with which program the file has been created, and which program you can use to open the file.
Install	Copy a program to your computer's hard disk. During this operation all the files will be copied to the correct folder, and the program will be included in the program list.
Nudge	In *Messenger* this is a vibration of the window. You can send a nudge to a contact while you are chatting.
Offline	In this chapter it means that a contact is not signed in with *Messenger* and is therefore not available for a chat session.
Online	In this chapter it means that a contact is signed in with *Messenger*, and is available for a chat session.
Profile	A summary of information about yourself, your interests, activities and contact information, which you can share with others.

- Continue reading on the next page -

Taskbar	Horizontal bar at the bottom of the desktop, where you can view the programs that have been opened, among other things.
Voiceclip	A brief voice recording in *Messenger*, which you can send to a contact.
Windows account	A collection of data which informs *Windows* of the user privileges and access privileges a user has on a specific computer. The user account contains the user name, the password, and a unique account ID.
Windows Live Messenger	This program allows you to chat with other users who have a *Windows Live ID* and who have installed *Messenger*. *Windows Live Messenger* used to be called *MSN Messenger*.
Wink	Short flash clips that you can send to a contact in *Messenger*, and which start playing right away.

Source: Help for Windows Live Essentials, Windows Help and Support, Wikipedia

5. Windows Live Photos

Windows Live Photos offers various features to save, organize, and share your photos with others. You can set up a new photo album and determine who is allowed to see these pictures. Then you can start adding photos to the album. You can send an e-mail link to all your friends and let them know that you have added photos to your album. You will be able to view your own pictures on any computer connected to the Internet. And you can download photos that other people share with you to your own computer.

You can exhibit your pictures as a slide show. You can move or copy your photos to other folders and add comments to them. People in your contact list can also be added to a photo. This is called 'tagging somebody'.

Photos integrates well with other *Windows Live Essentials* products. The photos you store with *Windows Live Photos* are saved in *SkyDrive*, which is the free storage space in *Windows Live Essentials*. Furthermore, you can send a link with *Hotmail*, which will enable the recipient to view the photos online. With *Mobile* you can publish photos from your cell phone to *Photos*, and in *Groups* you can view and add shared photos.

In this chapter we will first explain how to create a new album and determine with whom you want to share this album. Next, we will explain how to add photos to the album. Later we will handle how to send an e-mail link and how to modify your collection. Last of all, we will show you how to delete a photo and how to modify the access rights.

In this chapter you will learn how to:

- create a photo album;
- add photos;
- send an e-mail link;
- edit your collection and modify settings.

 Please note:

To work through this chapter effectively you will need to have a *Windows Live ID*. If you do not yet have a *Windows Live ID,* go to *section 1.2 Create a Windows Live ID* and you can read how to get one.

5.1 Creating a Photo Album

You are going to start with the creation of a photo album. While you are doing this, you can decide who will have access to this album. You can only set access rights that are applicable to an entire album; you cannot set access rights for photos individually.

☞ **Open** *Internet Explorer* ⬮¹

☞ **Open the home.live.com website** ⬮³

☞ **Sign in with your** *Windows Live ID* ⬮⁴

⊕ **Click** Photos

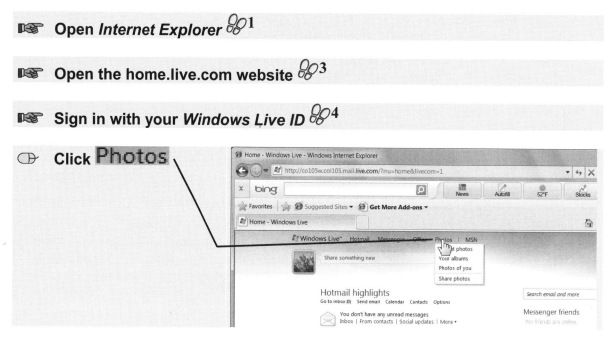

🍂 **Please note:**

In this book we will open all *Windows Live Essentials* products from the *Home Page*. If you want, you can also access *Photos* directly by typing http://photos.live.com in the address bar of your Internet browser.

You see the album that you have send in *Chapter 3 Windows Live Mail*:

⊕ **Click**

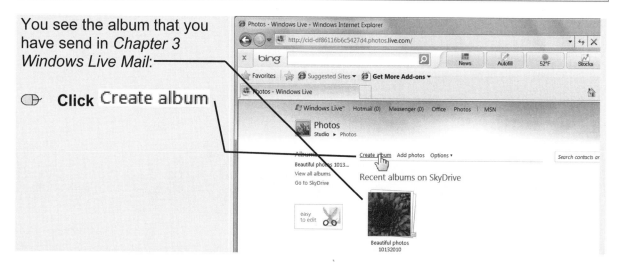

Type a name for the new album ———

⊕ **Click** Change

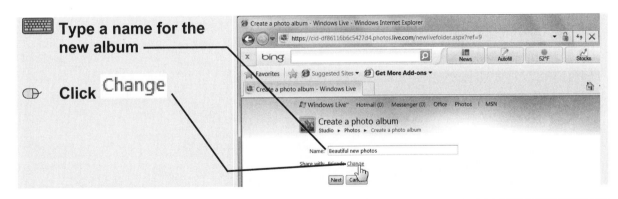

Now you can select the people with whom you want to share this album. You can choose from *everyone, my friends and their friends, friends, some friends,* and *just me*:

In this example we have chosen **Some friends**:

⊕ **Drag the slider** ▭ **to Some friends**

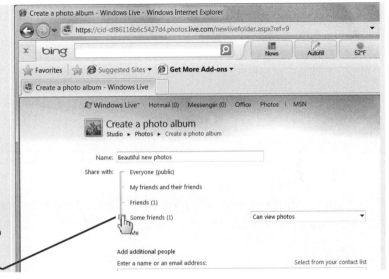

 Tip

Share an album with people who are not in your contact list
You can also share an album with people who are not listed in your contact list:

By Add additional people, **type one or more e-mail addresses** ———

The e-mail addresses have to be separated from each other by a comma or a blank space.

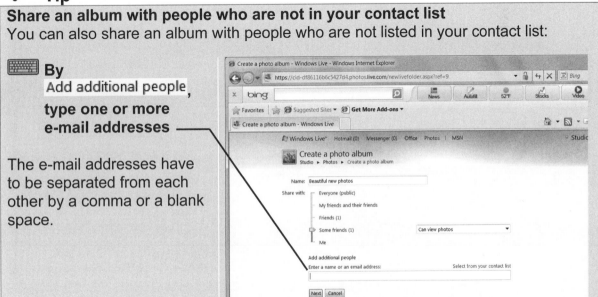

Click Next

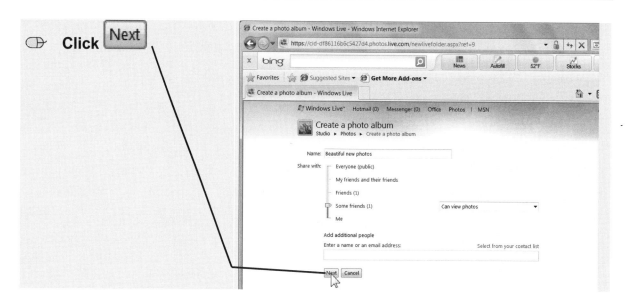

5.2 Adding Photos

Please note:

After you have created a new photo album, you will automatically see the *Add photos* window. When you want to add photos later on, just click the album and then click Add photos.

You can drag photos from a different window to the *Add photos* window. You can also select photos from a folder. In this example we have selected photos from a folder:

Click
select photos from your

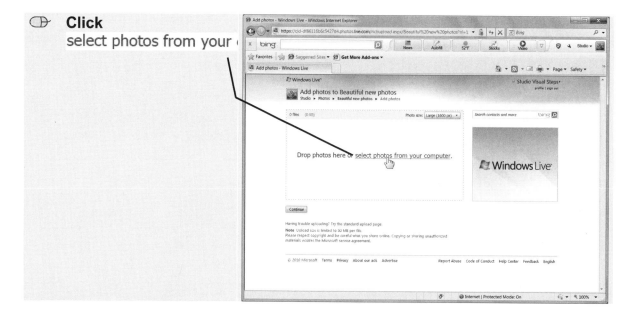

In this example we will use photos from the *Sample Pictures* folder:

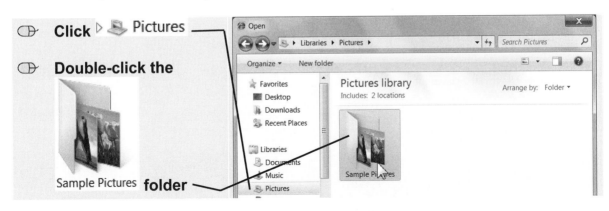

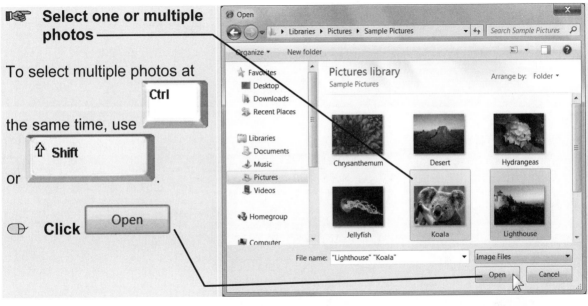

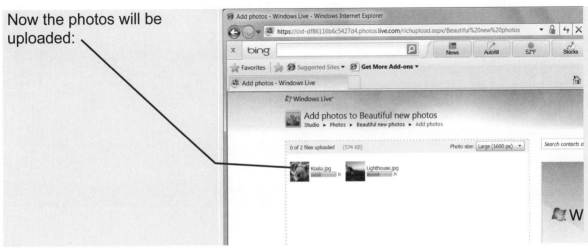

Tip

Determine the size of the pictures

You can select the size of the photos you want to add:

⊕ **Click**

Large (1600 px) ▼

⊕ **Click a size**

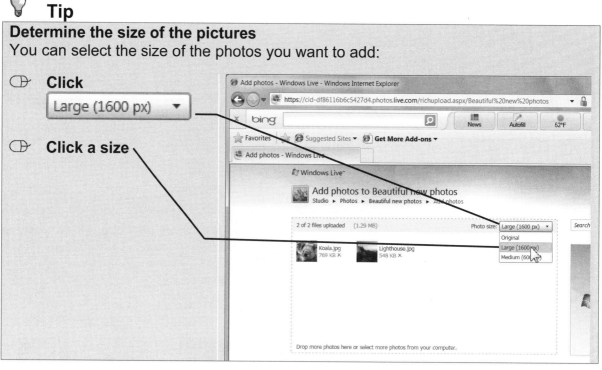

⊕ **Click** Continue

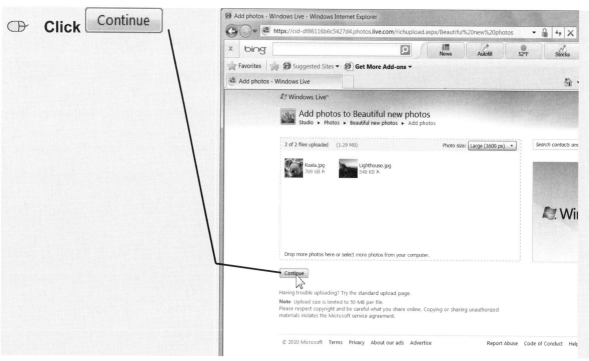

Now the photos have been added to the album:

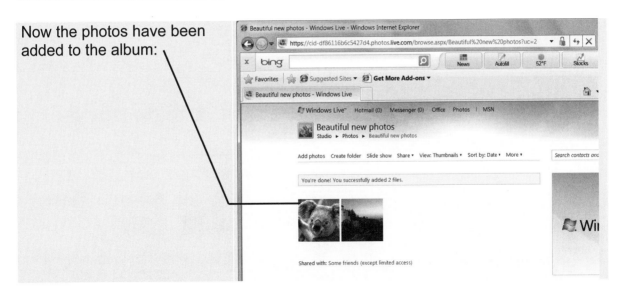

The photos have been stored in *Windows Live SkyDrive.* You can use up to 25 GB of storage space on the *Windows Live Essentials* server. You can read more about *SkyDrive* in *Chapter 12 Windows Live SkyDrive.*
Now you are going to check how much storage space you have left.

Click Photos

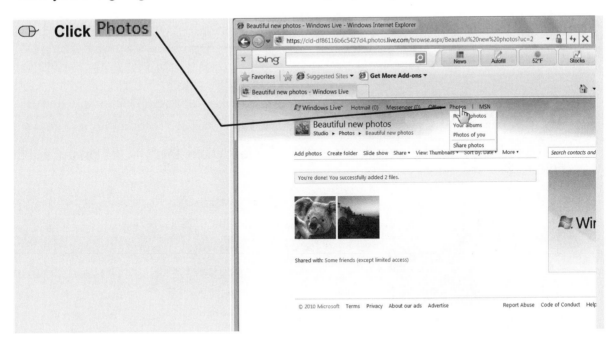

Click Go to SkyDrive

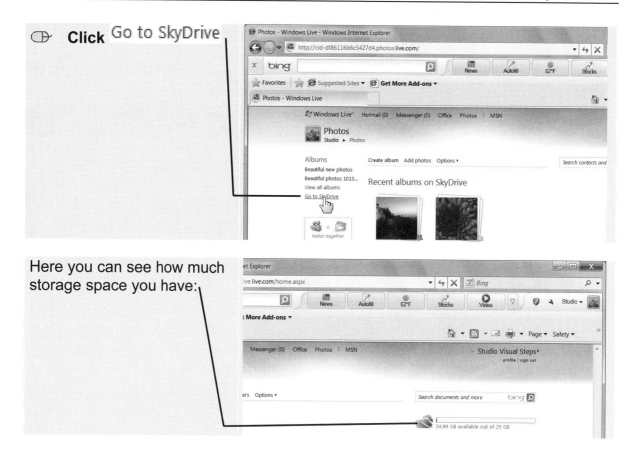

Here you can see how much storage space you have:

5.3 Sending an E-mail Link

You can send a link by e-mail. When the recipient clicks this link, he or she will be able to view the photos online.

Click Beautiful new photos

Click Share ▼

Click Send a link

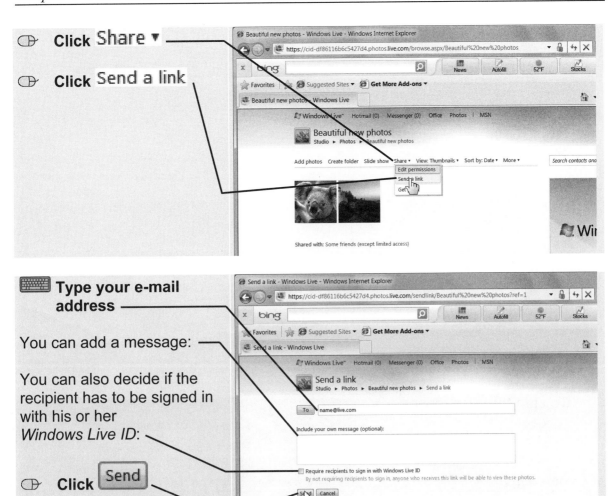

Type your e-mail address

You can add a message:

You can also decide if the recipient has to be signed in with his or her
Windows Live ID:

Click Send

Now you are going to take a look at the e-mail message:

Click Hotmail

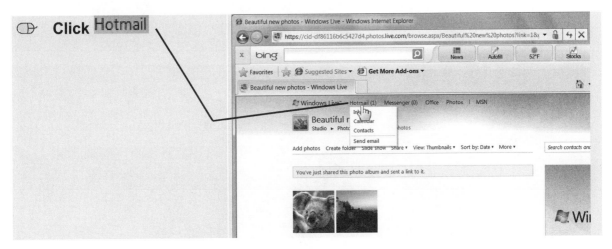

☞ **Open the e-mail message that contains the photo album** ✂10

This e-mail could also be stored in the *Family* or *Junk* folder.

⊕ **Click**

View album

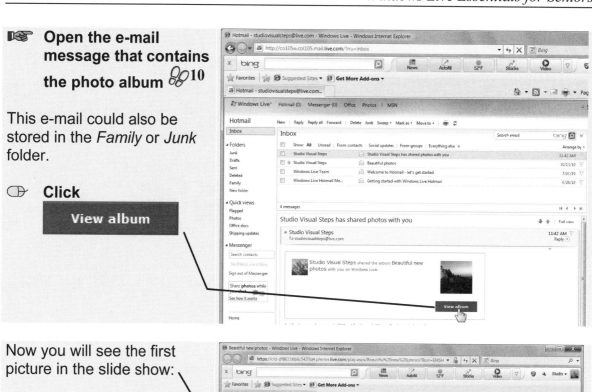

Now you will see the first picture in the slide show:

To start the slide show:

⊕ **Click**

You can also view the slide show on a full screen:

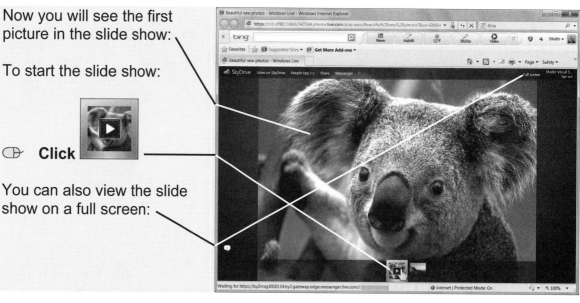

⊕ **Click** SkyDrive

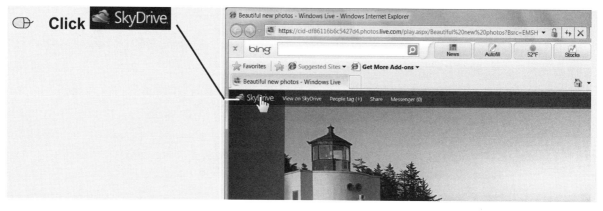

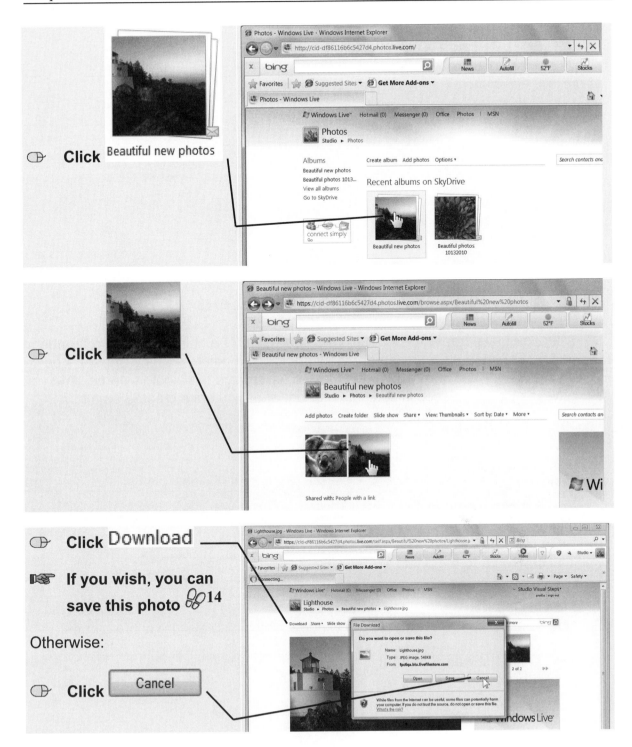

HELP! I see a safety warning

At the top of the window you might see this warning message:

⊕ **Click**

  🖼 To help protect your sec

⊕ **Click** Download File...

In *Internet Explorer 9* you
might see a separate window
with this message.

5.4 Editing Photos and Changing Settings

After you have created a photo album, you will still be able to change a number of
things. For instance, you can add new photos and delete existing photos. You can
also move photos and change their name, or change the album's name. And you can
always modify the access settings later on, after you have created an album.

⊕ **Click** More ▼

You can move a photo:

You can copy a photo to a
different folder: ⸻

You can rename the photo:

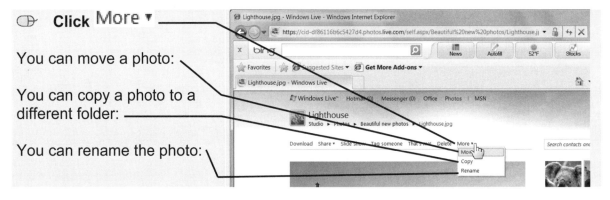

Now you are going to return to the window which displays the entire album:

⊕ **Click the name of your
album**

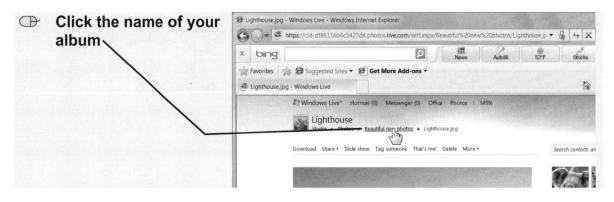

You can add new photos: ——

Within the photo album, you can create a new folder: ——

You can change the photos' display mode: ——

You can sort the photos in a different order: ——

🖰 **Click** More ▾ ——

You can also delete the entire album: ——

You can change the photo album's name: ——

To add a description of the photo album:

🖰 **Click** Properties

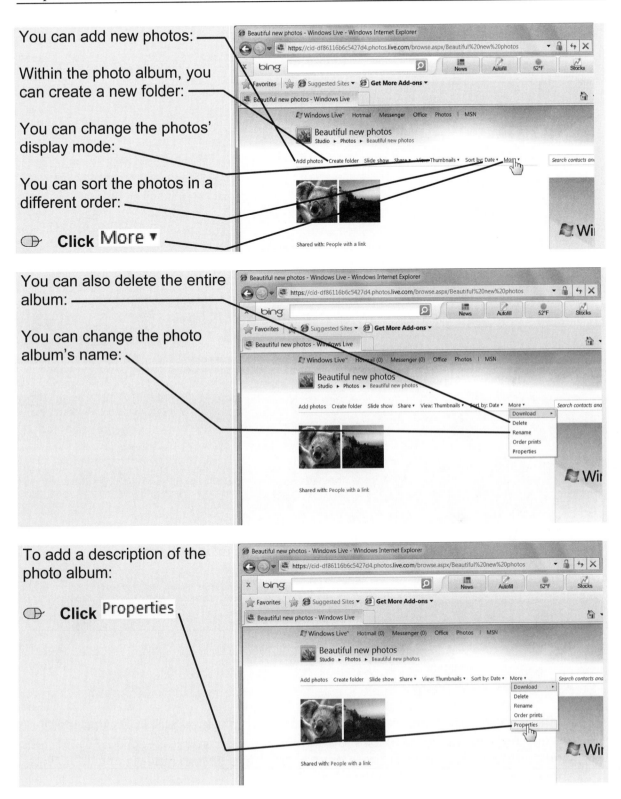

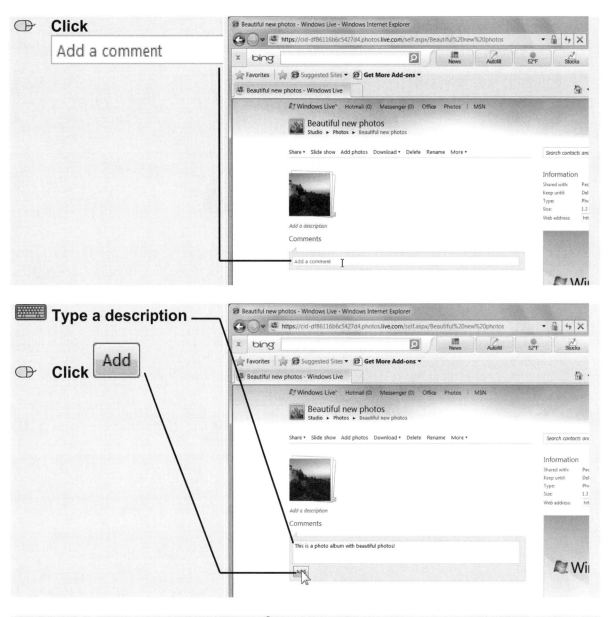

Click

Add a comment

Type a description ———

Click Add

☞ **Sign out with** *Windows Live* ⚹²

☞ **Close all windows** ⚹⁶

In this chapter you have learned how to create a photo album in *Photos*, and how to determine who will have access to this album. Later, you learned how to add photos, and send an e-mail link to others. Finally, we have shown how easy it is in *Photos* to modify your album or even delete it.

5.5 Background Information

Dictionary

Access rights	You can always determine which people are allowed to share your albums in *Windows Live Photos*, by setting the access rights.
Contact	A collection of data about a specific person, which contains at least the person's e-mail address. This data is stored in the *Contact* folder. There are different types of contacts: the contact you can use in *Messenger*, *Mail* and *Hotmail*, and the contacts who can view your profile.
Download	Copy a file from another computer or from the Internet to your own computer.
Link	Also called *hyperlink*. *Link* refers to a connection. It is a navigational tool that lets the user move or 'jump' to a new page of information after clicking the link.
Tag	*Tag* means to attach something to a photo. If you tag somebody, you attach his or her name to a specific photo, so it will be easier to identify the person or persons depicted in the photo.
Upload	Copy a file from your own computer to another computer or to the Internet.
Weblog	Also called Blog. It is a website that is updated on a regular basis and which display the information in reverse chronological order (the most recent message will appear at the top of the list).
Windows Live Photos	An online *Windows Live Essentials* product that allows you to save, organize, and share your photos. The photos you store with *Windows Live Photos*, will be stored in *SkyDrive*, the free storage space offered by *Windows Live Essentials*.

Source: Help for Windows Live Essentials, Windows Help and Support, Wikipedia

5.6 Tips

 Tip

Additional information
In this chapter you have been introduced to the most important features in *Windows Live Photos*. In the help pages of this program you will find additional information about *Photos.* You can open the help pages by clicking **Help Center** .

Tip

Tagging someone
Tagging a photo means that you can indicate who or what is depicted in the photo:

☞ **Click** Tag someone

You can select your own name, or somebody else from your contact list: ——

You can also add a different name: ——

Underneath the photo you can see who is in this picture: ——

To remove the tag:

☞ **Click** ✕

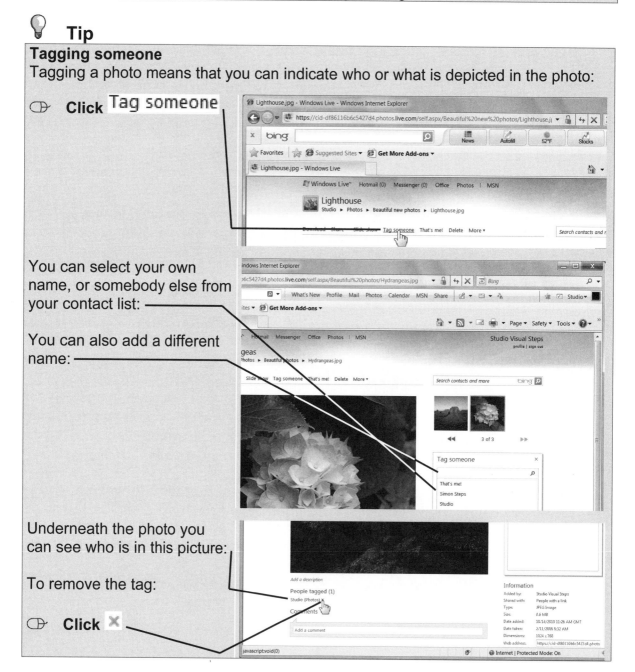

6. Windows Live Photo Gallery

You can use the *Windows Live Photo Gallery* program to organize, edit, and share your photos. All photos that reside in the *My Pictures* folder of your computer will be displayed automatically. You can add new folders, or import photos from an external device, such as a digital camera or scanner. You can also use *Photo Gallery* to organize and share video files, but you cannot edit them. In this chapter we will only discuss photos. But some of the same operations can be done on videos as well.

Photo Gallery offers various options for simple photo editing. For instance, you can remove red eye, adjust the exposure and crop a photo. Other *Photo Gallery* features allow you to view a slide show, burn photos to a CD or DVD, and send photos by e-mail. Furthermore, you can add tags to your photos, which makes it easier to organize and order them. You can also add tags to people to help correctly identify them when they are depicted in your photos.

Photo Gallery integrates well with other *Windows Live Essentials* products. For instance, you can use *Photo Gallery* to publish photos in *Windows Live Photos* and *Groups*. *Photo Gallery* allows you to directly add photos to *Movie Maker*, and to a weblog you have written with *Writer*. *Photo Gallery* is very similar to the *Photo Gallery* program in *Windows Vista*. But the *Vista Photo Gallery* program does not have the same integration with other *Windows Live Essentials* products as *Windows Live Photo Gallery* does.

In this chapter we will first explain how to add photos to *Photo Gallery*. Then we will show you how to work with the photo editing features and how to publish your photos. In the last section, we will take a look at some of the other things you can do with *Photo Gallery*.

In this chapter you will learn how to:

- add photos to *Photo Gallery*;
- edit photos in *Photo Gallery*;
- publish photos with *Photo Gallery*;
- use additional features in *Photo Gallery*.

Please note:

To work through this chapter effectively you will need to have a *Windows Live ID*. If you do not yet have a *Windows Live ID,* go to *section 1.2 Create a Windows Live ID* and you can read how to get one.

Please note:

If you want to be able to execute all the operations in this chapter, you will need to copy the *photos* folder from the website that goes with this book, and save the folder to the *My Documents* folder on your computer's hard drive. In *Appendix A Copy Photos Folder to Your Computer's Hard Drive* you can read how to do this.

6.1 Adding Photos

By default, *Photo Gallery* will display all of the photos in the *My Pictures* folder on your computer. You can add new folders that contain pictures to *Photo Gallery* yourself. You can also import photos from an external device, such as a digital camera or scanner.

☞ **Open** *Windows Live Photo Gallery* ℘8

☞ **Sign in with your** *Windows Live ID* ℘4

🖰 **Click** [Yes]

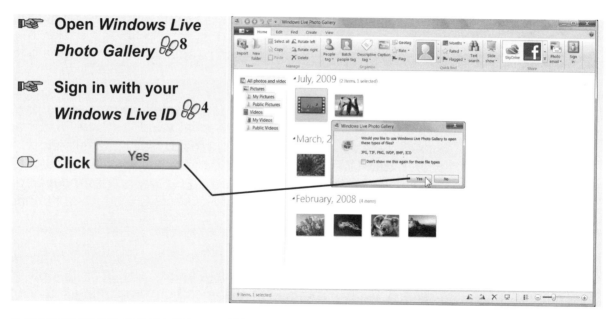

You can add a folder containing pictures to *Photo Gallery*:

🖰 **Click** [▤ ▼]

🖰 **Click** [Include folder]

Click Add...

Now select the folder you want to add:

Click ▷ Documents

In *Windows Vista* you need to click Documents .

Click Photos

Click Include folder

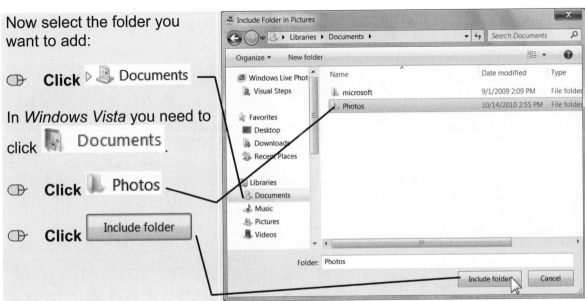

At the bottom of the window:

Click OK

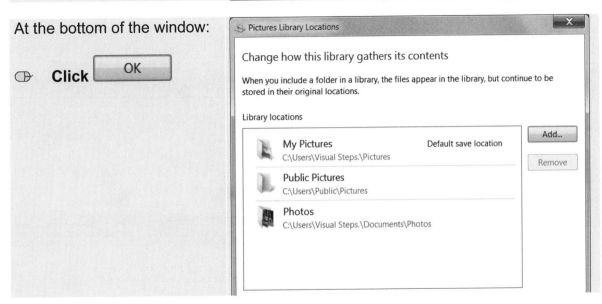

In this window you will see that the folder with pictures has been added:

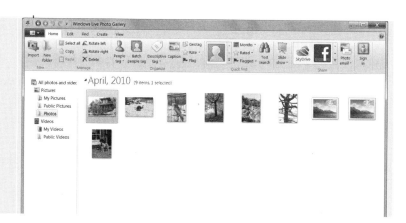

You can also import photos directly from an external device. In this example we will import photos from a memory card.

⊕ **Click** Import

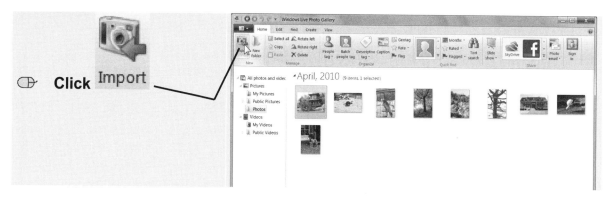

In the popup window, you will see the external device:

If you see more than one device, then click the one you want to use.

⊕ **Click** Import

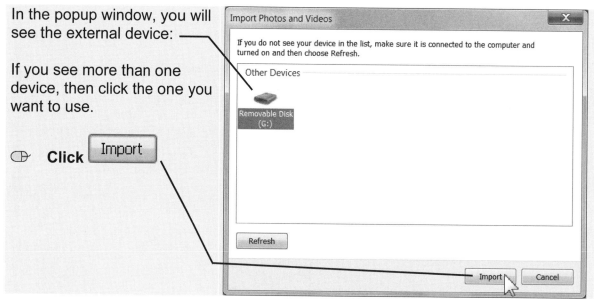

Now you can select the
photos you want: ——————

In this example we are going
to import all photos: ——————

⌨ **Type a name for the
photos** ——————

☞ **Click** Import ——————

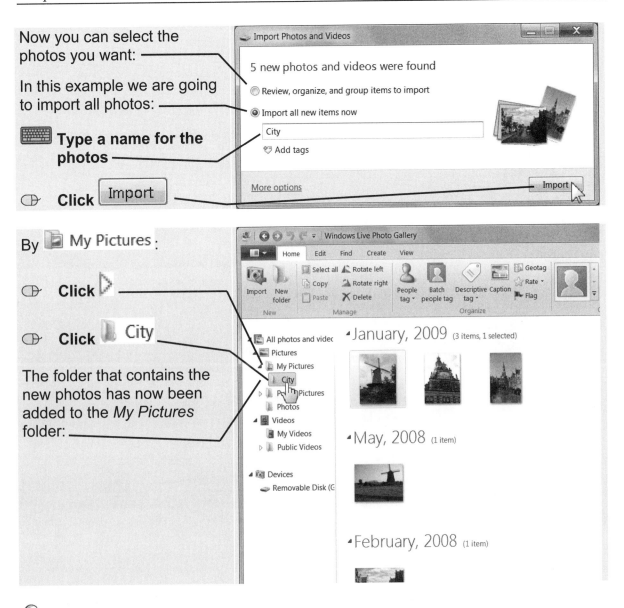

By 📁 My Pictures :

☞ **Click** ▷ ——————

☞ **Click** 📁 City ——————

The folder that contains the
new photos has now been
added to the *My Pictures*
folder: ——————

💡 **Tip**

Import to a different folder
The photos you import from an external device, will be stored in the *My Pictures*
folder. You can always choose on another location if you prefer:

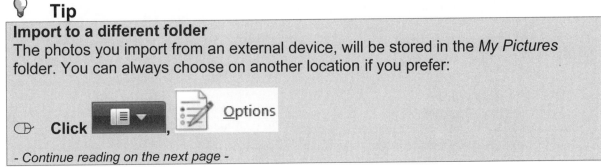

☞ **Click** 📋▾ , 📝 Options

- Continue reading on the next page -

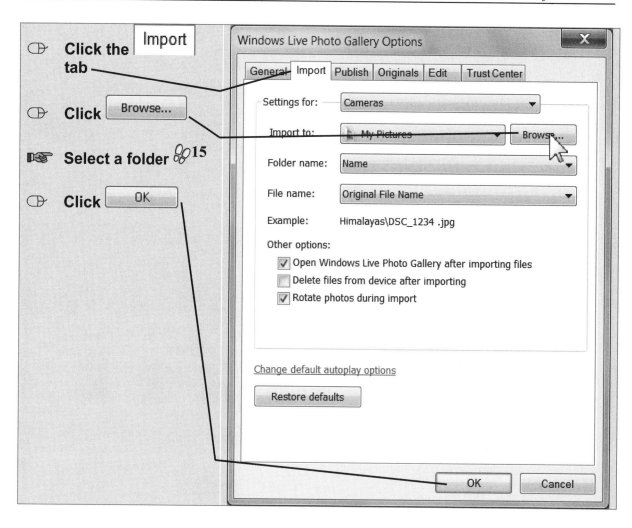

6.2 Editing Photos

Photo Gallery offers a few simple options for editing your photos. These include red eye removal, adjusting the exposure and cropping.

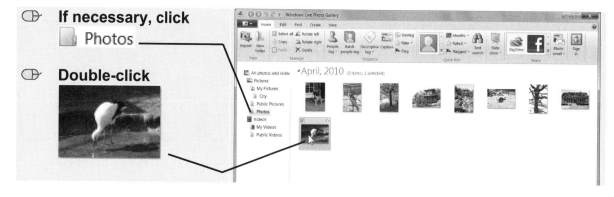

HELP! I cannot edit the photo

The photo file that you are working on may have been saved as a *read-only* file. It is also possible that *Photo Gallery* does not support the file format of a particular photo. You still can edit these photos if you do the following:

To remove the *read-only* attribute:

☞ **Right-click the photo**

☞ **Click** Properties

You will see this window:

☞ **Click the** General **tab**

☞ **Uncheck the box** ☑ **next to** Read-only

At the bottom of the window:

☞ **Click** OK

To change the file type:

☞ **Click** Make a copy

It is recommended that you select the JPG file type.

You will now be able to edit the copy.

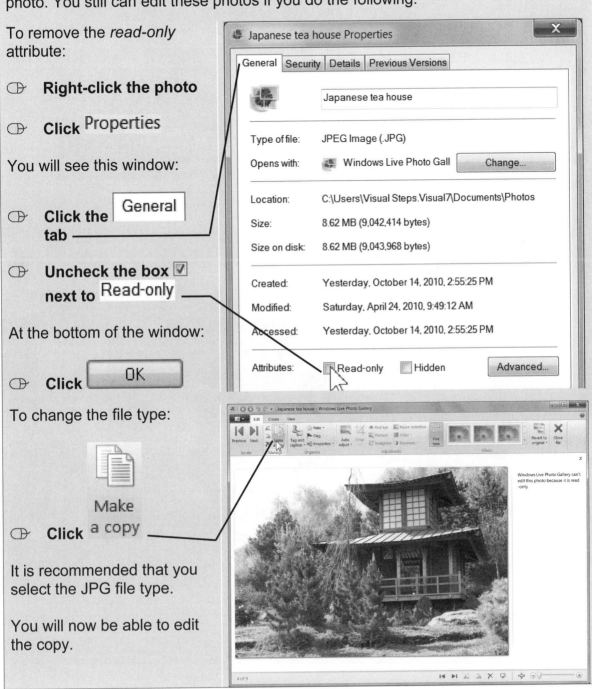

On the ribbon and to the right of your window and you will see the editing options that are available: ——

In the bottom of the window you will see various buttons you can use for rotating a photo:

In this exercise you are going to crop the photo:

By 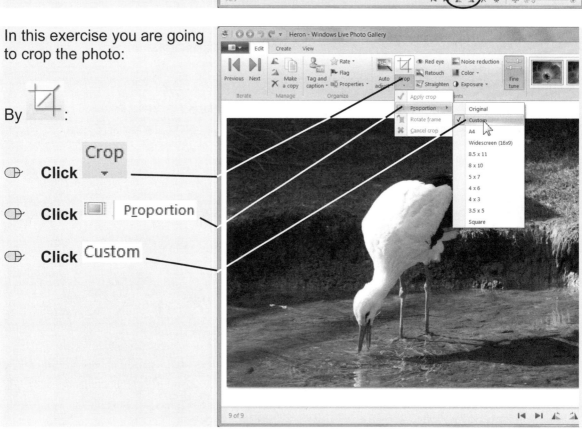 :

🖱 **Click** Crop ▾ ————

🖱 **Click** 🖼 Proportion

🖱 **Click** Custom

Usually, you will still need to adjust the picture manually. This is how you do that:

☞ **Place the mouse pointer in the bottom right corner** ——

The pointer will turn into ⬊:

☞ **Drag the bottom of the frame outwards diagonally** ——

You are trying to place the heron inside the frame:

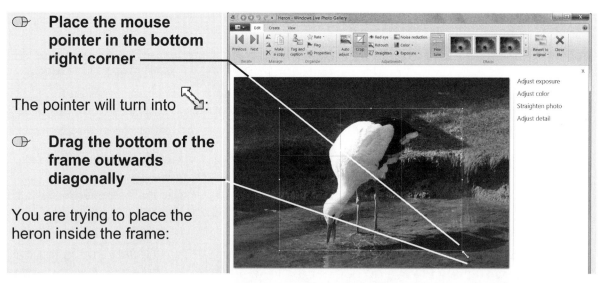

By :

☞ **Click** **Crop** ▾ ——

☞ **Click** ✓ Apply crop

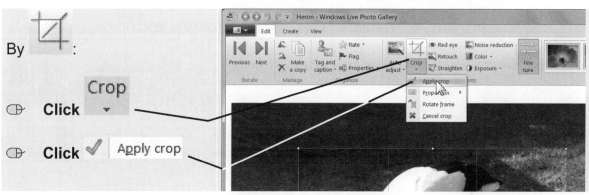

☞ **Click** ✖ Close file ——

Click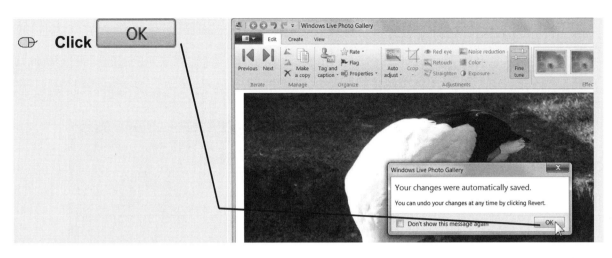

Please note:

The edited photo has now been saved. Fortunately, *Photo Gallery* keeps the original photo, so you can always go back at a later time to undo any edits you have made.

Now you are going to revert to the original version of the photo:

Double-click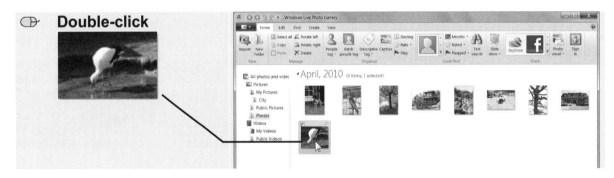

Click

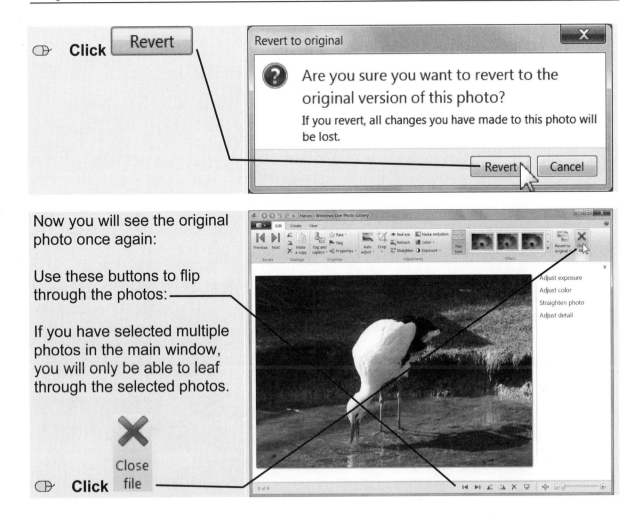

☞ **Click** Revert

Now you will see the original photo once again:

Use these buttons to flip through the photos:

If you have selected multiple photos in the main window, you will only be able to leaf through the selected photos.

☞ **Click** Close file

6.3 Publishing Photos

You can use *Photo Gallery* to publish photos in *Photos* and *Groups*. In this section we will show you how to publish photos in *Windows Live Photos*. However, you will need to be signed in with a *Windows Live ID* in order to do this.

The first step in publishing is to select the desired photos:

☞ **Select the photo(s) you want to publish** 𝒫𝒫5

☞ **Click** SkyDrive

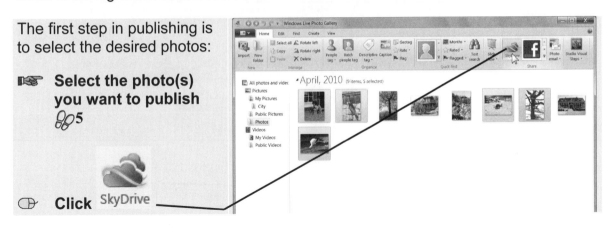

HELP! I am no longer signed in

This is how you sign in with *Windows Live Photo Gallery*:

In the upper right corner of the window:

☞ **Click Sign in**

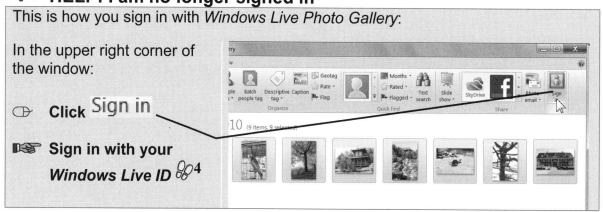

☞ **Sign in with your Windows Live ID** ∞⁴

You can add the photos to an existing album:——————

In this example we will create a new album:

⌨ **Type a name** ——————

You can determine the size of the photos: ——

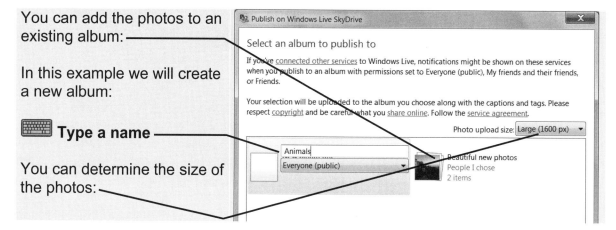

Next you can determine who is allowed to view the photos:

☞ **Click**
Everyone (public)

☞ **Click an option** ——

☞ **Click Publish**

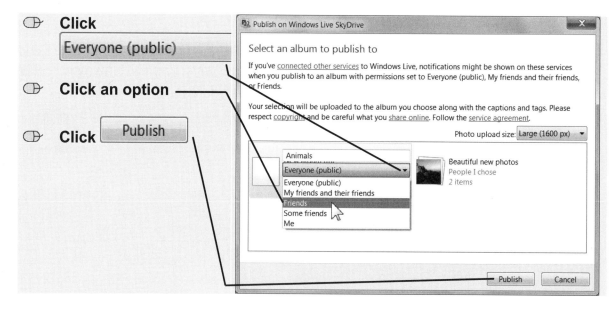

Now the photos will be published. Depending on the number of photos in your selection, this may take a little time.

You can view the album in *Windows Live Photos* by clicking View album :

☞ **Click** Close

6.4 More Photo Gallery Features

In the previous sections you have learned how to edit and publish your photos. *Photo Gallery* offers a few more interesting options.

☞ **Click a photo**

☞ **Click the** Edit **tab**

You can delete photos:

You can rename photos:

You can resize photos:

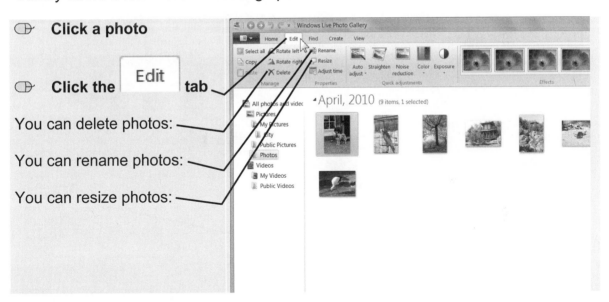

 Please note:

If you delete photos, these photos will not only be deleted from *Photo Gallery*, but also from your computer!

Tip

Delete folders

You can however delete a folder from *Photo Gallery*, without deleting this folder from your computer:

☞ **Right-click the folder**

☞ **Click**
Remove from the gallery

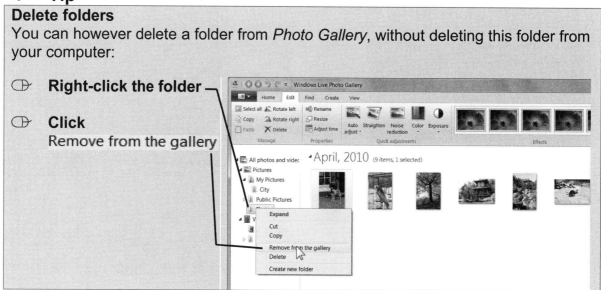

☞ **Click the** Home **tab**

☞ **Click** Caption

In this window you can add and edit information regarding the selected photo:

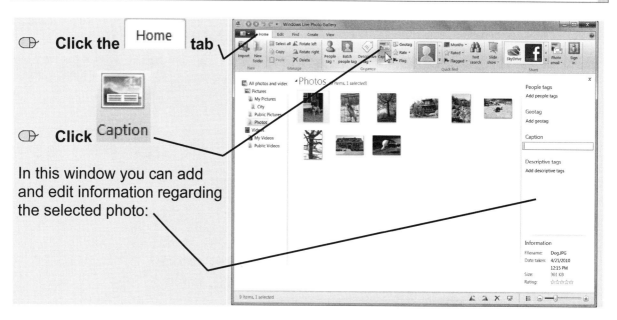

Among other things, you can add *People tags* and *Descriptive tags*. With *People tags* you can add the names of the people that are depicted in the picture. *Descriptive tags* are keywords which will help you organize your photos more easily.

☞ **Click** Add people tags

You can add a new name:

You can also select a name from your contact list. Your contacts will only be displayed if you have signed in with *Windows Live Essentials*.

To close the information window:

☞ **Click** ☒

You can view a slide show:

You can send an e-mail with one or more pictures:

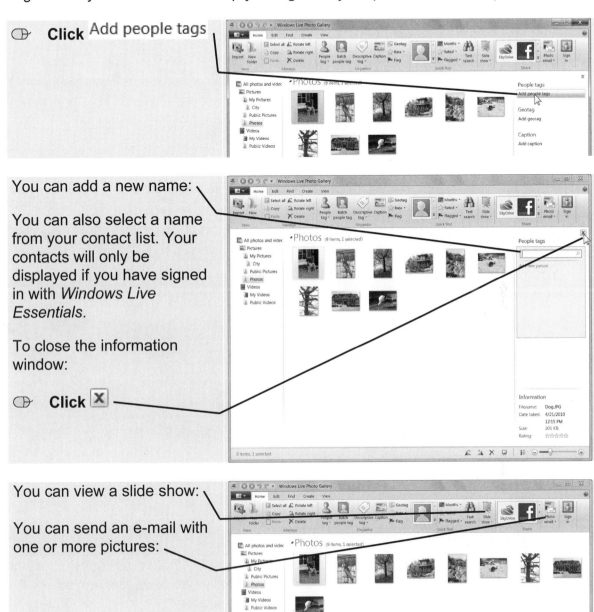

☞ **Click the** **Create** **tab**

You can add photos to a blog:

You can add photos to *Movie Maker.*

☞ **Click**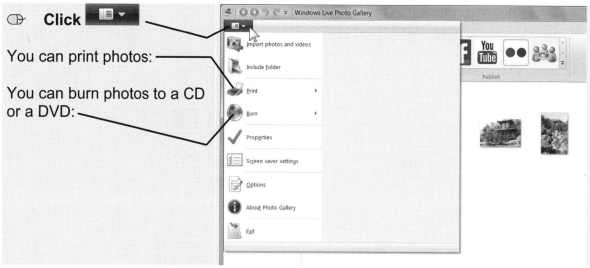

You can print photos:

You can burn photos to a CD or a DVD:

☞ Sign out with *Windows Live* 🐾²

☞ Close *Windows Live Photo Gallery* 🐾⁶

In this chapter you have learned how to add photos to *Photo Gallery*. Next, we have explained how to edit and publish photos. And finally, we have shown you some of the additional features that are available in *Photo Gallery*.

💡 **Tip**

Addition information
In this chapter you have been introduced to the basic features in *Windows Live Photo Gallery*. In the help pages of this program you will find additional information about *Photo Gallery*. You can open these help pages by clicking .

6.5 Background Information

Dictionary	
File type	The formatting of a file. The file type indicates the program with which the file was created and which program you can use to open it.
Publish	In *Photo Gallery* this means that you are displaying your photos on the Internet.
Tag	A tag is a kind of label. In *Photo Gallery* you can add *People tags* and *Descriptive tags* to photos.
Windows Live Photo Gallery	With *Windows Live Photo Gallery* you can organize, edit, and share photos. Also, you can import photos from an external device to *Photo Gallery*.
Wizard	A part of a computer program that helps the user execute a specific task. The user receives step-by-step instructions for modifying certain settings and receives information on the progress of the task.

Source: Help for Windows Live Essentials, Windows Help and Support, Wikipedia

Learn More
In this chapter you have learned about the main features of *Photo Gallery*. In the book **Digital Photo and Video Editing for Seniors** (ISBN 978 90 5905 167 6) however you will learn much more about the extensive options and functions of this program. This book will be available in spring 2011.
You can find more information about the Visual Steps books at
www.visualsteps.com

6.6 Tips

💡 Tip

Arranging and grouping
You can order and group your photos in the following ways:

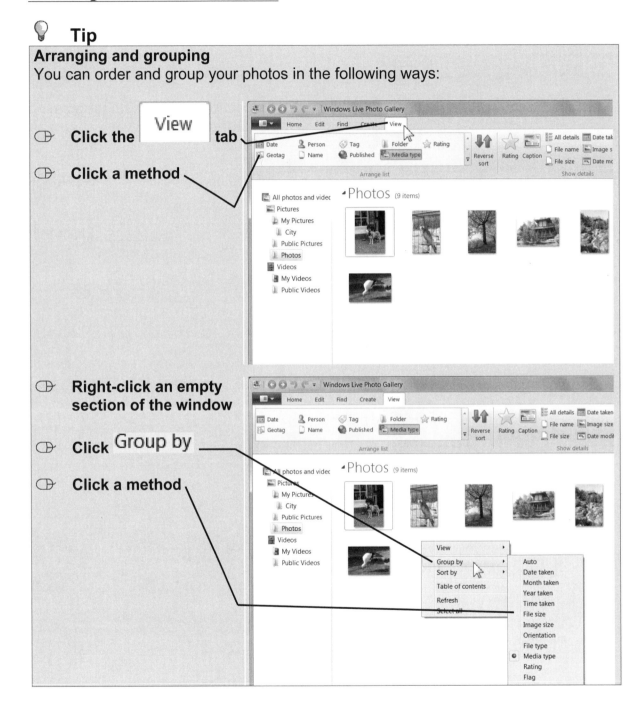

☞ **Click the** View **tab**

☞ **Click a method**

☞ **Right-click an empty section of the window**

☞ **Click** Group by

☞ **Click a method**

7. Windows Live Movie Maker

You can use the *Windows Live Movie Maker* program to easily create a movie of your photos and videos. You can enhance your movie any way you like by adding a soundtrack, visual effects, or text. You can store the movie on your computer, or you can publish your movie online.

Movie Maker also integrates well with other *Windows Live Essentials* products. For instance, you can add photos and videos from *Photo Gallery* to *Movie Maker*. If you save the movie as a movie file, you can send this movie to somebody else with *Messenger* or *Hotmail*, or you can store the movie in *SkyDrive*. *Windows Live Movie Maker* looks very similar to the *Movie Maker* program that comes with *Windows Vista*. But the *Vista Movie Maker* program does not have the same integration with other *Windows Live Essentials* products as *Windows Live Movie Maker* does.

In this chapter we will first explain how to add photo, video, and audio files to *Movie Maker*. Next, you will learn how to edit and save a movie, and finally you will learn how to publish it on the Internet.

In this chapter you will learn how to:

- add photo, video, and audio files;
- edit a movie;
- save a movie;
- publish a movie.

 Please note:

If you want to publish a movie you will need to have a *Windows Live ID*. If you do not yet have a *Windows Live ID,* go to *section 1.2 Create a Windows Live ID* and you can read how to get one.

7.1 Adding Photo, Video, and Audio Files

In *Movie Maker*, you start by adding photos and/or videos.

☞ **Open** *Windows Live Movie Maker* 👣8

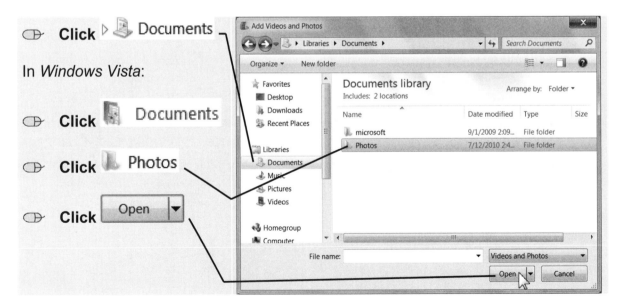

☞ **Click** and photos / Add videos

In this example we have selected the images from the *Photos* folder in the *Documents* folder.

☞ **Click** ▷ 💻 Documents

In *Windows Vista*:

☞ **Click** 📁 Documents

☞ **Click** 📁 Photos

☞ **Click** Open ▼

☞ **Click one or more photos**

To select multiple photos at once, use the **Ctrl** or **⇧ Shift** keys.

☞ **Click** Open ▾

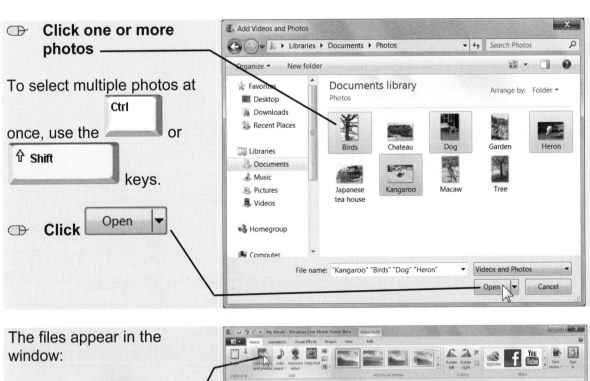

The files appear in the window:

☞ **Click** Add videos and photos

☞ **Click** 🖳 Videos

☞ **Double-click** Sample Videos

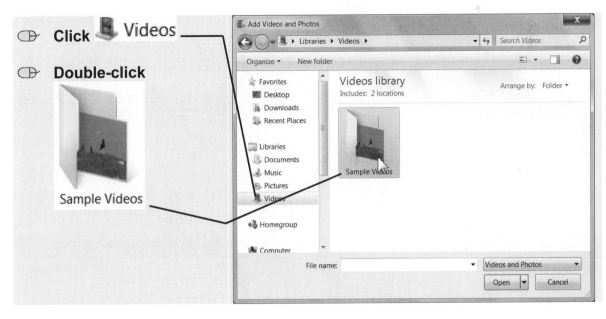

☞ **Click one or more
video files**

In this example we have
selected the *Wildlife* video
from the *Sample videos* folder
in *Windows 7*:

☞ **Click** Open ▼

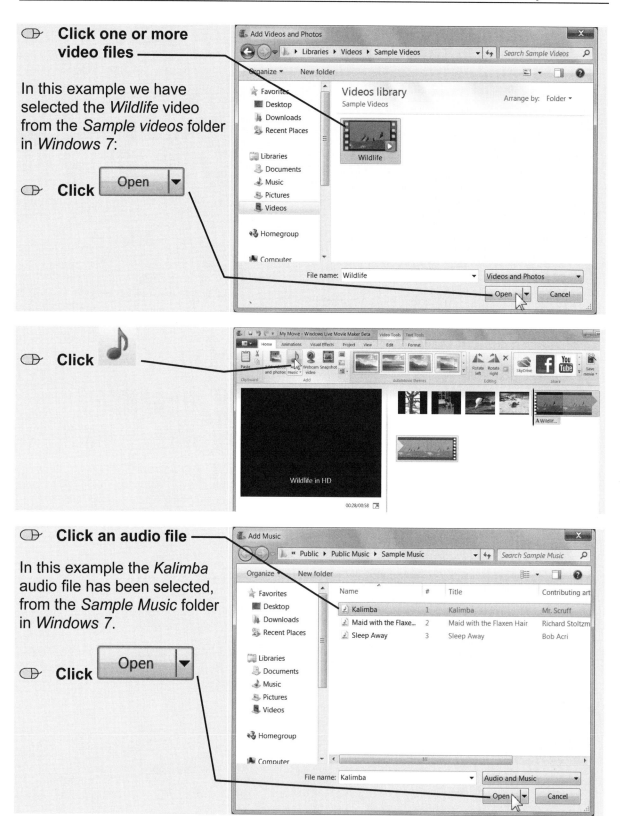

☞ **Click** ♪

☞ **Click an audio file**

In this example the *Kalimba*
audio file has been selected,
from the *Sample Music* folder
in *Windows 7*.

☞ **Click** Open ▼

Now the audio file appears in the window:

All of the files you have just added are shown here in the *Windows Live Movie Maker* window:

File types
You can add the following file types to *Movie Maker*:

Video file types	**File extensions**
Windows Media Video	.WMV
Windows Media file	.ASF and .WM
DV-AVI file	.AVI
Microsoft recording of a TV program	.DVR-MS
MPEG1 movie files	.M1V
MPEG2 movie file	.MPEG, .MPG, .MPE, .M1V, .MP2, .MPV2, .MOD, or .VOB
MPEG4 movie files	.MP4, .MOV,.M4V, .3GP, .3G2, and .K3G
Motion JPEG files	.AVI and .MOV

Photo file types	**File extensions**
Joint Photographic Experts Group	.JPG and .JPEG
Tagged Image File Format	.TIF and .TIFF
Graphics Interchange Format	.GIF
Bitmap	.BMP
Portable Network Graphics	.PNG
HD Photo	.WDP

Audio file types	**File extensions**
Windows Media Audio file	.ASF, .WM and .WMA
Pulse-code Modulation file	.AIF, .AIFF, and .WAV
Advanced Audio Coding file	.M4A
MP3 audio file	.MP3

7.2 Editing Movies

By adding files and joining them in one folder, you have already made a kind of (simple) movie. Now you can start editing the movie by adding transitions, effects, and text.

Click the

Visual Effects tab

Click the third photo

Click

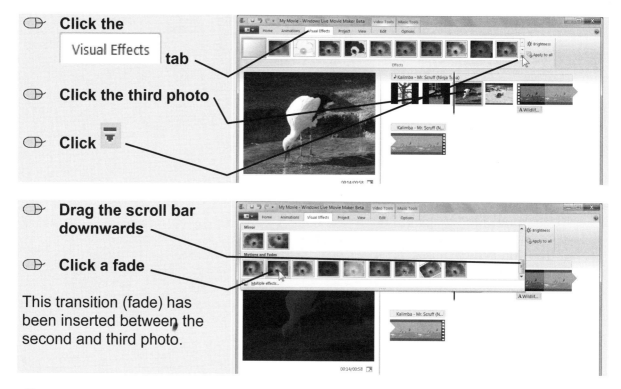

Drag the scroll bar downwards

Click a fade

This transition (fade) has been inserted between the second and third photo.

 Tip

Use the same fade between all the photos
If you want to insert the same fade for all the photos, first select all the photos, and then you can select the type of fade you want to use.

Click a photo

Click an effect type

Now the effect will be applied to the photo:

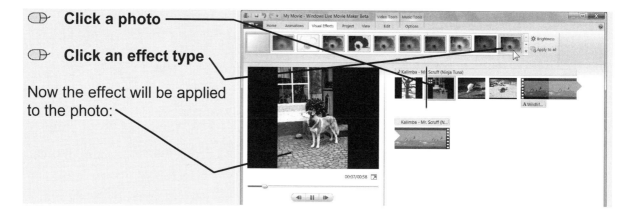

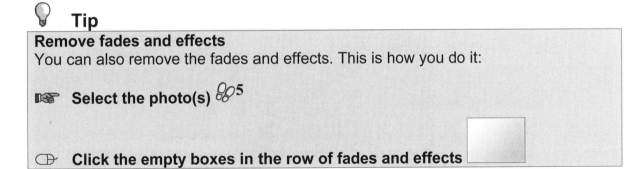

☺ Tip

Remove fades and effects
You can also remove the fades and effects. This is how you do it:

☞ **Select the photo(s)** 5

☞ **Click the empty boxes in the row of fades and effects**

➥ Please note:

If you edit photos and videos in *Windows Live Movie Maker*, the original files will not be affected. These files will remain stored on your computer.

☞ **Click the** Edit **tab**

You can adjust the duration of the photos:

☞ **Click a video**

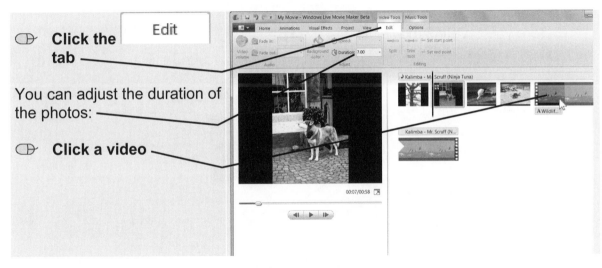

You can hide or cut the beginning or the end of a video:

You can adjust the volume of the video:

Here you see that the title has automatically been added to the movie:

☞ **Click the** Format **tab**

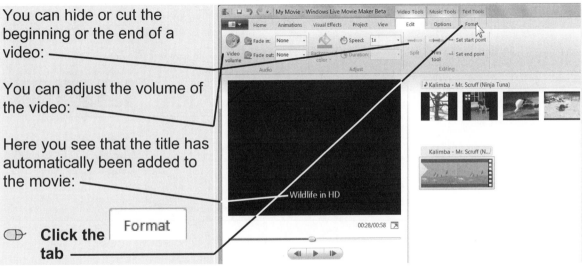

Now you can edit the text:

You can change the duration of the text:

You can also add an effect to the text:

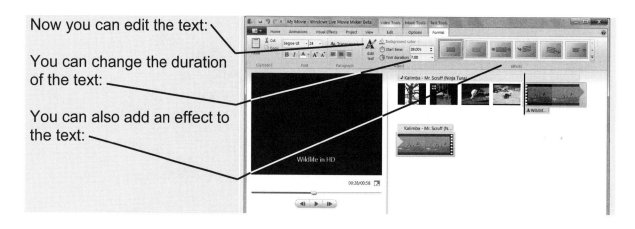

7.3 Saving a Movie

Before you save the movie, it is a good idea to take a look at it first:

- Click the first photo

- Click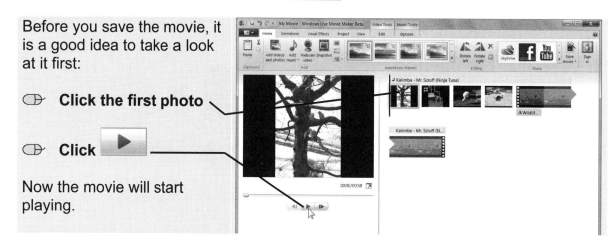

Now the movie will start playing.

To save the movie:

- Click

- Click   Save project

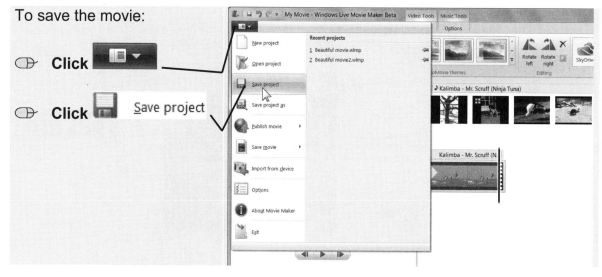

Type a file name

Click Save

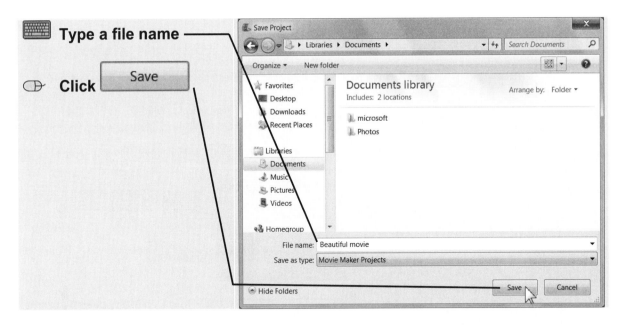

Now the movie has been saved as a *Movie Maker project* with the file extension .WMLP. You can only view and edit this file in *Windows Live Movie Maker*.

You can also save the movie as a single video file, with the .WMV file extension. This video file can then be viewed in a media player, such as *Windows Media Player*. But once you give the file this extension, it is no longer editable in *Windows Live Movie Maker*.

If necessary, click the

Home **tab**

Click

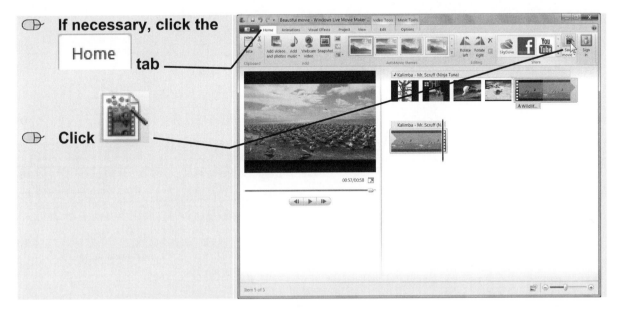

Tip

Smaller size

You can save the video file with a smaller file size, in order to play this file on a mobile media device:

At 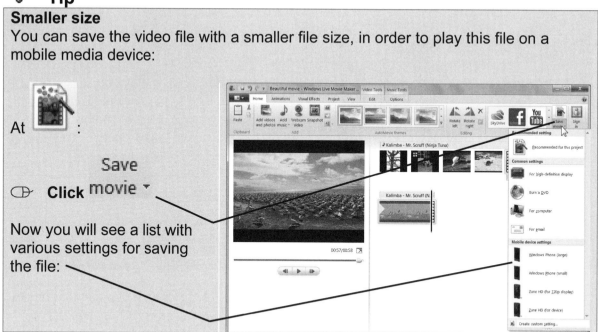 :

⊂⊐ **Click** Save movie ▾

Now you will see a list with various settings for saving the file:

⌨ **Type a different file name, if you wish**

Here you can see where the movie will be stored:

⊂⊐ **Click** Save

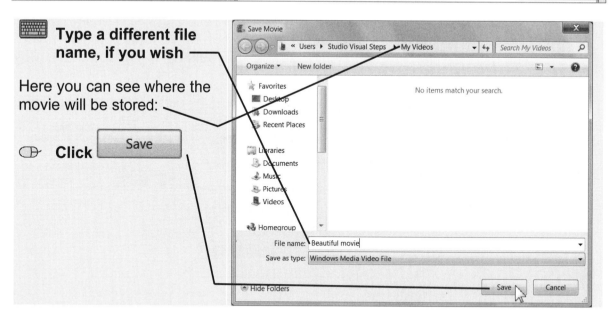

Now the movie will be compiled. This may take a while. When the movie is done, you will see this window:

⊂⊐ **Click** Close

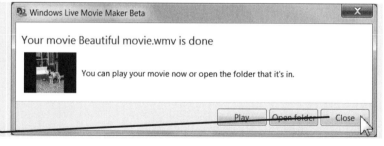

7.4 Publishing Movies

You can share your movie with others by publishing the movie on *YouTube*. This is a website where anybody can publish his or her movies. After you have published your movie, you can send your friends an e-mail which contains a link to the video on *YouTube*.

Click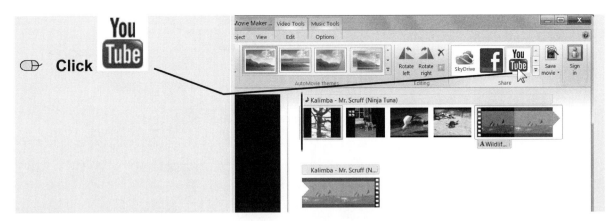

Choose the resolution for your movie. In this example we have chosen the recommended resolution:

Click

➜ 960 x 720 (recommende

Estimated size: 37.04 MB

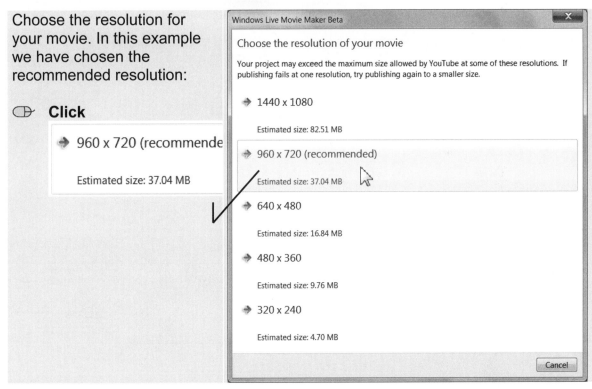

Choose the resolution of your movie

Your project may exceed the maximum size allowed by YouTube at some of these resolutions. If publishing fails at one resolution, try publishing again to a smaller size.

➜ 1440 x 1080

Estimated size: 82.51 MB

➜ 960 x 720 (recommended)

Estimated size: 37.04 MB

➜ 640 x 480

Estimated size: 16.84 MB

➜ 480 x 360

Estimated size: 9.76 MB

➜ 320 x 240

Estimated size: 4.70 MB

Cancel

☞ **Sign in with your *Windows Live ID*** ✂️4

To publish a movie on *YouTube*, you will need to create a *YouTube* account.

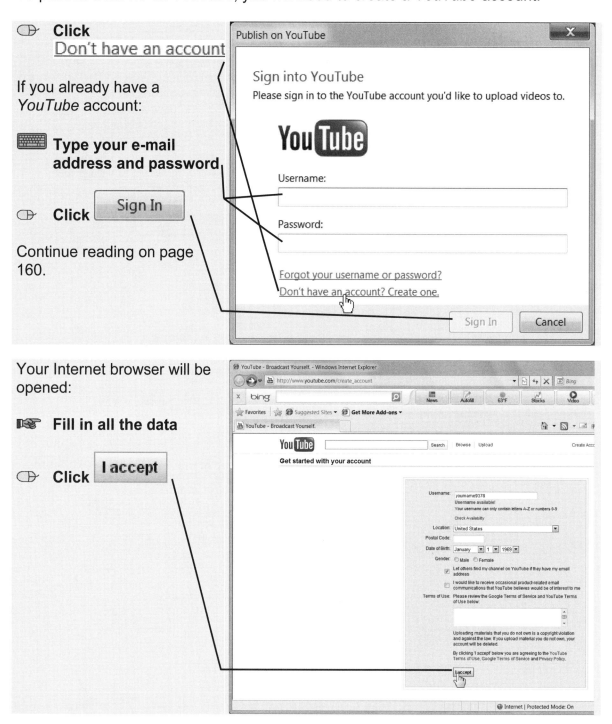

⊕ **Click**
Don't have an account

If you already have a
YouTube account:

⌨ **Type your e-mail
address and password**

⊕ **Click** | Sign In |

Continue reading on page
160.

Your Internet browser will be
opened:

☞ **Fill in all the data**

⊕ **Click** | I accept |

If you have a *Google* account:

Type your e-mail address and password

Click **Sign in**

If you do not have a *Google* account. At the right-hand side of the window:

☞ **Fill in all the data**

Click **Create my new accou...**

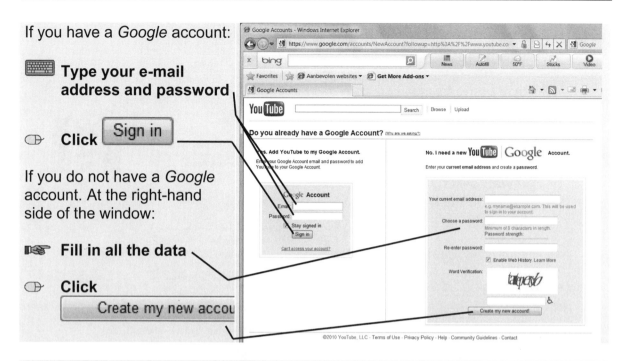

☞ **Close *Internet Explorer*** ✂6

Type your e-mail address and password

Click **Sign In**

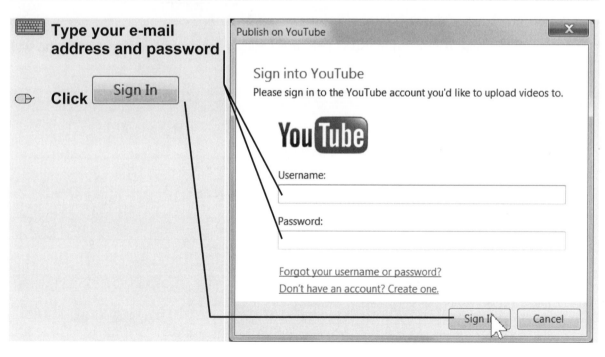

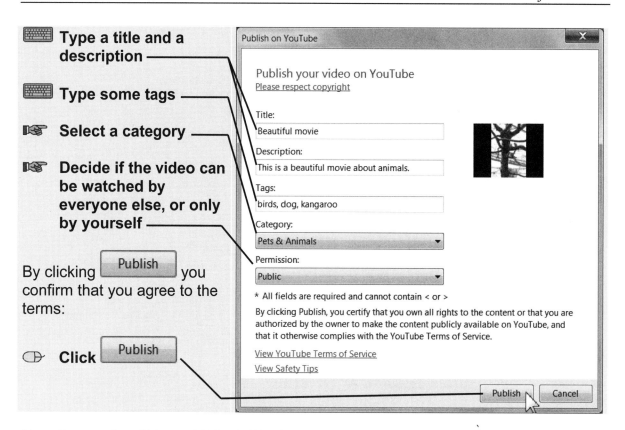

Type a title and a description

Type some tags

☞ **Select a category**

☞ **Decide if the video can be watched by everyone else, or only by yourself**

By clicking Publish you confirm that you agree to the terms:

⊙ **Click** Publish

Now the movie will be published. This may take a little while. Afterwards, you will see the following window:

⊙ **Click** Watch online

The *Internet Explorer* window will be opened:

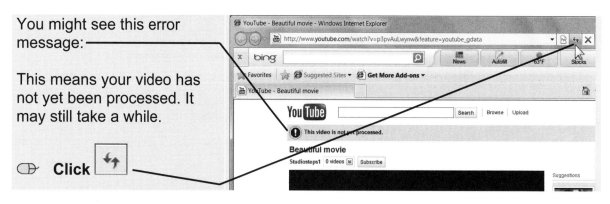

You might see this error message:

This means your video has not yet been processed. It may still take a while.

⊙ **Click** ⟳

If *YouTube* has finished
processing your video, the
movie will be played at once:

You can also send the movie to someone else, by e-mail:

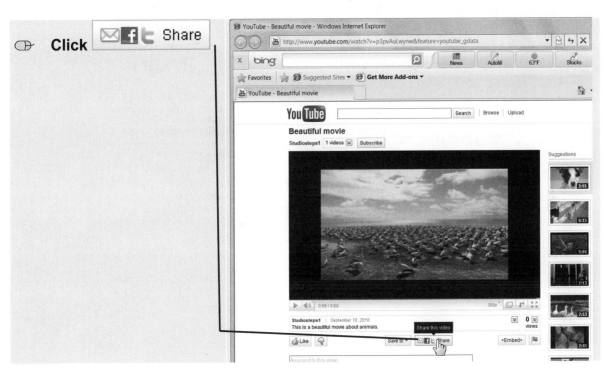

☞ **Drag the scroll bar downwards**

☞ **Click** Email

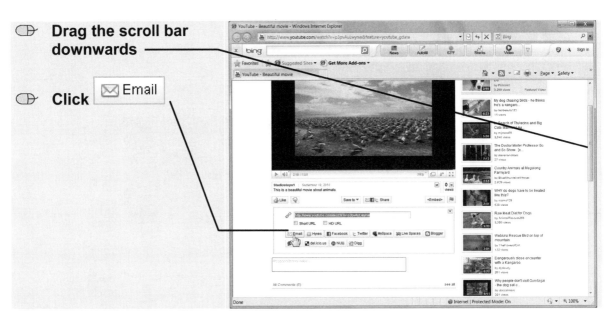

You might see a login window. To send the movie you will need to sign in to *YouTube* first:

☞ **Enter your *YouTube* username**

☞ **Enter your password**

☞ **Click** Sign in

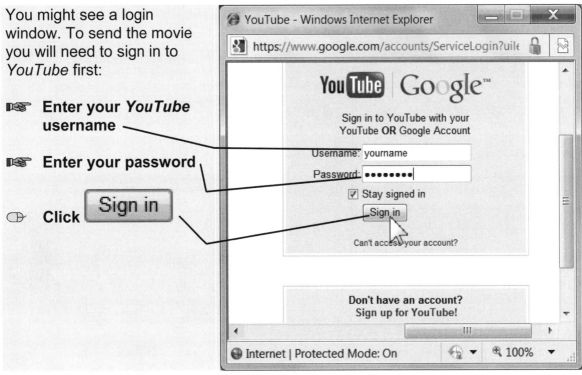

Type your e-mail address

Click Send

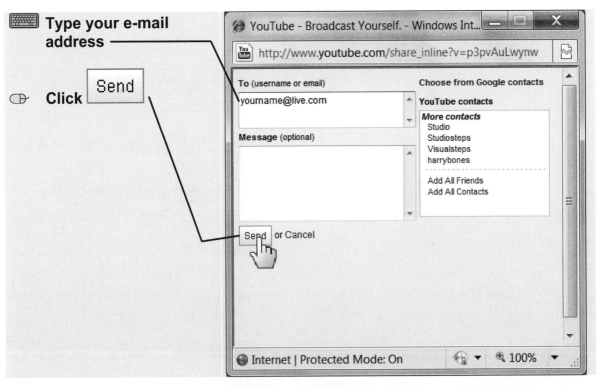

The e-mail message has been sent successfully:

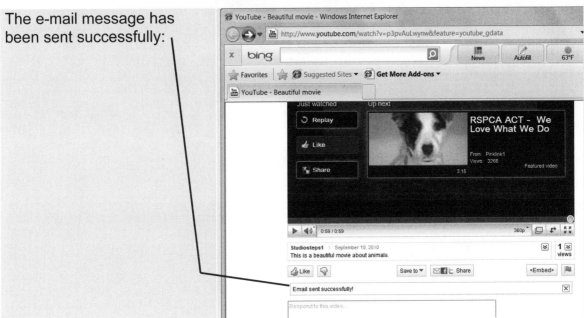

☞ **Open the e-mail message in** *Hotmail* 🦶10

Click **Show content**

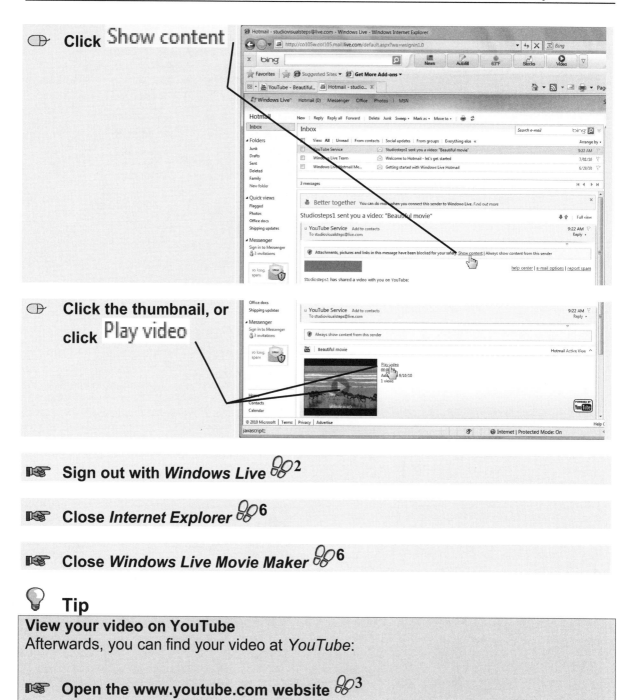

Click the thumbnail, or click **Play video**

👉 Sign out with *Windows Live* 👣2

👉 Close *Internet Explorer* 👣6

👉 Close *Windows Live Movie Maker* 👣6

💡 Tip

View your video on YouTube
Afterwards, you can find your video at *YouTube*:

👉 Open the www.youtube.com website 👣3

- Continue reading on the next page -

If you have not yet signed in with your *YouTube* account:

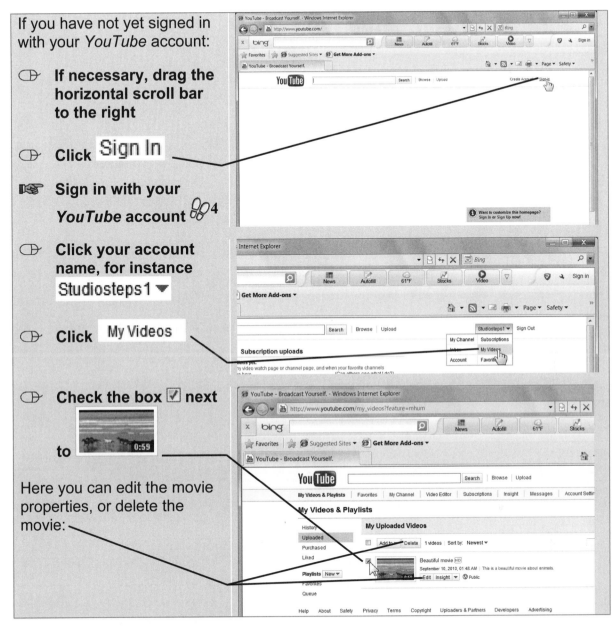

☞ **If necessary, drag the horizontal scroll bar to the right**

☞ **Click** Sign In

☞ **Sign in with your *YouTube* account** 🐾4

☞ **Click your account name, for instance** Studiosteps1 ▼

☞ **Click** My Videos

☞ **Check the box ☑ next to** 0:59

Here you can edit the movie properties, or delete the movie:

In this chapter you have learned how to make a movie in *Movie Maker*, by adding photos and videos. Next we explained how you can edit this movie by adding fades, effects, and text. Finally, we have shown you how to save your movie in various formats and how to publish it on *YouTube*.

Tip

Additional information

In this chapter you have learned the basics of the *Windows Live Movie Maker* program. In the help pages of this program you will find additional information on *Movie Maker*. You can access these help pages by clicking ⊕.

7.5 Background Information

Dictionary	
File	A general name for everything that is stored on your computer. For example, a file can consist of a program, a text, or a photo.
File extension	A string of characters that is added at the end of a file name, and by which you can recognize the file type.
File type	The formatting of a file. The file type indicates the program with which the file was created and which program you can use to open it.
Online	Publishing something online means that you have put it on the Internet.
Publishing	In *Movie Maker* this means you are transferring a movie to the Internet.
Tag	In *Movie Maker* you need to add tags to a video, if you want to publish this video on for example *YouTube*. Tags are keywords that you can use to search for the video later on.
Windows Live Movie Maker	With *Windows Live Movie Maker* you can create a movie of your photos and videos. You can store the movie on your computer, or you can publish your movie online.

Source: Help for Windows Live Essentials, Windows Help and Support, Wikipedia

Learn More
In this chapter you have learned about the main features of *Movie Maker*. In the book **Digital Photo and Video Editing for Seniors** (ISBN 978 90 5905 167 6) however you will learn much more about the extensive options and functions of this program. This book will be available in spring 2011.
You can find more information about the Visual Steps books at
www.visualsteps.com

8. Windows Live Writer

Windows Live Writer is a program that enables you to create blog messages offline, and publish them to a blog later on. *Windows Live Writer* supports a large number of web services, such as *SharePoint, Wordpress, Blogger, LiveJournal, TypePad*, and *Moveable Type Community Server*. In this chapter we will mainly discuss publishing blog messages to *WordPress*.

In *Writer* you can preview your blog message first before you publish it. You can also determine when your message will be published. In this way, you can post blog messages to the Internet even when you are not online yourself. You can add photos, videos, road maps, and hyperlinks to your blog messages. Furthermore, *Writer* will detect the theme of your blog and will adapt your blog message accordingly.

Writer integrates well with other *Windows Live Essentials* products. For instance, you can add photo albums from *Photos* to your blog message. In *Writer* you can also add a new photo album to *Photos*. The blog messages you have created in *Writer*, can be published to a web service later on.

In this chapter we will first explain how to add a blog account to *Windows Live Writer*. Then we will show you how to create and publish a blog message.

In this chapter you will learn how to:

- add a blog account;
- create a blog message;
- publish a blog message.

 Please note:

To work through this chapter effectively you will need to have a *Windows Live ID*. If you do not yet have a *Windows Live ID*, go to *section 1.2 Create a Windows Live ID* and you can read how to get one.

8.1 Adding a Blog Account

If you have not yet added a blog account in *Writer*, you will be guided automatically through the following process.

☞ **Open *Windows Live Writer*** 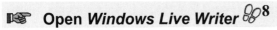⁸

Click Next >

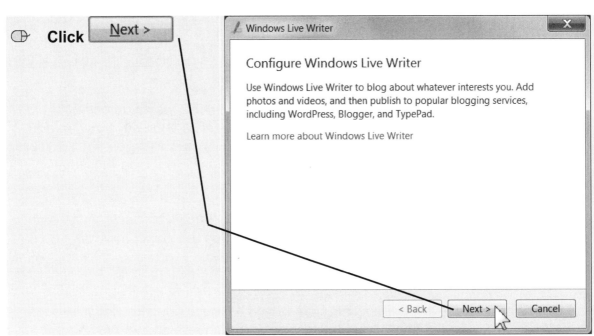

Click the radio button ⦿ **next to**
Create a new blog

You can also select a different blog service:

Click Next >

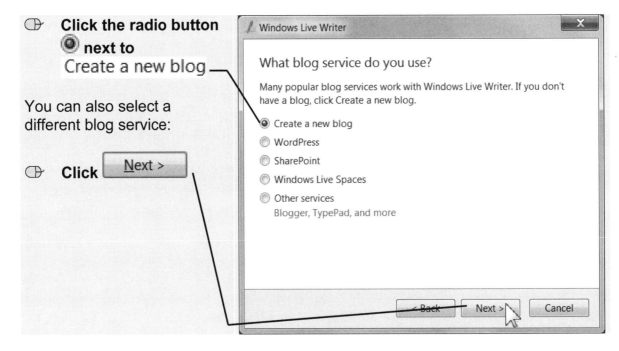

First you will need to create your blog online. *Windows Live Essentials* is partnering with WordPress.com:

☞ **Click** www.WordPress.com

If you want to create a blog with a different service:

☞ **Click** < Back

☞ **Choose a different blog service in the *What blog service do you use?* window**

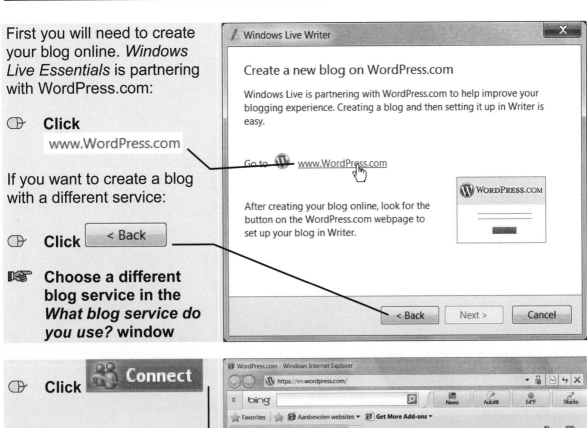

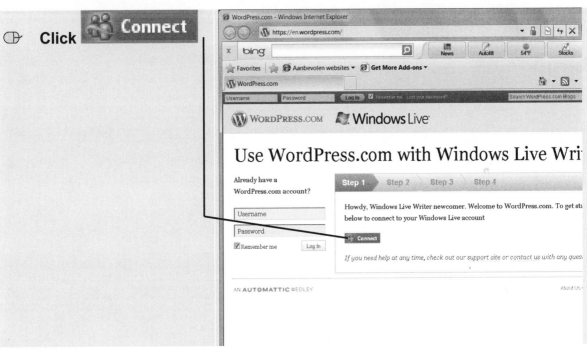

☞ **Click** Connect

☞ **Fill in all the data**

⊕ **Check the box ☑ next to**
I have read and agree to

⊕ **Click**
Next →

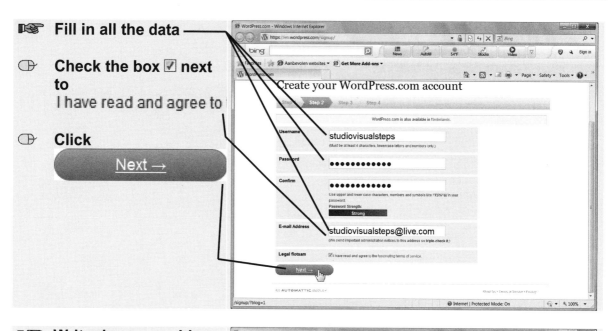

☞ **Write down your blog domain on paper for safekeeping**

⊕ **Click**
Signup →

An e-mail has been send to your e-mail address:

☞ **Open the e-mail message** ✂10

☞ **Click the link in the message**

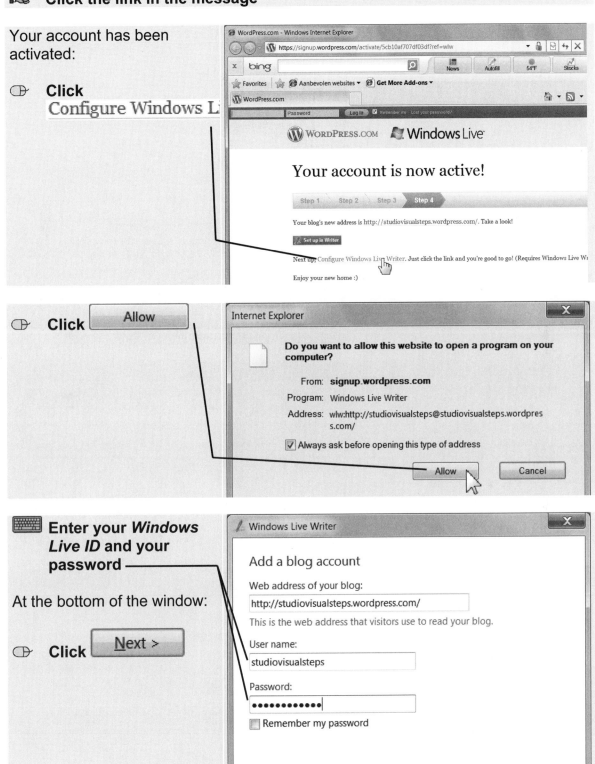

Your account has been activated:

⊕ **Click**
Configure Windows Li

⊕ **Click** `Allow`

⌨ **Enter your *Windows Live ID* and your password**

At the bottom of the window:

⊕ **Click** `Next >`

When your blog account has been created, you will see the following window:

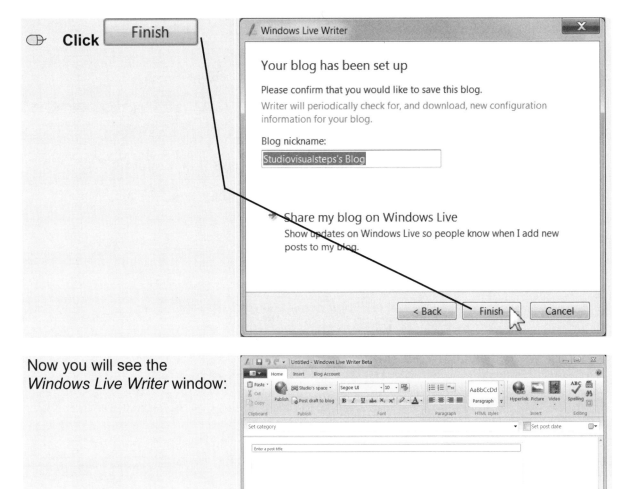

Now you will see the
Windows Live Writer window:

8.2 Creating a Blog Message

Now you are going to create a blog message.

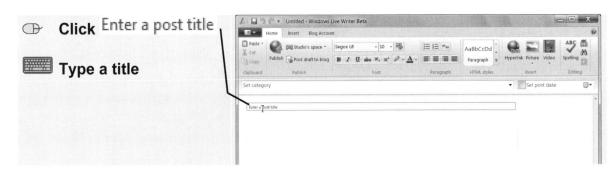

Click below the title

Type a message

You can use the layout toolbar to edit the text:

☞ **If you wish, change the layout of the text**

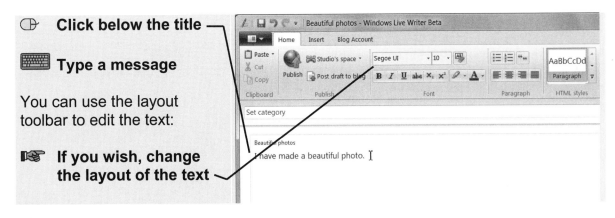

➥ **Please note:**

Pressing **Enter ←** will move the cursor to a new paragraph.
If you want to insert a line break instead of starting a new paragraph, then you need

to simultaneously press **⇧ Shift** and **Enter ←** .

You can add a picture to your blog message:

Click

Click **From your computer**

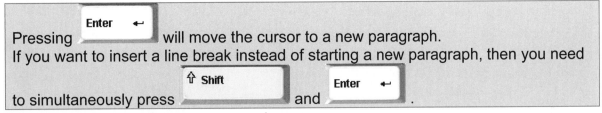

☞ **Open one or more photos** 𝄖5

The photos will be added to *Windows Live Photos* as well.

You can use the options on

the **Format** tab to edit the pictures:

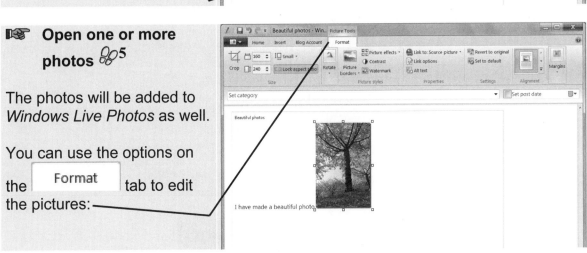

Tip

Insert an Internet picture
You can also insert a picture from the Internet. To do this, you will need to copy the picture's web address:

In *Internet Explorer*:

- **Right-click the picture**
- **Click** Properties
- ☞ **Select the address** ✇**17**
- **Right-click the selected address**
- **Click** Copy

In *Writer*:

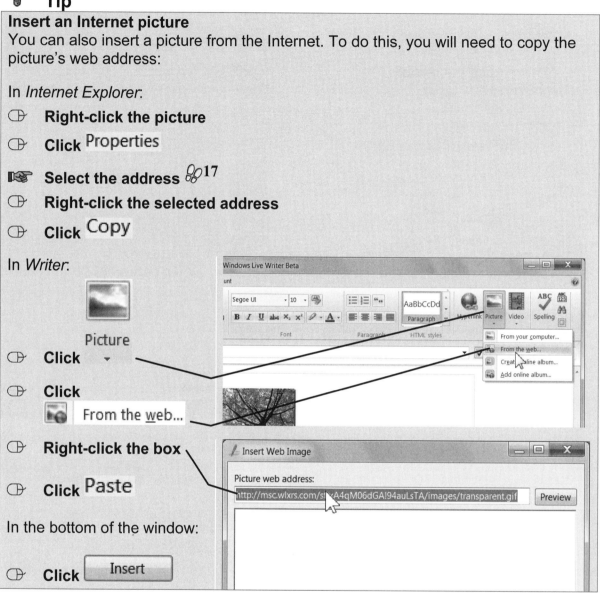

Picture
- **Click** ▼
- **Click**
  🖼 From the *w*eb...

- **Right-click the box**

- **Click** Paste

In the bottom of the window:

- **Click** Insert

You can also add other items to your blog message:

- **Click the** Insert **tab**

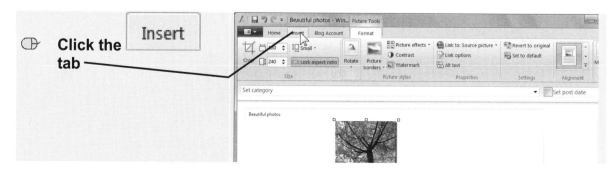

You can insert a hyperlink:

You can insert a photo album:

You can add an existing photo album from *Photos*, or you can create a new album. This new album will be added to *Photos*.

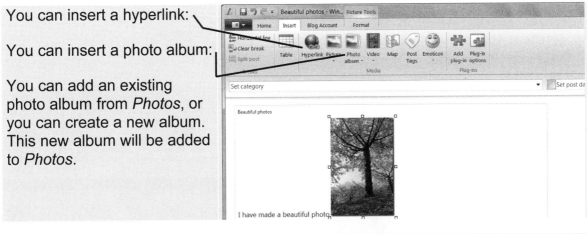

You can insert a table:

You can insert a map:

You can add tags:

Tags are keywords that are used for searches by certain websites.

Click Video

You can look for a video on the Internet, and copy the link:

You can add a video file from your own computer:

You can add a video from a video service, such as *YouTube*:

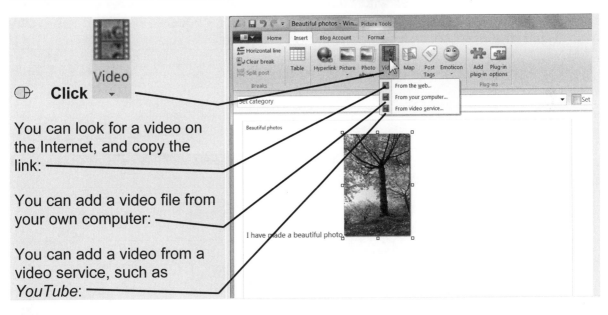

Please note:

If you insert a video from your own computer, it will be uploaded automatically to *YouTube*.

8.3 Publishing a Blog Message

Before you publish your blog message, you can preview it:

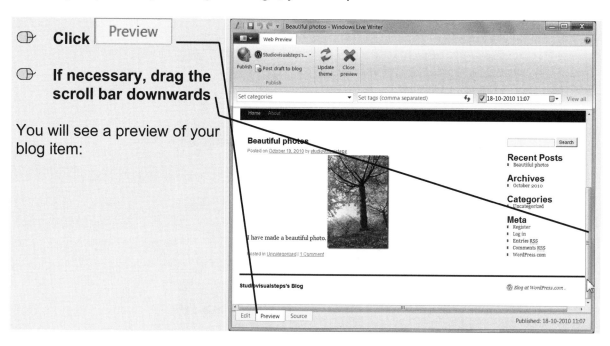

- ⬚ **Click** Preview

- ⬚ **If necessary, drag the scroll bar downwards**

You will see a preview of your blog item:

You can modify the *publication date* of the message. If you choose a date from the past, this date will be added to the message. If you choose a data that lies in the future, the message will be published on that date.

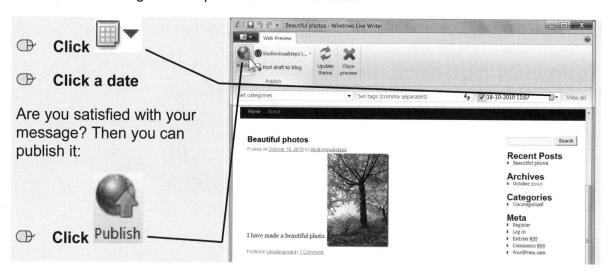

- ⬚ **Click** 🗓️ ▼

- ⬚ **Click a date**

Are you satisfied with your message? Then you can publish it:

- ⬚ **Click** Publish

☞ **Sign on with your *Windows Live ID*** 🦶4

Now the message will be published.

Tip

Remove the publication date
You can remove the publication date by unchecking the box ☑ next to the date.

☞ **If necessary, sign in with your *Windows Live ID* ℘℘⁴**

Now you will see your blog
message: ──────────

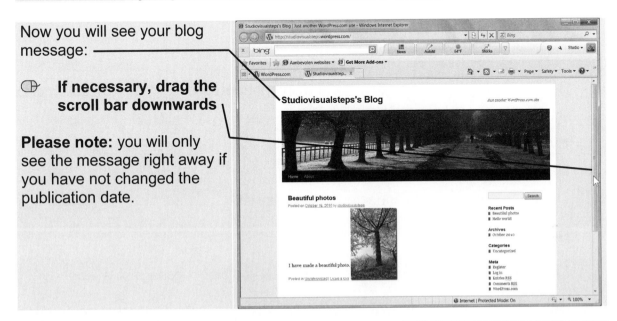

⊕ **If necessary, drag the
scroll bar downwards** ＼

Please note: you will only
see the message right away if
you have not changed the
publication date.

☞ **Sign off with *Windows Live* ℘℘²**

☞ **Close all the windows ℘℘⁶**

 Tip

Additional information
In this chapter we have covered the basic operations for working with *Windows Live Writer*. You will find additional information in the help pages. You can access the help pages by clicking Help.

In this chapter you have learned how to create a blog account in *Writer*. You then learned how to create a blog message, how to add various items to your message, and how to publish it.

8.4 Background Information

Dictionary	
Blog	Website where you can find regularly updated posts, and where the information is presented in reverse chronological order (the most recent message will be displayed first.
Blog account	Information about a blog that is used by *Writer* to publish blog messages.
Hyperlink	Also called link. This is a navigational tool that automatically leads the user to the relevant information when the link is clicked.
Offline	Not connected to the Internet.
Online	Connected to the Internet.
Publish	In *Writer* this means posting a blog message to a blog.
Upload	Copying a file from your own computer to another computer or to the Internet.
Windows Live Writer	Program that allows you to create offline blog messages, which you can post later on to blog.
WordPress	*WordPress* is an online blogging service. *Writer* is collaborating with *WordPress*.

Source: Help for Windows Live Essentials, Windows Help and Support, Wikipedia

9. Windows Live Calendar

Windows Live Calendar is an online version of a calendar system that can be shared with other people. You can create multiple diaries and view them all at once, in the same overview. This means you can manage different types of appointments and keep your schedule well organized. You can view the calendar per day, per week, or per month.

You can determine with whom you want to share your calendar. You can invite people for an appointment and monitor their replies. You can determine if and when you want to receive reminders for your appointments. You can also keep track of birthdays. You will receive a reminder when one of your contacts has his or her birthday. And finally, *Calendar* also gives you the ability to manage a list of tasks to be completed.

Calendar integrates well with other *Windows Live Essentials* products. For instance, you can share a calendar with people from your contact list and you can use *Hotmail* to invite people to view calendar entries. You can have reminders sent to *Hotmail* or *Messenger*. And you can access a shared *Windows Live Calendar* from *Groups*.

In this chapter we will first explain how to manage calendars and set the permissions. Next, we will explain how to add an appointment. Last of all, we will show you how to adjust some of the additional options available in *Calendar*.

In this chapter you will learn how to:

- manage calendars;
- set permissions;
- add an appointment;
- modify additional options.

 Please note:

To work through this chapter effectively you will need to have a *Windows Live ID*. If you do not yet have a *Windows Live ID,* go to *section 1.2 Create a Windows Live ID* and you can read how to get one.

9.1 Managing Calendars

Calendar automatically creates three calendars: a personal calendar, a calendar with all the US holidays, and a birthday calendar. The birthday calendar contains the birthday of your contacts, if you entered this information at the time you added a new contact.

You can add, edit, and delete calendars yourself. You can also determine which calendars you want to show in the calendar overview, and which calendars you want to hide (temporarily). You can view the calendar overview per day, per week, or per month.

☞ **Open** *Internet Explorer* 🦶¹

☞ **Open the home.live.com website** 🦶³

☞ **Sign in with your** *Windows Live ID* 🦶⁴

👉 **Click** 🪟 Windows Live™

👉 **Click** All services

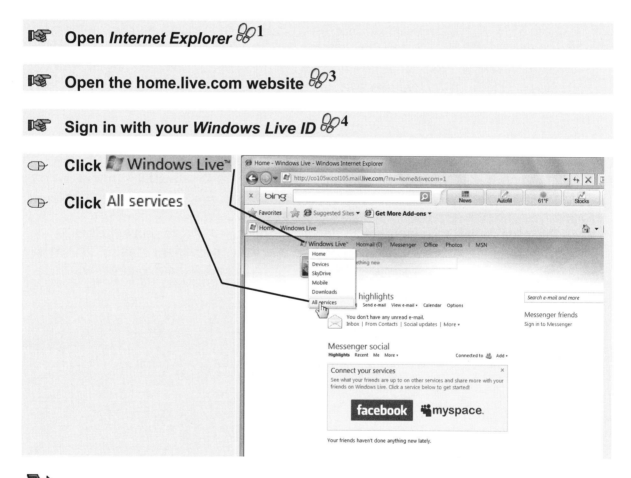

🔖 **Please note:**

In this book we will open all *Windows Live Essentials* products from the *Home Page*. If you want, you can also access *Calendar* directly by typing http://calendar.live.com in the address bar of your Internet browser.

☞ **Click** Calendar

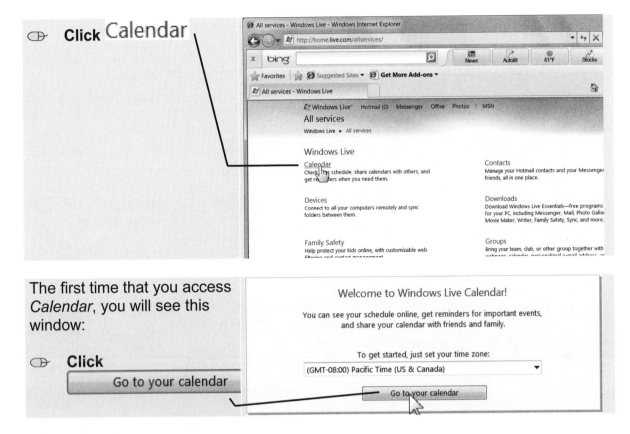

The first time that you access *Calendar*, you will see this window:

☞ **Click**

Go to your calendar

First, you are going to add a new calendar:

You will see three calendars:

☞ **Click**
Add a new calendar

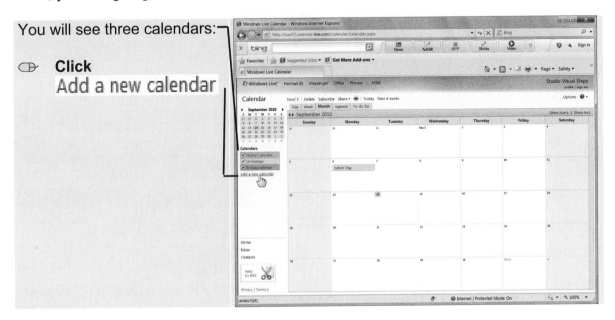

Type a name

Click a color

Click Save

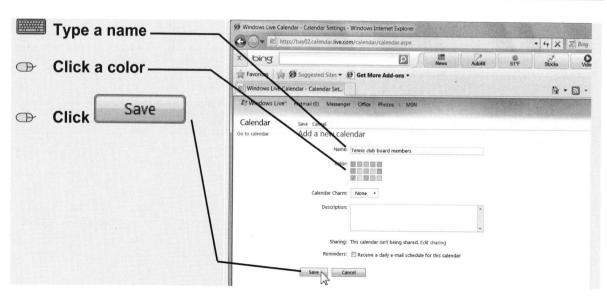

To edit the calendar:

Click the calendar's name

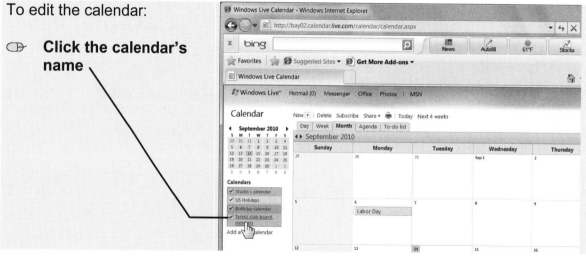

Now you can edit the calendar.

You can also delete the calendar:

You can also simply return to the overview:

Click Cancel

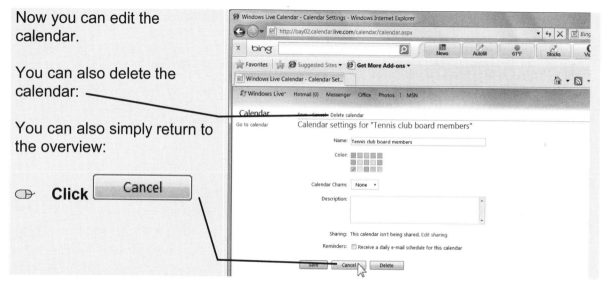

You can choose which calendars you want to display in the calendar overview:

Uncheck the box ✔
next to US Holidays

Now this calendar will no longer be displayed.

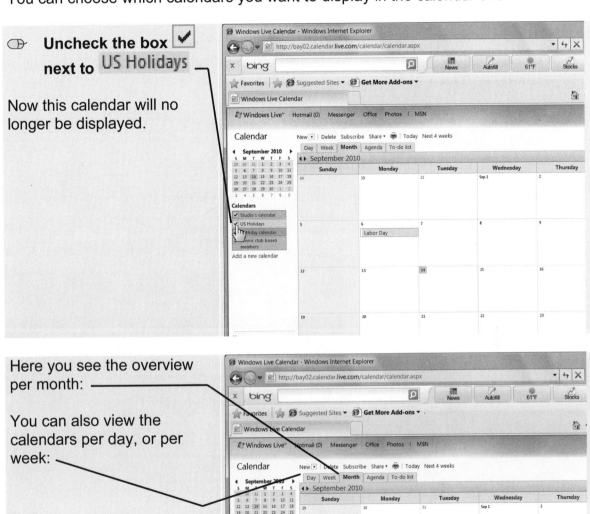

Here you see the overview per month:

You can also view the calendars per day, or per week:

9.2 Setting Permissions

Initially, you will only be able to view and edit your calendars yourself. But you can share a calendar with others, if you wish. You can set the access rights for the people with whom you want to share your calendar.

Click Share ▼

Click the new calendar

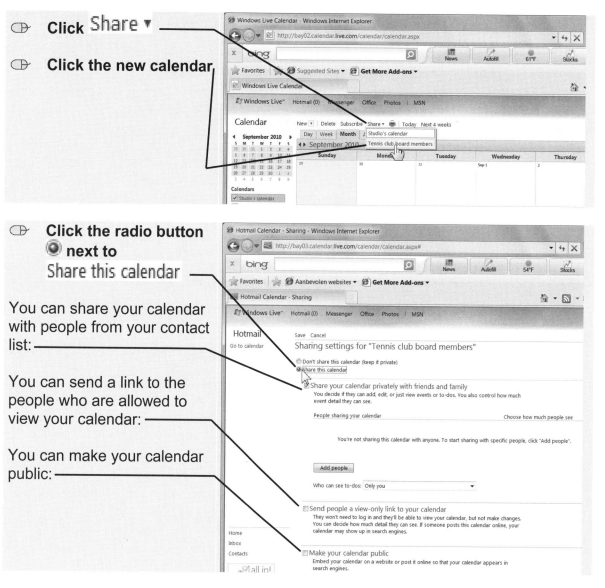

Click the radio button ◉ next to
Share this calendar

You can share your calendar with people from your contact list:

You can send a link to the people who are allowed to view your calendar:

You can make your calendar public:

 Please note:

If you make your calendar public, the web address of your calendar will be posted on the Internet. This means that anyone can view your calendar, and that your calendar can be found by a search engine. If you decide to change a public calendar into a private calendar once more, you calendar's web address may still be found by a search engine.

☞ **If necessary, check the box ☑ next to** Share your calendar w

☞ **Click** Add people

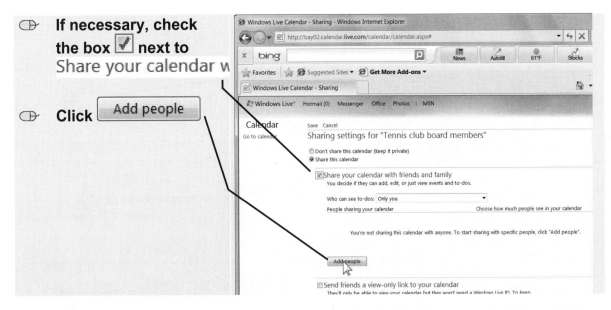

☞ **Check the box(es) ☑ next to one or more contacts**

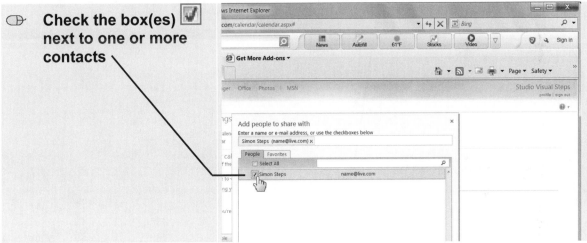

Now you can set the permissions. You can select one of the following options.

- **Co-owner**: a co-owner can create, edit, and delete events, and can edit the settings for sharing the calendar. A co-owner cannot delete the calendar.
- **View, edit, and delete items**: other users can view event details and change existing entries.
- **View details**: other users can view event details.
- **View free/busy times, titles and locations**: other users can see if you have scheduled an event, and they can view the title and location of this appointment.
- **View free/busy times**: other users can see if you are available for an event.

If necessary, drag the scroll bar downwards

By View details, click ▼

Click an access level

Click Add

Click Save

Click OK

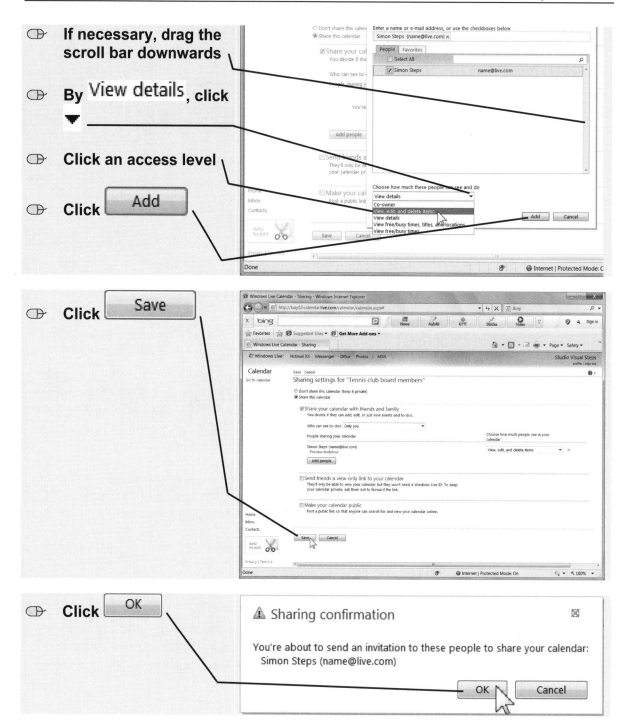

Tip

Stop sharing a calendar

If you do not want to share a calendar any longer with a particular contact:

☞ **Click Share ▼**

☞ **Click the calendar you want to stop sharing**

In the window where you see the data for this contact:

☞ **Click ✖**

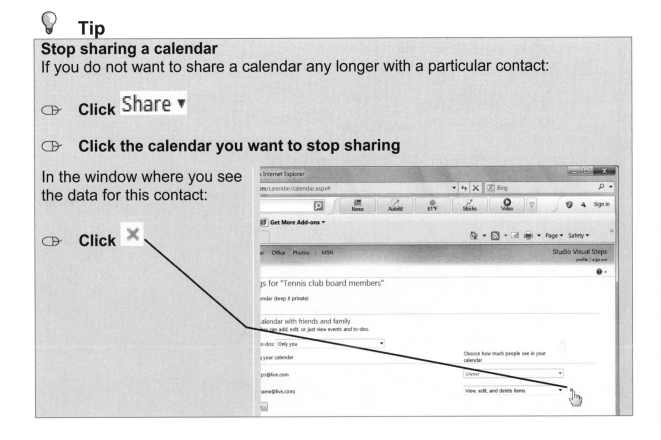

9.3 Adding an Event

☞ **If necessary, drag the scroll bar upwards**

☞ **Click New**

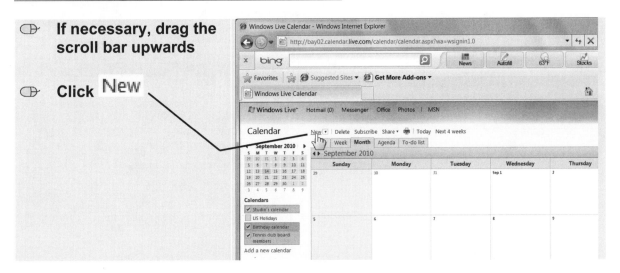

💡 Tip

Alternative ways of adding an event
You can also add an event in a different way:

☞ **Select one or more days**

To select multiple days, you need to hold the mouse button down and drag the mouse pointer over the days you desire.

👉 **Click ➕ Add**

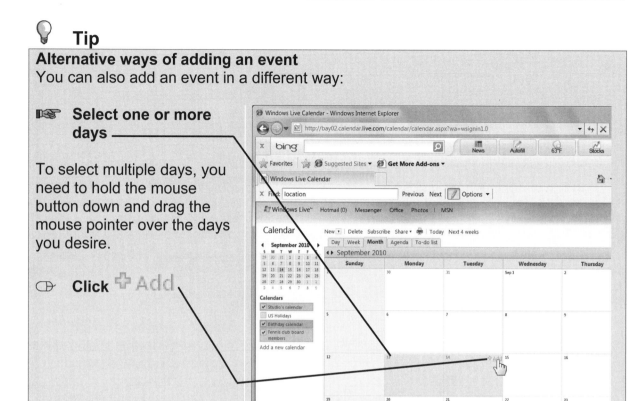

⌨ **Type a subject**

⌨ **Type a location**

👉 **By Calendar: click ▼**

👉 **Select a calendar**

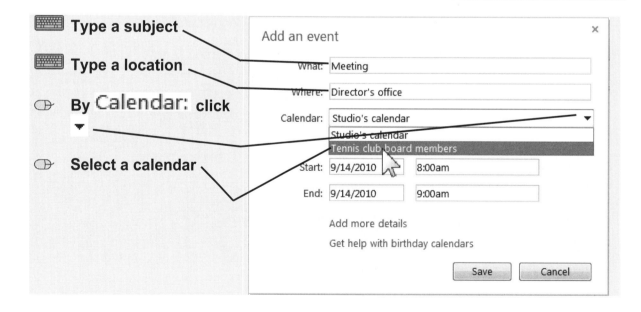

By Start: type a date and a time

By End: type a date and a time

If you have previously selected the correct date in the overview, this date will already be filled in here.

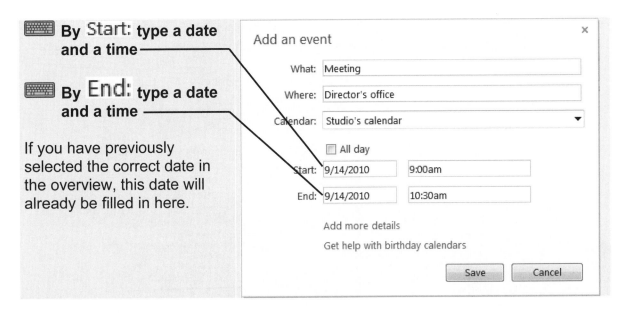

You can even add more details to an event. For instance, you can set a recurrence. Or you can determine when you want to receive a reminder, and you can invite other people to the event.

Click
Add more details

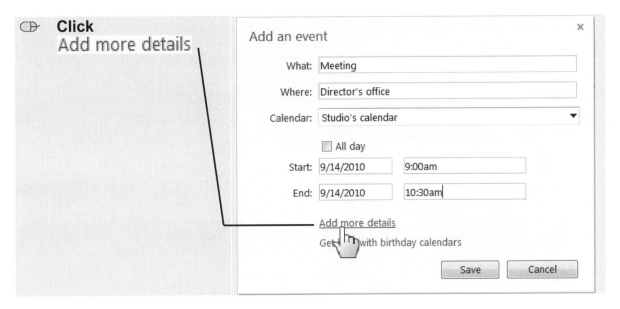

You can hide the event from the other users of this calendar:

You can add a charm:

You can select a different time zone:

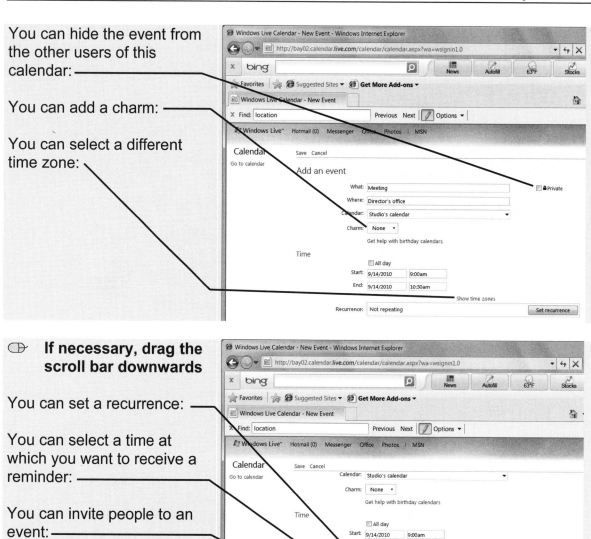

⊕ **If necessary, drag the scroll bar downwards**

You can set a recurrence:

You can select a time at which you want to receive a reminder:

You can invite people to an event:

These may also include persons who are not listed in your contacts.

You can add a detailed
description to your event:

You can state your availability
for this event:

By this item, others can tell if
you are available for an
appointment.

Click **Save**

After a while, the event will be
included in the calendar
overview:

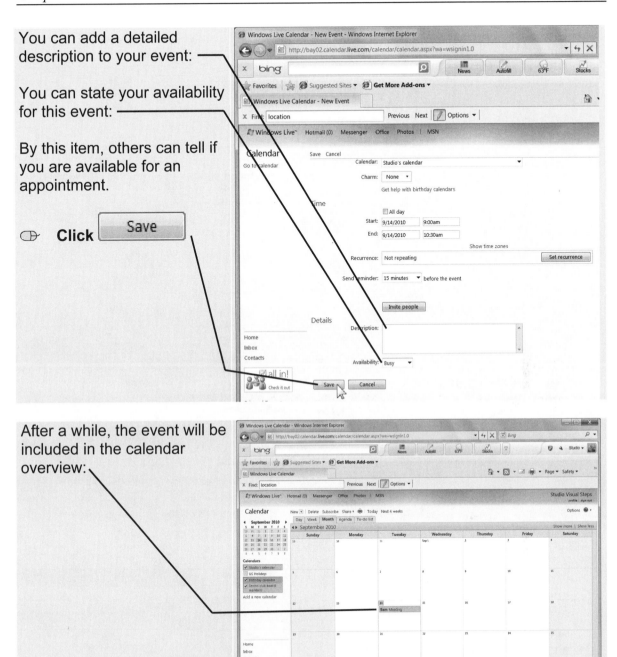

Tip

Edit or delete an event
Afterwards, you can edit the event, or delete it:

☞ **Click the event title**

Now you can edit this event:

You can also delete the event:

If you have already sent an invitation for a particular event, you can also send an update, if anything has changed:

You can also cancel the event as well and send a notice of cancellation:

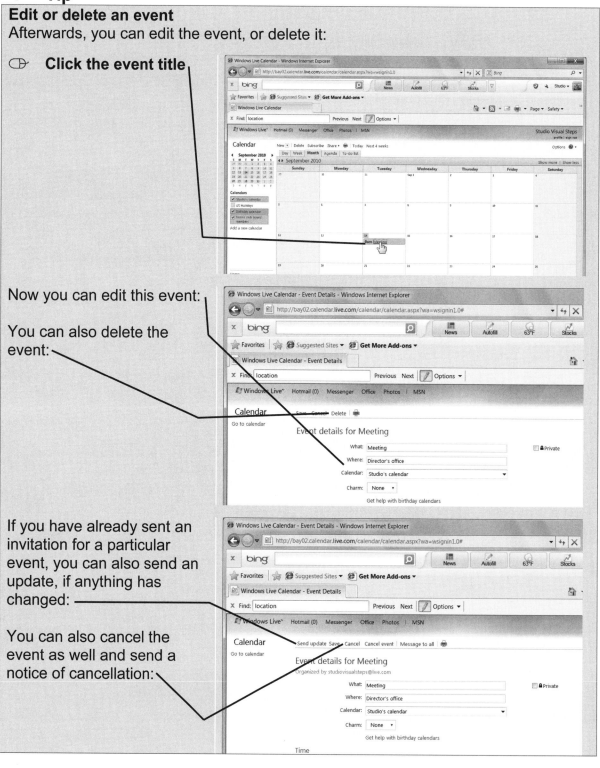

💡 Tip

View people who will be attending the event
If you have sent invitations for an event, you can view the reactions to this invitation:

Here you can see how many people have responded to your invitation:

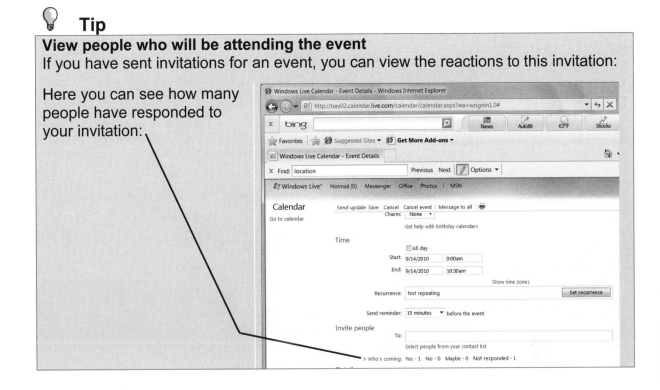

9.4 Modifying other Options

In *Calendar*, you can modify several additional options. For example, you can set Sunday as the first day of the week, instead of Monday and you can change the starting time for all the days. You can modify the default period for receiving reminders, and you can select a different primary calendar. While adding an event, the primary calendar will always be displayed first.

At the right-hand side of the window:

☞ **Click** Options

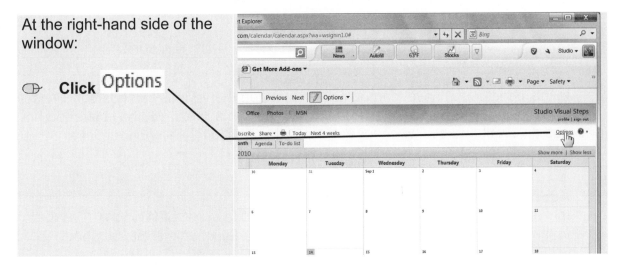

⊕ **If necessary, drag the scroll bar downwards**

You can change the first day of your calendar week:

You can change the time your calendar day starts:

You can set your default reminder time:

While adding an event, you will still be able to change this time setting.

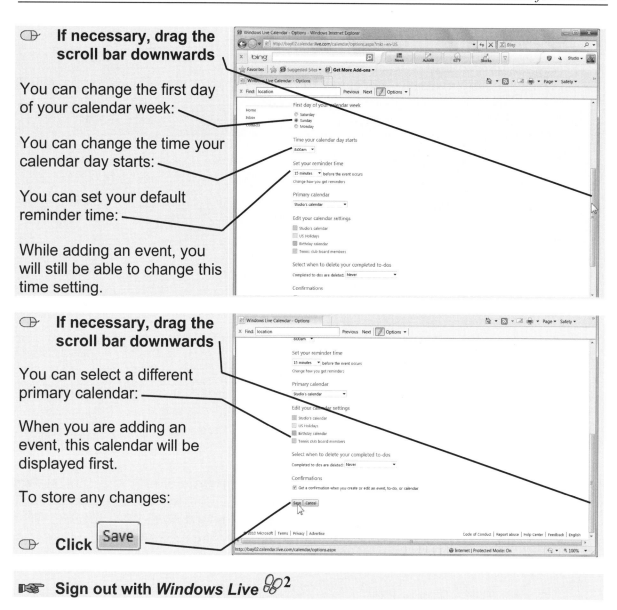

⊕ **If necessary, drag the scroll bar downwards**

You can select a different primary calendar:

When you are adding an event, this calendar will be displayed first.

To store any changes:

⊕ **Click** Save

☞ **Sign out with** *Windows Live* 🦶²

☞ **Close** *Internet Explorer* 🦶⁶

In this chapter you have learned how to manage the various calendars in *Windows Live Calendar*, and how to change the access rights. Next, you have learned how to add an event and how to change some of the additional *Calendar* options.

💡 **Tip**

Additional information
In this chapter you have learned about the basic features of *Windows Live Calendar*. In the help pages for this program you will find additional information about *Calendar*. You can access the help pages by clicking and Help.

9.5 Background Information

Dictionary

Contact	A collection of data about a specific person, which contains at least the person's e-mail address. This information is stored in the *Contacts* folder.
Online	Connected to the Internet.
Permission	A setting which you can use to determine who is allowed to view your profile, the comments of others about your profile, your files, your calendar, or a photo album. You can decide for yourself which people are allowed to view this data in *Windows Live*.
Search engine	A web service which searches all text on the web for the keywords you have entered.
Windows Live Calendar	An online calendar you can share with others.

Source: Help for Windows Live Essentials, Windows Help and Support, Wikipedia

9.6 Tips

 Tip

To do list
In *Calendar*, you can also maintain a to-do list:

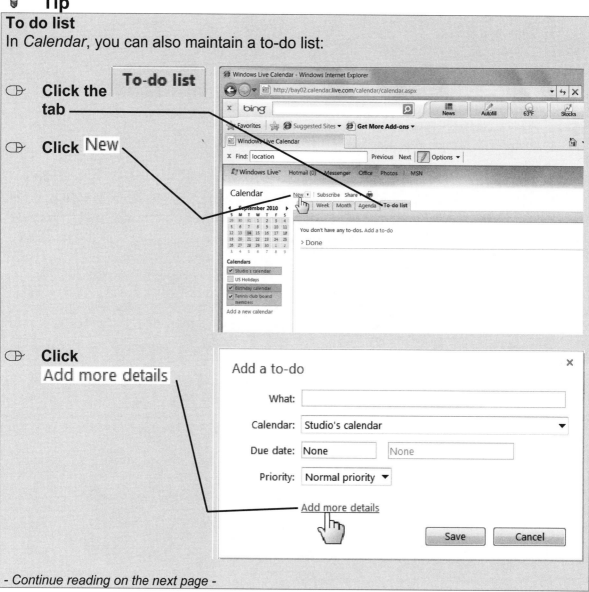

☞ **Click the** | **To-do list** tab

☞ **Click** New

☞ **Click** Add more details

- Continue reading on the next page -

☞ Enter the items you want to list

⊕ Click Save

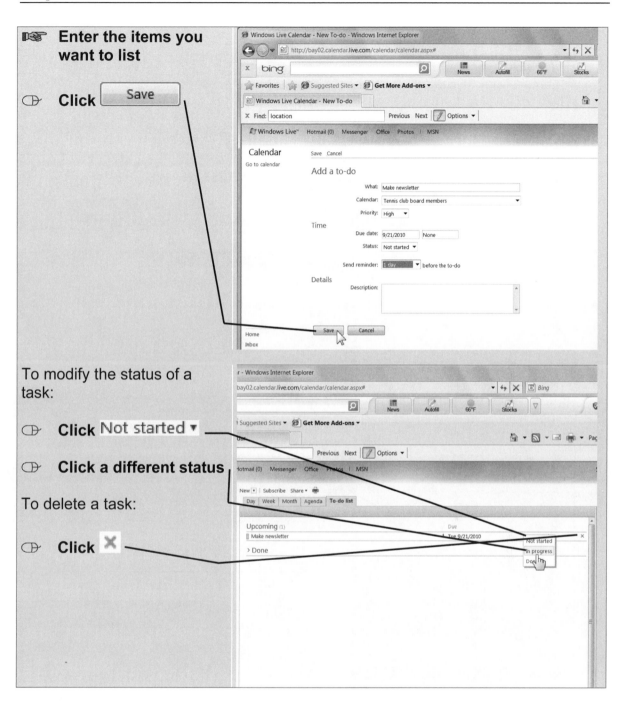

To modify the status of a task:

⊕ Click Not started ▼

⊕ Click a different status

To delete a task:

⊕ Click ✖

Tip

Printing

You can print the calendar overview, as well as the event list, or the to-do list. *Calendar* will automatically produce a print version of the selected items.

For example, if you want to print an event list:

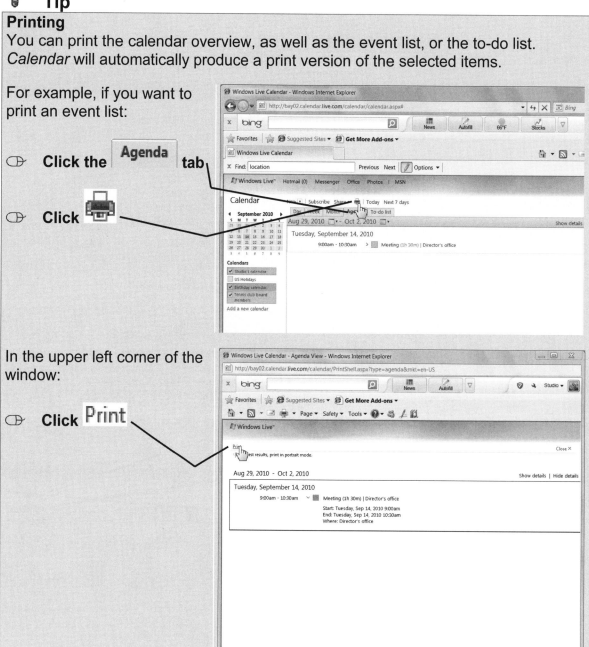

☞ **Click the** **Agenda** **tab**

☞ **Click** 🖨

In the upper left corner of the window:

☞ **Click** **Print**

10. Windows Live Groups

Windows Live Groups allows you to create a group of contacts with whom you can communicate in various ways. You can share photo files or other types of files, and you can share a calendar. You can send e-mail messages to the group members and conduct group conversations. In this way, you can use *Windows Live Essentials* to keep up-to-date with all of the activities of your group members.

Groups also integrates well with other *Windows Live Essentials* products. Both *Hotmail* and *Mail* allow you to send e-mail messages to group members. In *Messenger* you can conduct group conversations. You can use *Groups* to exchange photos with *Windows Live Photos*, and you can manage a group calendar in *Calendar*. You can also use *SkyDrive* to exchange files with other users.

In this chapter we will first show you how to create a group, and how to invite people to become a member of the group. Next, we will discuss how to set up your group's access rights. Then we will explain more about the various *Groups* features, and finally we will show you how to modify several additional options.

In this chapter you will learn how to:

- create a group;
- invite people;
- modify access rights;
- use additional *Groups* features;
- modify other options.

 Please note:

To work through this chapter effectively you will need to have a *Windows Live ID*. If you do not yet have a *Windows Live ID,* go to *section 1.2 Create a Windows Live ID* and you can read how to get one.

10.1 Creating a Group

When you create a group in *Windows Live Groups*, you become the owner of this group. As the owner, this means that you can determine who is allowed to become a group member. You can also set permissions (access rights) for all group members. Moreover, you are the only person who can delete this group.

☞ **Open *Internet Explorer*** ¹

☞ **Open the home.live.com website** ⬗³

☞ **Sign in with your *Windows Live ID*** ⬗⁴

⬗ **Click** 🪟 Windows Live™

⬗ **Click** All services

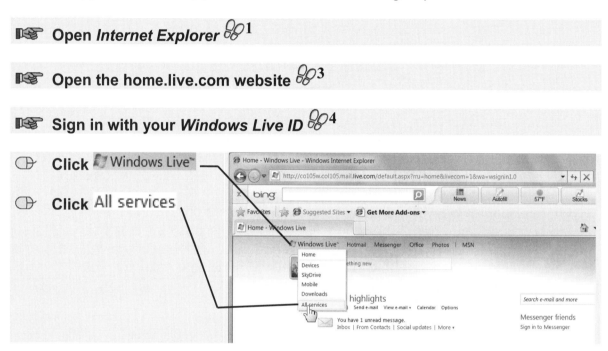

➥ **Please note:**

In this book we will open all *Windows Live Essentials* products from the *Home Page*. If you want, you can also access *Groups* directly by typing http://groups.live.com in the address bar of your Internet browser.

⬗ **Click** Groups

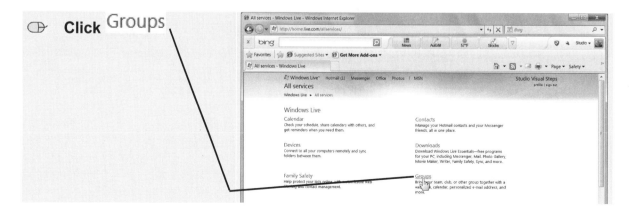

⊕ Click

Create a group

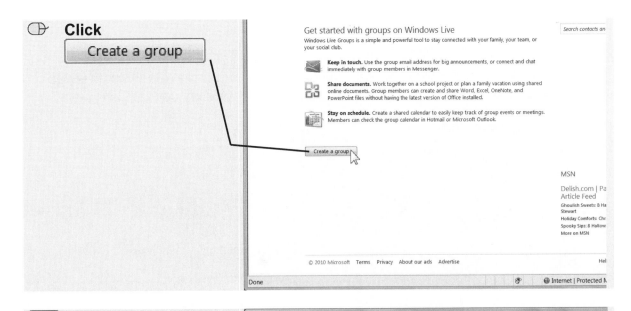

⌨ Type a name for the group

A unique web address will be created automatically. You can change this web address, if you want to:

⊕ Click
Check availability

If the web address is not available, choose a different web address.

⊕ Click Create

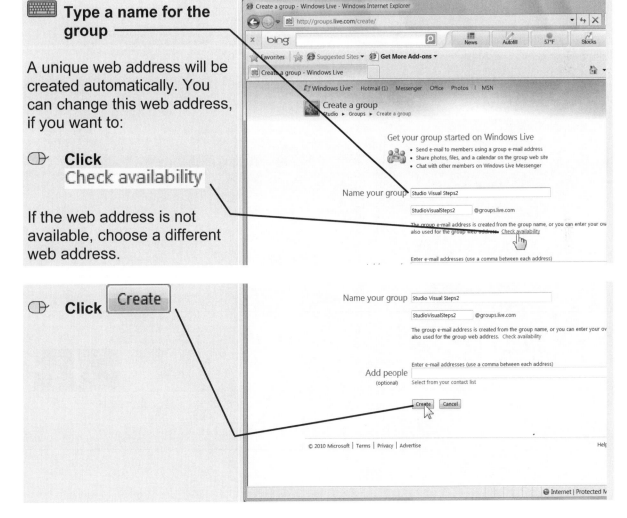

Tip

Delete a group

As the owner of a group, you can delete it. Once you have done this, the web address of the deleted group will not be available for sixty consecutive days.

Click Options

Click Delete group

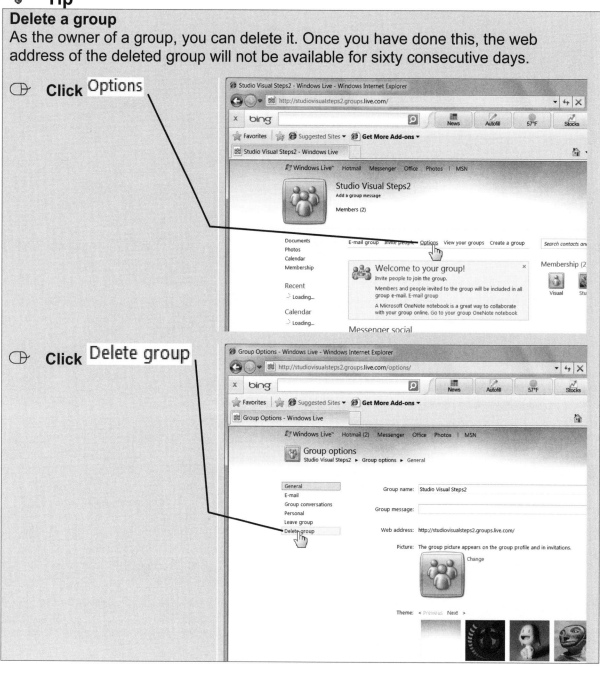

10.2 Inviting People

You can invite somebody to join your group. If this person accepts your invitation, he or she will become a group member.

Click Invite people

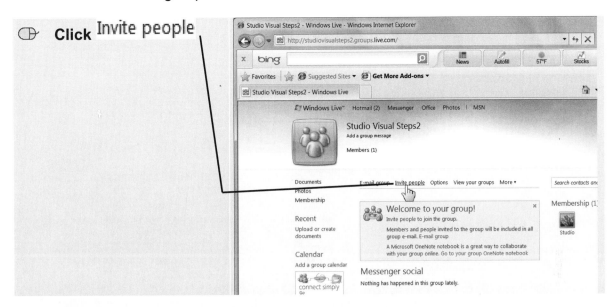

If you know somebody's e-mail address, you can enter this address. But you can also select somebody from your contacts list:

Click To

Click the people you want to invite

Click Send

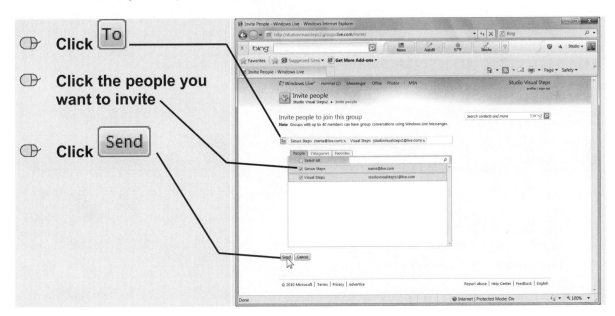

All the people you have invited will receive an e-mail message. Before deciding to accept the invitation, these people will be allowed to view the group.

This is what a group invitation looks like in *Hotmail*:

The recipient of the e-mail message can view the group by clicking

View group:

Please note: this message may possibly be moved to the *Junk* folder.

Next, the recipient can click

Join or

Decline Invitation :

☞ **Reopen the group**
👣**11**

If somebody has become a member, you will see a message here:

⊕ **Click** Studio Visual Steps2

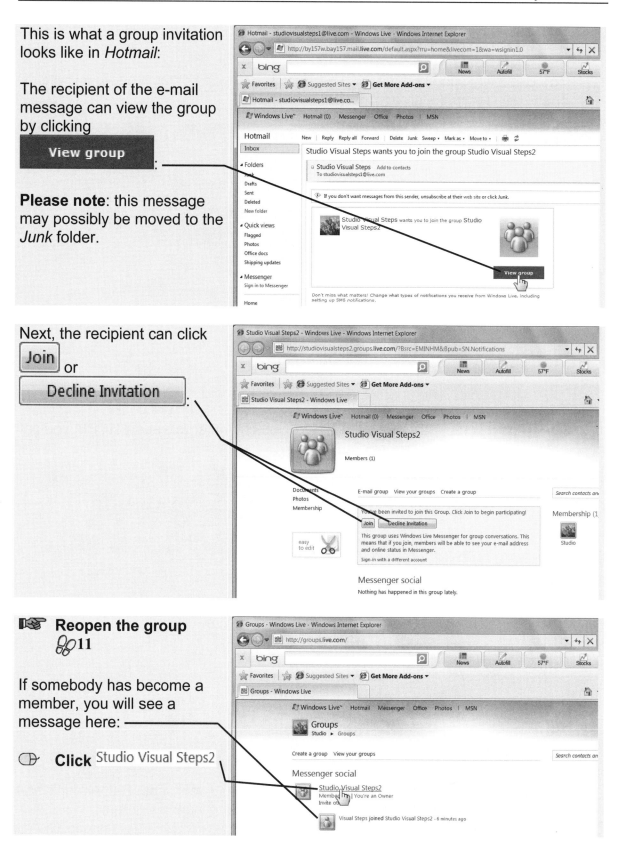

💡 Tip

Delete a group member

As owner, you can delete a group member. After you have clicked Remove, you will not see a message, but the member will immediately be removed.

⟜ **Click** Membership

⟜ **Click the member**

⟜ **Click** Remove

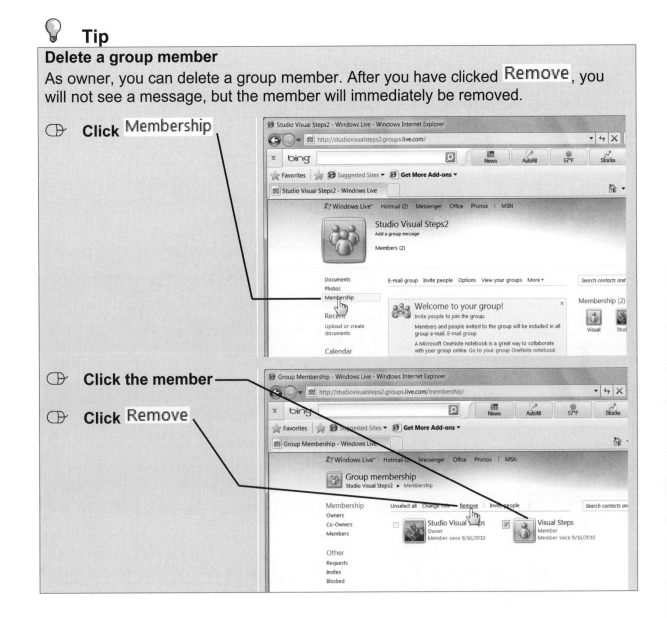

10.3 Modifying Permissions

You can change the role of a group member, from *Member* to *Owner*, or *Co-owner*.

A member is allowed to execute the following tasks:
- view the group page;
- take part in conversations;
- exchange photos and other documents;
- add events to the group calendar.

A co-owner can execute all the tasks of a regular member, but is also allowed to:

- delete items from the updates list;
- change the roles of group members;
- invite new members;
- accept or refuse applications for group membership;
- block persons;
- delete members;
- modify group options.

The owner of a group is allowed to execute the same tasks as a co-owner. But an owner is the only person who is allowed to delete a group.

Click **Membership**

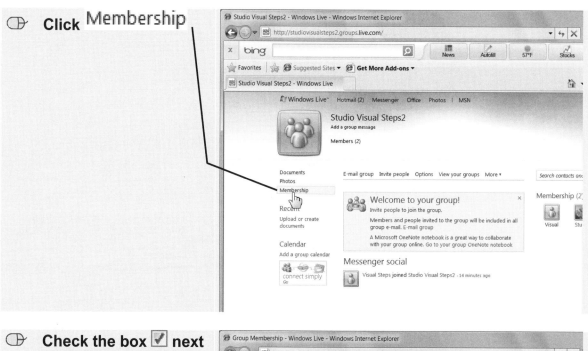

Check the box ☑ next to the member whose role you want to change —

Click **Change role ▾**

Click the desired role

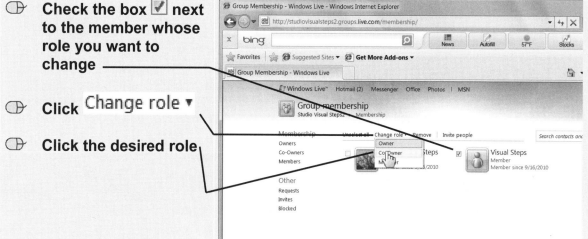

Now the role has been
changed:

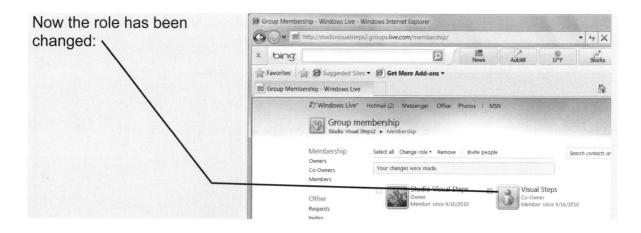

10.4 Groups Features

You have now created a group and this group may already have a number of
members. Now you can start using all of the *Groups* main features. For instance, you
can exchange a photo, or another document or you can create a group calendar:

To return to the group:

☞ **Click the group name**

Here you can add documents
and photos:

The files will be stored in the
group's *SkyDrive*. In *Chapter
12 Windows Live SkyDrive*
we will explain how *SkyDrive*
works.

Here you can create a
calendar:

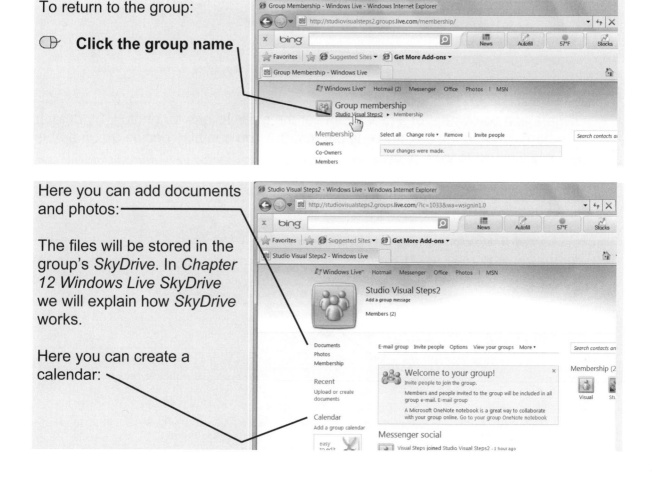

Click Photos

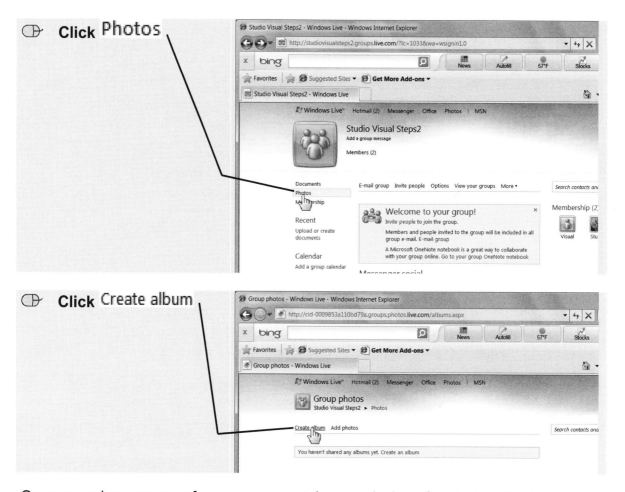

Click Create album

Owners and co-owners of a group can set the permissions for photos. By default, members can add, delete, and edit photos. But you can also decide that members are only allowed to view photos.

Here you can modify the photo permissions: ⎯

In *Chapter 5 Windows Live Photos* you can read how to add photos to an album.

To return to the group:

Click the group name

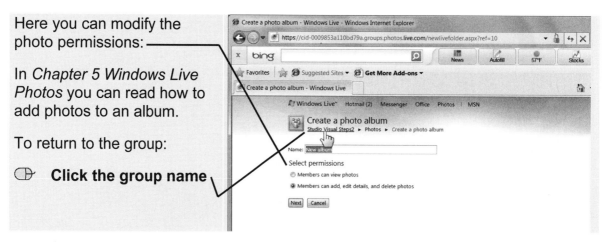

Click
Add a group calendar

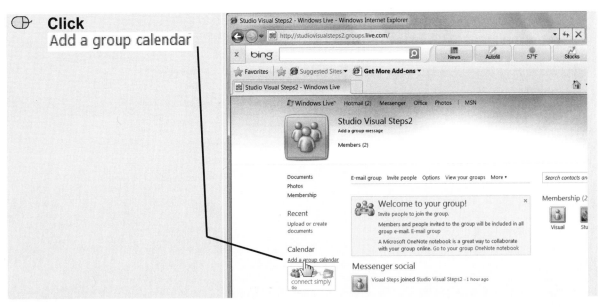

Click
Add calendar

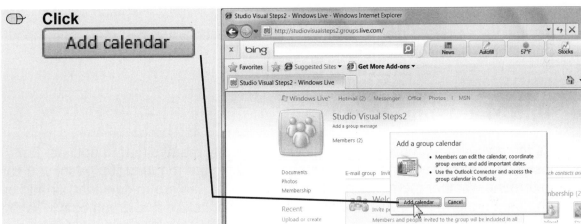

In *Calendar,* a group calendar has already been created:

In *Chapter 9 Windows Live Calendar* you can read how to use *Calendar.*

To return to the group:

Click the group name

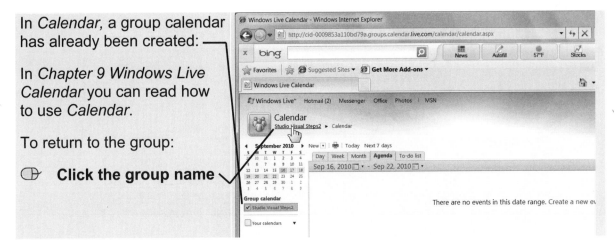

From *Hotmail*, you can send
an e-mail message to the
entire group: ───────

In *Chapter 2 Windows Live
Hotmail* you can read how to
use *Hotmail*.

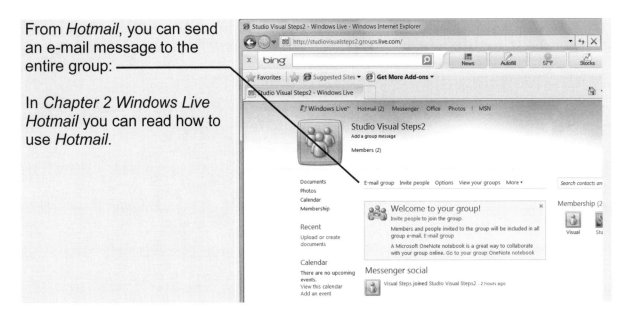

Members can choose not to receive group e-mails. Owners and co-owners can
disable the group's e-mail function. In the next section, you can read more about this
option and about some of the other options.

10.5 Modifying Options

As the owner of a group, you are allowed to modify many different options. For
instance, you can add a group message and a picture to the group. Also, you can
determine whether members are allowed to modify the group calendar, or add or edit
photos. Furthermore, you can disable the e-mail function and group conversations in
Messenger.

Click Options

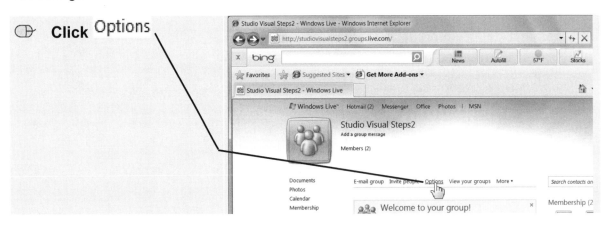

You can type a group
message:

You can add a picture of the
group:

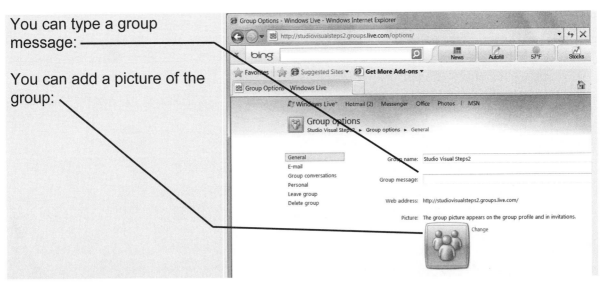

⊕ **If necessary, drag the
scroll bar downwards**

You can select a different
theme:

You can determine whether
members are allowed to edit
the group calendar:

You can determine whether
members are allowed to add
and edit photos:

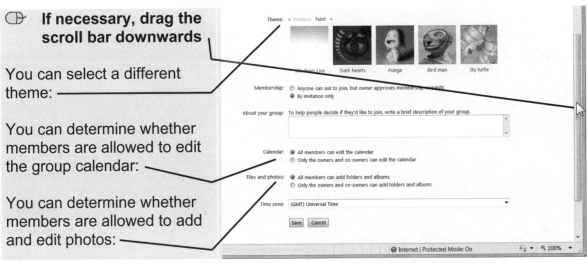

⊕ **Click E-mail**

You can disable the e-mail for
the entire group:

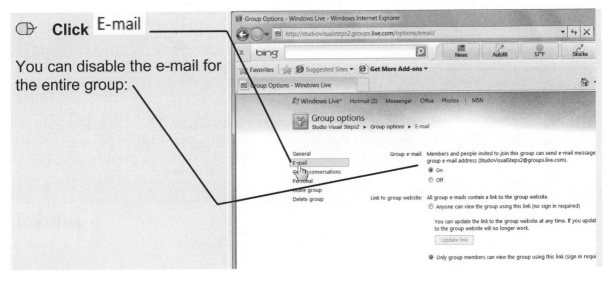

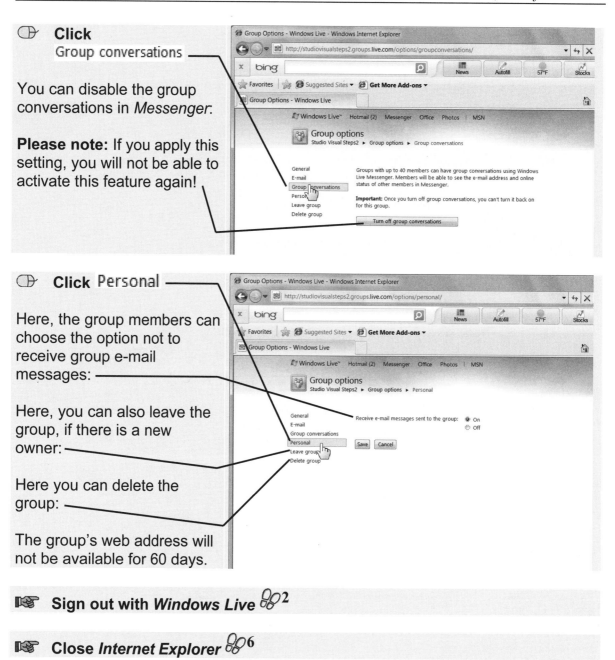

☞ **Click**
Group conversations

You can disable the group conversations in *Messenger*.

Please note: If you apply this setting, you will not be able to activate this feature again!

☞ **Click Personal**

Here, the group members can choose the option not to receive group e-mail messages:

Here, you can also leave the group, if there is a new owner:

Here you can delete the group:

The group's web address will not be available for 60 days.

☞ **Sign out with** *Windows Live* 👣²

☞ **Close** *Internet Explorer* 👣⁶

In this chapter you have learned how to create a group and how to invite people to join it. Next, you have learned how to modify permissions. Last of all, we took a look at some of the additional modifications you can make with the *Groups* service.

10.6 Background Information

Dictionary	
Contact	A collection of data about a specific person, which contains at least the person's e-mail address. This information is stored in the *Contacts* folder.
Permission	As owner or co-owner of a group, you can determine the roles of the group members.
Publish	In *Groups,* this means you are posting a discussion message in *Group discussions.*
Web address	A website's address, also known as the URL.
Windows Live Groups	With *Windows Live Groups* you can create a group of contacts, with whom you can conduct conversations, among other things.

Source: Help for Windows Live Essentials, Windows Help and Support, Wikipedia

10.7 Tips

 Tip

Addition information
In this chapter you have learned about the basic features of *Windows Live Groups*. In the help pages for this program you will find additional information about *Groups*. You can access the help pages by clicking Help Center .

11. Windows Live Family Safety

With *Windows Live Family Safety* you can monitor the Internet behavior of your children or grandchildren. You can block or allow specific websites. You can also filter the content of websites according to various categories. The default settings for these filters are developed in collaboration with many professional organizations.

In *Family Safety* you can also see an overview of the online activities of your children, and you can manage your children's contact list. You can access the *Family Safety* website from any computer connected to the Internet, and monitor what your children are doing, or modify the settings. But first, you will need to install the *Family Safety* component to your computer.

Family Safety integrates well with other *Windows Live Essentials* products. Not only can you manage your children's contact list, but you can also determine whether your children are allowed to use *Messenger* or *Hotmail*.
In this chapter we will first explain how to create a parental account. Next, we will explain how to create accounts for the children. Then we will discuss filtering web content, viewing the activity reports, and managing contacts. Finally, we will explain how to handle requests.

In this chapter you will learn how to:

- create a parental account;
- add accounts;
- filter web content;
- view the activity report;
- manage contacts;
- handle requests.

 Please note:

To work through this chapter effectively you will need to have a *Windows Live ID*. If you do not yet have a *Windows Live ID,* go to *section 1.2 Create a Windows Live ID* and you can read how to get one.

11.1 Creating a Parental Account

When you have downloaded and installed *Family Safety*, as explained in section *1.4 Download Windows Live Essentials Products*, the *Family Safety Filter* will be installed to your computer.

☞ **Open** *Windows Live Family Safety* 🐾 **8**

Your screen may now turn dark and you will be asked to give permission to continue:

☞ **Click** Yes

☞ **Sign in with your** *Windows Live ID* 🐾 **4**

Now you are signed to *Windows Live Family Safety*. In this window you can select the accounts you want to monitor:

☞ **Check the box** ☑ **next to the relevant account**

☞ **Click** Save

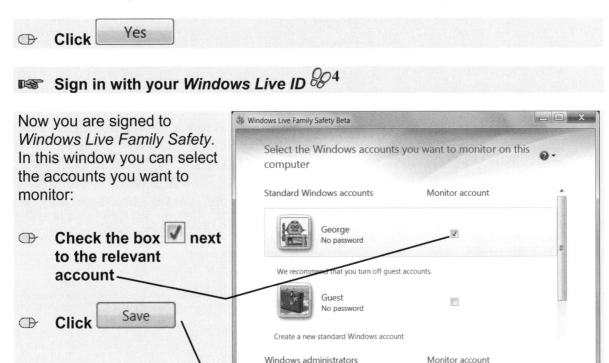

To apply the correct *Family Safety* settings to the correct person, you will need to match the correct names to their *Windows* accounts:

☞ **Select the correct name for this account**

☞ **Click** Save

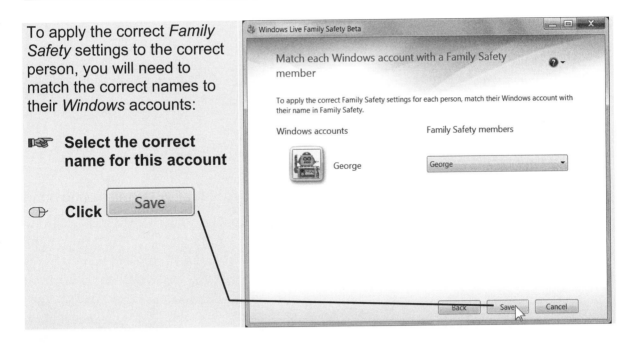

🔙 **Please note:**

Family Safety works best if each family member has his or her own account. If everybody uses the same account, you will not be able to view an activity report.

To prevent children from getting around *Family Safety*, you will need to create a password for each account:

☞ **Click** Add passwords

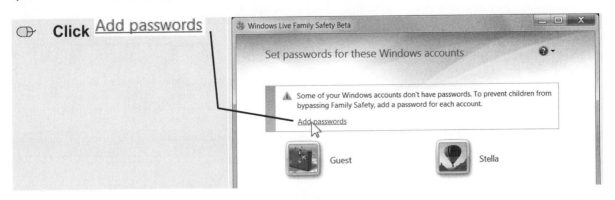

☞ **Create password for all the accounts** 🐾20

You cannot add a password to a guest account. To prevent your children (or grandchildren) from using the guest account to access the Internet, you can disable the guest account.

☞ **Disable the guest account** 🐾21

☞ **Close the *Manage Accounts* window** ∂∂6

 Click [Next]

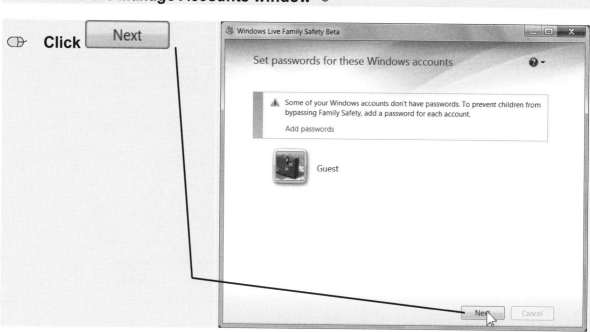

➥ Please note:

It is best to create separate accounts for each child. This way, you can add different security settings to each specific account. If your children (or grandchildren) are using the same *Windows account* as you, you will not be able to view an activity report, and the children will have access to all websites.

To go to the *Family Safety* website:

☞ **Click**
   familysafety.live.com

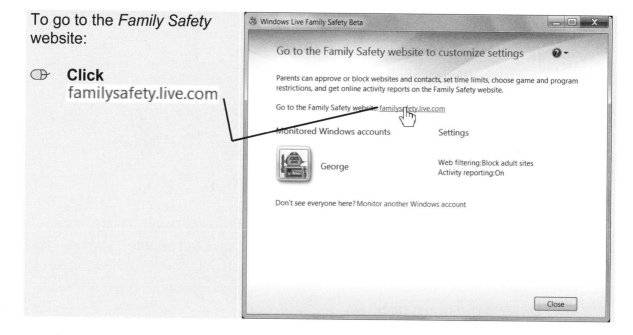

You will see the family summary:

Family members who are added to *Family Safety*: ⎯⎯⎯⎯

You can view the activity report: ⎯⎯⎯⎯

You can add a (grand)parent: ⎯⎯⎯⎯

You can remove a family member from *Family Safety*: ⎯⎯⎯⎯

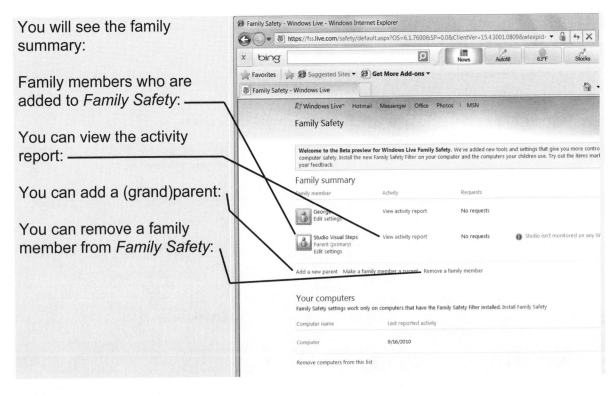

Tip

Multiple child and parental accounts

If you want each child to have his or her own safety settings, or if you want to individually manage the contact list for each child, you will need to give each child his or her own child account.

You can also add an extra parental account. People who have parental accounts can modify the *Family Safety* settings, and add and delete accounts.

To add a child account:

⊕ **Click** Add a new child ⎯⎯⎯⎯

To add a parental account:

⊕ **Click** Add a new parent ⎯⎯⎯⎯

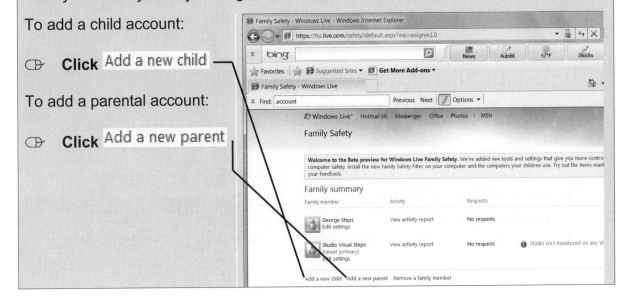

Tip

Delete an account

You can also remove an account from *Family Safety*. If you do this, you will not remove the entire *Windows Live ID*.

👉 **Click**
Remove a family member

👉 **Check the box ☑ next to the account you want to remove**

👉 **Click** Remove

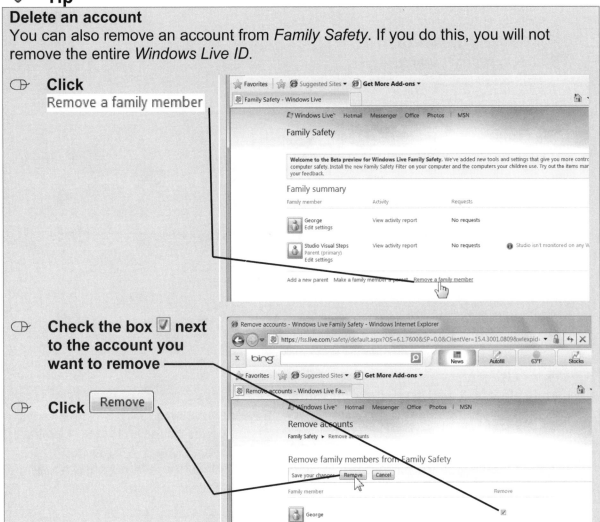

11.2 Filtering Web Content

Family Safety can filter web content by category. You can set the filter level to *Allow list only*, *Child-friendly*, *General interest*, *Online communication (basic)*, or *Warn on adult*.

- The setting *Allow list only*, only allows websites that a parent has added to the Allow list.
- The setting *Child-friendly* also allows websites in the child-friendly category. Blocks adult sites.

- The setting *General interest* also allows websites that are of general interest. Still blocks adult sites.
- The setting *Online communication (basic)* also allows social networking, web chat, and web mail. Still blocks adult sites.
- The setting *Warn on adult* allows all websites but warns when the sites contain suspected adult content.

Click the account image

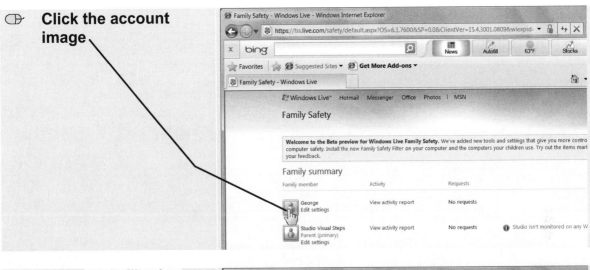

Click Web filtering

Drag the slider to the web filter you have selected

Click Save

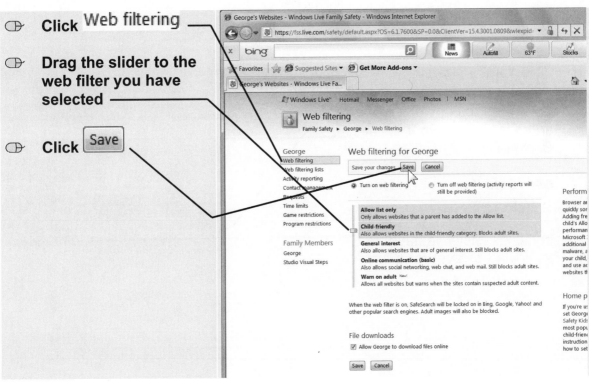

Please note:

Family Safety may arrange websites in a different way than what you normally expect. That is why it is recommended to regularly view your child's activity report, and modify the settings if you think it necessary.

Besides setting a filter on categories you can also allow or block certain specific websites.

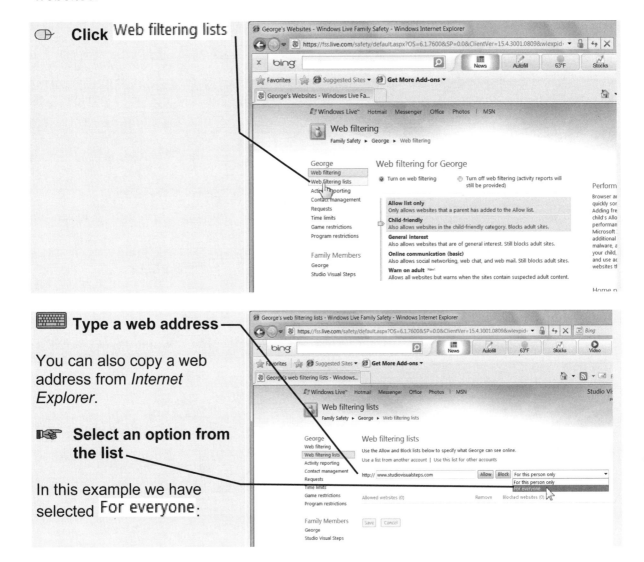

Click Web filtering lists

Type a web address

You can also copy a web address from *Internet Explorer*.

☞ **Select an option from the list**

In this example we have selected For everyone:

Click

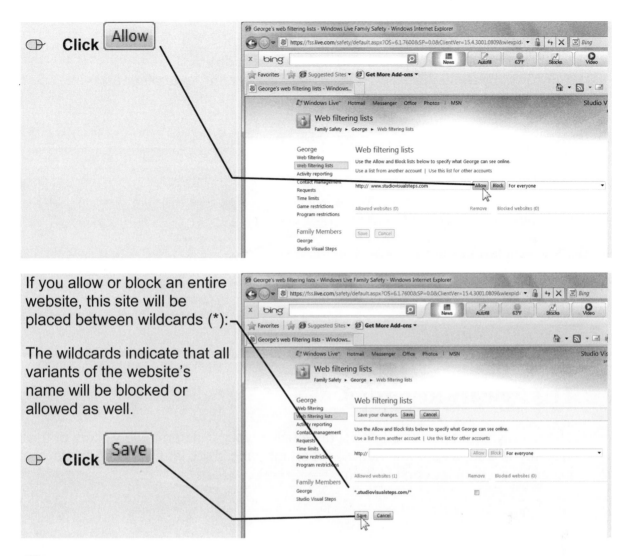

If you allow or block an entire website, this site will be placed between wildcards (*):

The wildcards indicate that all variants of the website's name will be blocked or allowed as well.

Click Save

➥ Please note:

Make sure you always sign out with your *Windows* account before your child or grandchild uses the computer, otherwise he or she may use your account to surf the Internet.

Tip

Use a list of websites from or for a different account
You can copy a list of blocked and allowed websites from another account. You can also copy the current list to another account.

Click
Use a list from another
or
Use this list for other a

☞ **Select the account you want to use for copying the list**

Click OK

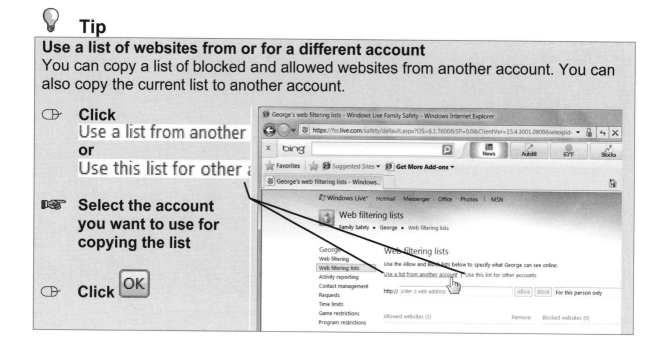

11.3 Activity Reporting

The activity report consists of a list of websites your children have visited, or tried to visit. If you want a separate activity report for each child, you will need to create a separate account for each of them.

Click Activity reporting

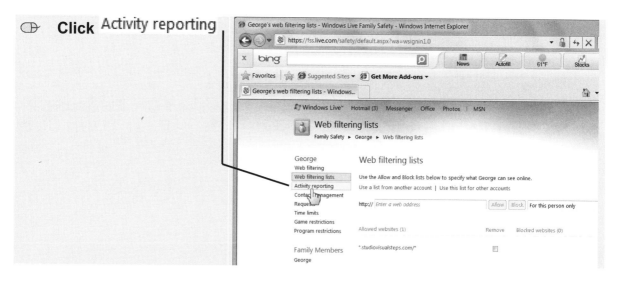

In this example you will see a list of the websites your child has visited, or tried to visit:

Please note: you will only see these websites if your child has visited a number of websites, after you have installed *Family Safety*.

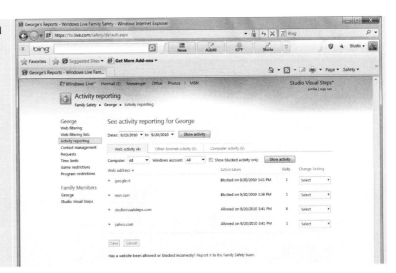

You can add websites to the list of allowed or blocked websites:

☞ **Click** Select ▼

☞ **Click the desired option**

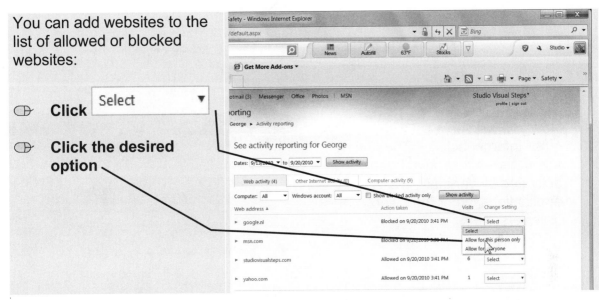

Do not forget to store your changes:

☞ **Click** Save

☞ **Click** Other Internet activity (

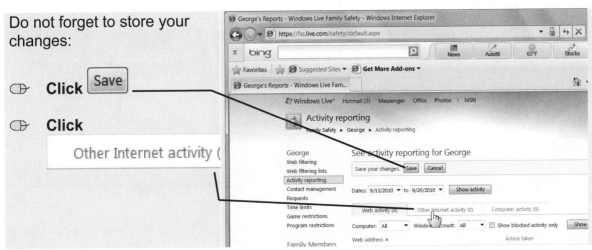

Tip

View another list

If you have installed *Family Safety* to multiple computers or *Windows accounts*, you can view this list here as well:

☞ **Select a different computer, another *Windows* account, or another date** ─────

⊕ **Click** [Show activity]

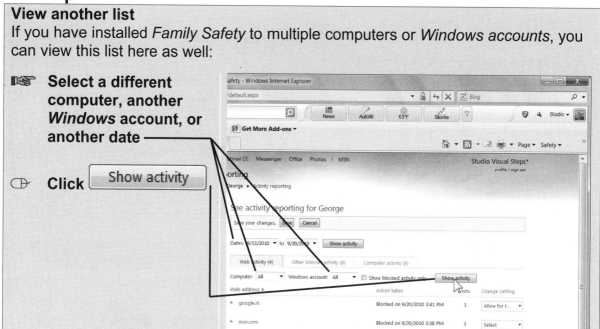

Now you will see a list with other Internet activity. These are websites that have been activated by various applications, other than web browsers:

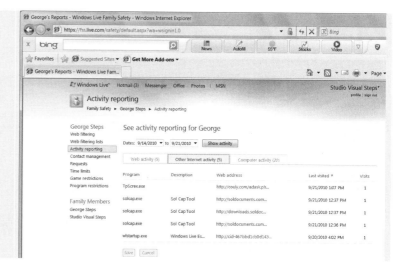

⭑ Tip

Order
You can sort the websites according to a specific column:

For instance, if you want to sort the websites according to the number of visits:

☞ **Click** Visits

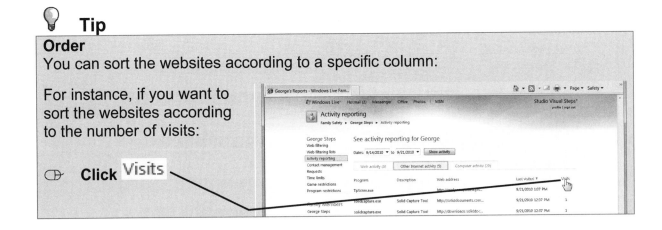

11.4 Managing Contacts

You can also manage your child's contact list. If you want to manage each child separately, you will need to create a separate account for each child. But you can also decide to let your children manage their own contact lists.

☞ **Click** Contact management

☞ **Click** add your child's Windo

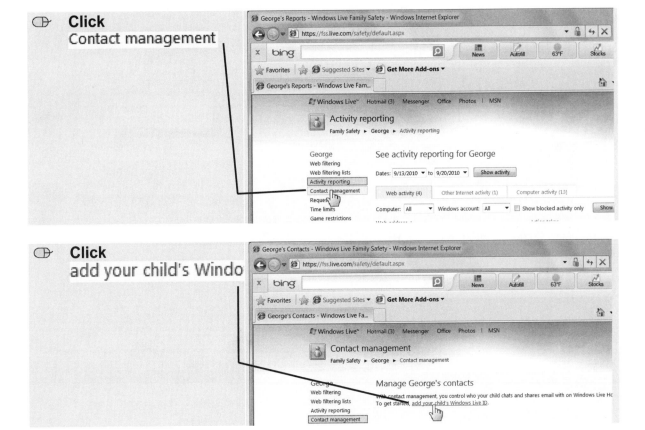

If your child (or grandchild) already has his or her own *Windows Live ID*:

⊕ **Click** Sign in

If this child does not yet have his or her own *Windows Live ID*, you can create one:

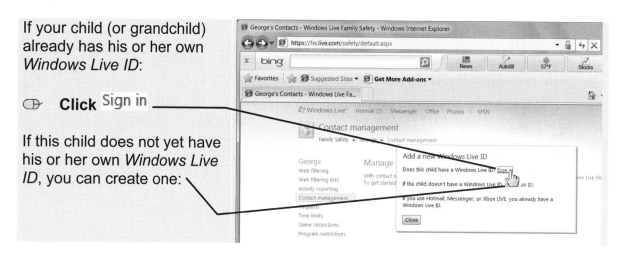

☞ **Sign your child (or grandchild) in with his or her *Windows Live ID* 🐾4**

To add a contact:

⌨ **Type a first name, a last name, and an e-mail address**

The last name is optional.

⊕ **Click** Add

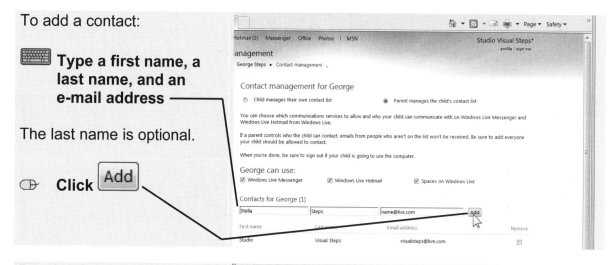

Do not forget to store the changes:

⊕ **Click** Save

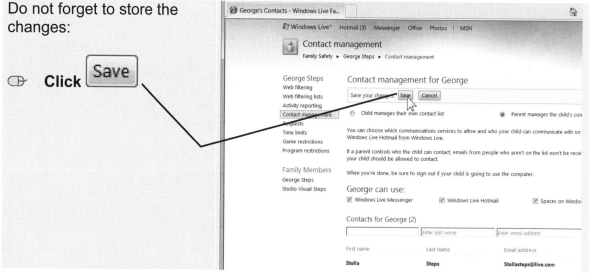

Tip

Family Safety messages
If you want your child to receive *Family Safety* messages, you will need to add the fsafety@live.com e-mail address to the list of contacts.

To remove a contact:

Underneath Remove:

☞ **Check the box ☑ next to the contact you want to remove**

☞ **Click** Save

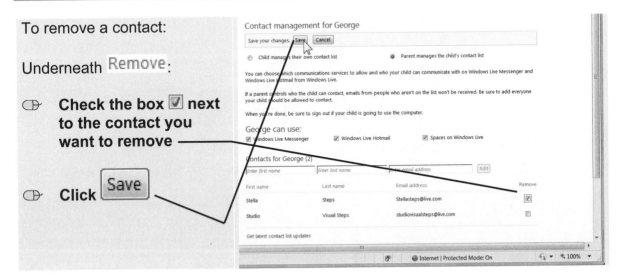

If you decide to let your child manage his or her own contact list, you will only be able to view the list. You will not be able to add or remove contacts.

To let your child manage his or her own contact list:

☞ **Click the radio button ◉ by** Child manages their own

☞ **Click** Save

Please note: Now this child will be allowed to add contacts to a program such as *Windows Live Messenger*.

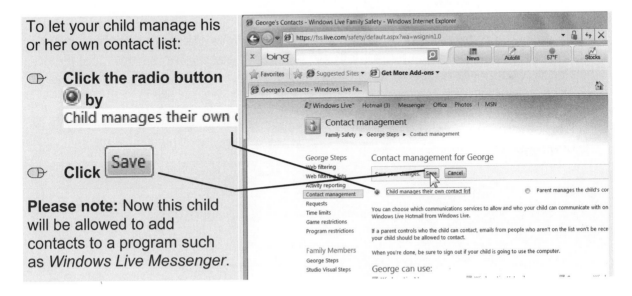

You can determine which products your child can use to communicate with their contacts. The programs are *Messenger*, *Hotmail*, and *Spaces*. By default these products have been disabled, but you can make sure your child cannot use these products:

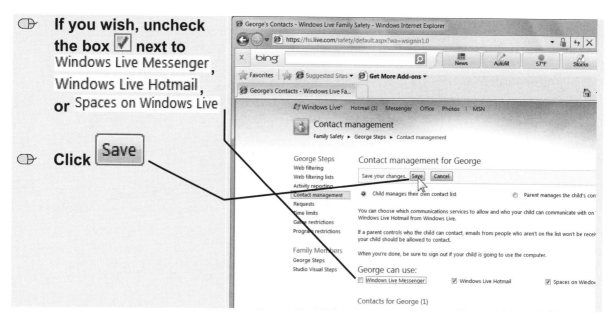

☞ **If you wish, uncheck the box** ✔ **next to** Windows Live Messenger , Windows Live Hotmail , **or** Spaces on Windows Live

☞ **Click** Save

🢂 **Please note:**

There are cases where *Family Safety* cannot detect the communication with a contact. For example, children can use *Windows Live Writer* to post blog messages on *Spaces*. Also, if a child manually adds *Messenger* contacts from local files, *Family Safety* will not be able to block this. Furthermore, if a cell phone is used to access *Messenger*, *Hotmail*, or *Spaces*, *Family Safety* cannot detect this. It is important to realize that the feature for managing contacts has its limitations.

11.5 Handling Requests

There are two ways for children to ask permission to visit a website or add a contact: by e-mail and in person.

A child who wants to visit a blocked website, will see this window:

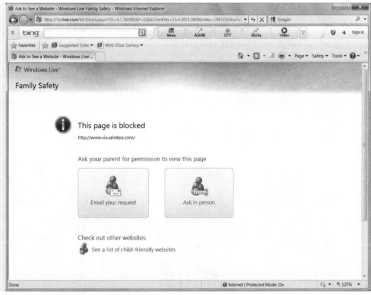

If the child has chosen to *E-mail the request*, you will receive an e-mail message containing a link to the *Family Safety* website:

☞ **Click** Requests page

You will see the requests page of the person who has sent you the request:

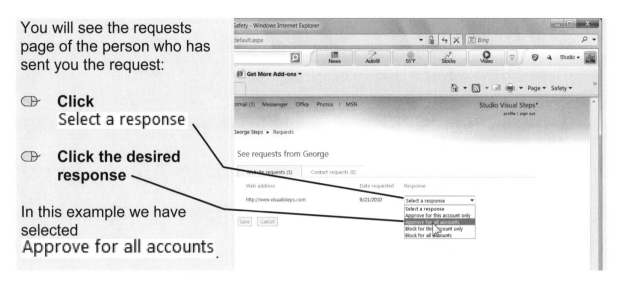

☞ **Click** Select a response

☞ **Click the desired response**

In this example we have selected Approve for all accounts.

☞ **Click** Save

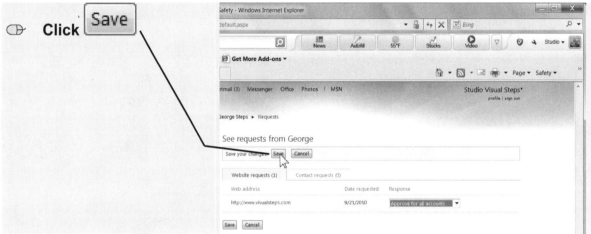

 Please note:

A request will be saved in the requests list for thirty days.

☞ **Sign off with** *Windows Live* ℰℰ²

If you are around, your child can also select the *Ask in person* option.

Type your password

Click Allow or Block

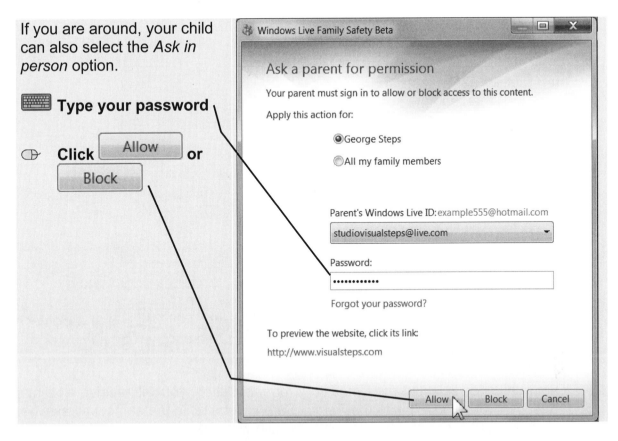

If a child wants permission to add a contact, he or she can do this from the *Messenger* program, for example:

In *Messenger*:

Click add ·

Click Add a friend...

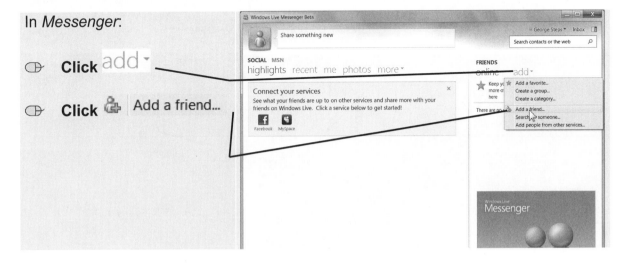

Your child (or grandchild) will see this window:

After the first name, last name (optional) and the e-mail address have been entered, the child can e-mail the request, or ask you in person:

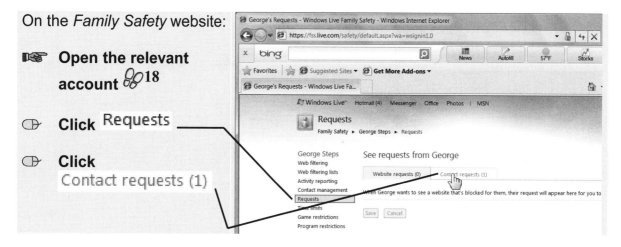

Please note:

If you have selected the option Child manages their own contact list in the *Contact management* window of the *Family Safety* website, the child will be able to add contacts without asking for permission.

If your child has selected the *Email your request* option, you will receive an e-mail message containing a link to the *Family Safety* website, in the same way as when your child asks for permission to visit a certain website.

On the *Family Safety* website:

☞ **Open the relevant account** **18**

◐ **Click** Requests

◐ **Click** Contact requests (1)

Click Select a response

Click the desired
response

In this example we have
selected Approve.

Click Save

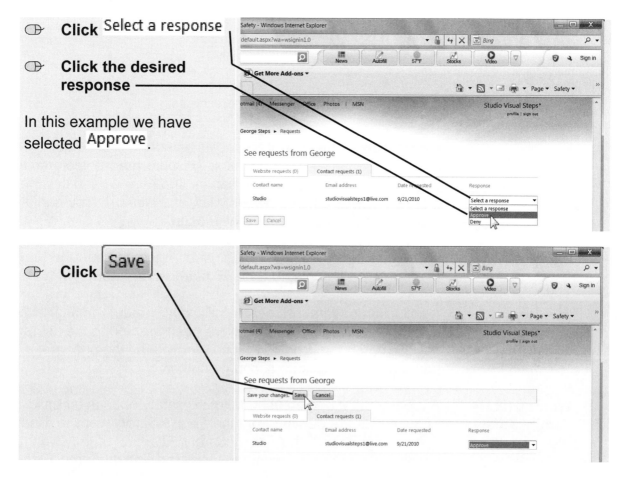

Your child will need to sign in with *Windows Live Essentials* once again, after which
the contact will be added to the contact list.
If you are around, your child can also select the *Ask in person* option to ask for
permission:

Sign in with your
Windows Live ID 🐾4

Click Approve or

Deny

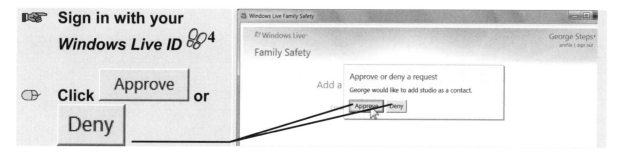

☞ If necessary sign out 🐾2 and close all windows 🐾6

In this chapter you have learned how to create a parental account in *Family Safety*,
and how to add child accounts. Next, you have learned how to change the settings
for filtering web content, for the activity report and for managing contacts. Finally, we
have discussed how to handle requests for viewing websites and adding contacts.

11.6 Background Information

Dictionary	
Contact	A collection of data about a specific person, which contains at least the person's e-mail address. This information is stored in the *Contacts* folder. Contacts can be added and used in various programs, such as *Messenger*, *Mail*, and *Hotmail*. You can also allow contacts to view your profile page.
Internet browser	A program that is used to render web pages and surf the Internet. For example, *Internet Explorer* is an Internet browser.
Windows account	A collection of data that enables *Windows* to determine which user rights and access rights have been granted to the users of a specific computer. The user account contains the user name, the password and a unique account number.
Windows Live Family Safety filter	A program that can be used to install safety options for children. The settings are derived from the *Family Safety* website. Users need to sign in with the *Family Safety Filter* first, if they want to use the Internet on a computer where the *Family Safety Filter* has been installed.

Source: Help for Windows Live Essentials, Windows Help and Support, Wikipedia

11.7 Tips

💡 Tip

Remove Family Safety
If you no longer want to use *Family Safety*, you will need to remove the *Family Safety Filter* from your computer. When you have done that, you can delete all the accounts on the *Family Safety* website.

👉 **Click** , Control Panel, Uninstall a program

👉 **Click** Windows Live Essentials , Uninstall/Change ,
→ Remove one or more Windows Live programs

👉 **Check the box ☑ next to** Family Safety

In the bottom of the window:

👉 **Click** Uninstall

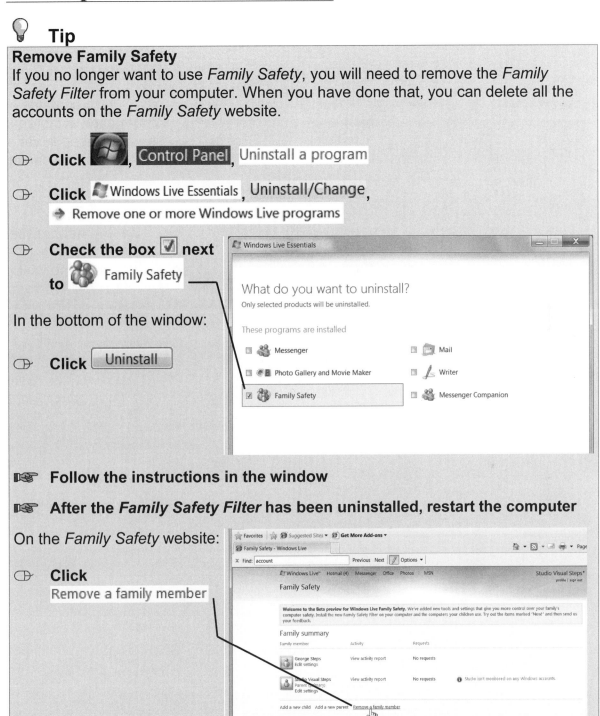

👉 **Follow the instructions in the window**

👉 **After the *Family Safety Filter* has been uninstalled, restart the computer**

On the *Family Safety* website:

👉 **Click** Remove a family member

- Continue reading on the next page -

⊕ **Check the boxes** ✓ **next to all the accounts**

⊕ **Click** Remove

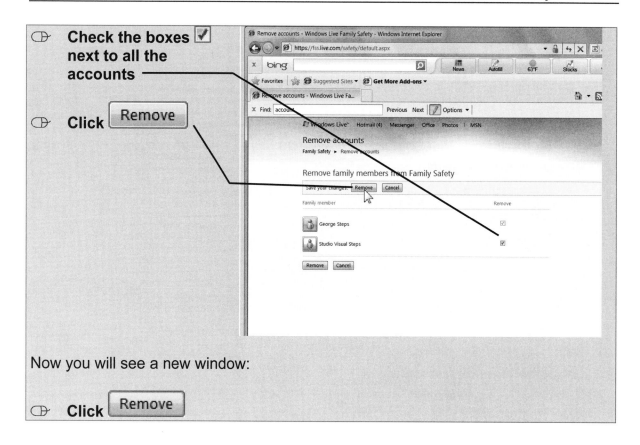

Now you will see a new window:

⊕ **Click** Remove

12. Windows Live SkyDrive

Windows Live SkyDrive makes it possible for you to store files online. You can then view them and share them with others. You can also determine who has access to the files. Think of *SkyDrive* as an additional hard drive with the extra advantage that you can open your files from any computer that is connected to the Internet!

You can use up to 25 GB of storage space on the *Windows Live Essentials* server, with a maximum file size of 50 MB per file. Each folder in *SkyDrive* has a unique web address, so you can include hyperlinks to this address in your blog, or in a chat message. You can also send an e-mail containing a link, to let others know that you have added files to a certain folder.

SkyDrive is integrated with others *Windows Live Essentials* products. The photos you store with *Photos* are stored in *SkyDrive* and vice versa, the photo folders that are stored in *SkyDrive* will be rendered in *Photos*. In *SkyDrive* you can use *Hotmail* to send a link to others and let them know that you want to share a file. And finally, you can use the *Toolbar* to save favorites in *SkyDrive*.

In this chapter we will first explain how to create a main folder, and how to determine with whom you want to share this folder. Next, you will learn how to add files and send hyperlinks to let others know that you want to share files. Finally, we will show you how to modify various options. This includes the option on how to change the type of the main folder.

In this chapter you will learn how to:

- create a main folder;
- add files;
- send a link;
- modify various options.

 Please note:

To work through this chapter effectively you will need to have a *Windows Live ID*. If you do not yet have a *Windows Live ID,* go to *section 1.2 Create a Windows Live ID* and you can read how to get one.

12.1 Creating a Main Folder

You are going to start by creating a main folder. While you are doing this, you have to decide who has access to this folder. You can only set the access rights for a main folder, not for a subfolder or for a file.

☞ **Open** *Internet Explorer* &&¹

☞ **Open the home.live.com website** &&³

☞ **Sign in with your** *Windows Live ID* &&⁴

👆 **Click** 🪟 **Windows Live**

👆 **Click** SkyDrive

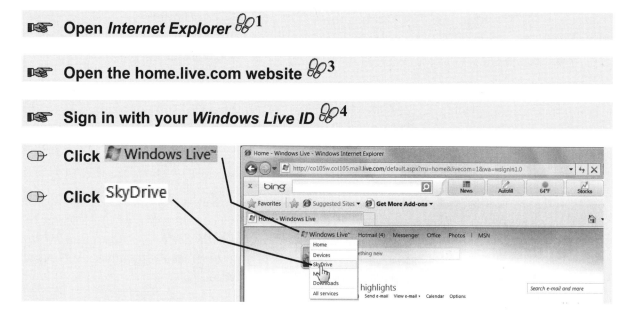

👉 **Please note:**

In this book we will open all *Windows Live Essentials* products from the *Home Page*. If you want, you can also access *SkyDrive* directly by typing http://skydrive.live.com in the address bar of your Internet browser.

You can add folders of the following types: *Documents*, *Favorites*, or *Photos*.

Under Documents you will see the default *My Documents* folder:

By Favorites you can create a folder for your favorites:

If you have added photos, you will see one or more photo albums under Photos:

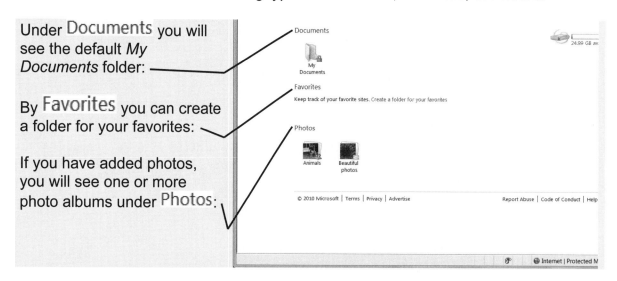

Tip

View the access rights for a folder
You can tell by the folder icon who has access to a folder: public folders are indicated by ⊕, shared folders use the 🚷 icon, and private folders use the 🔒 icon.

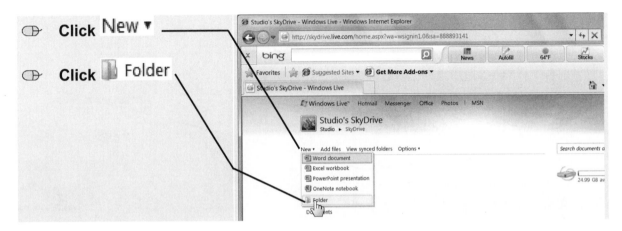

Tip

Create a subfolder
To create a subfolder, first you click the main folder, next you click New ▼ and then 📁 Folder.

You can decide with whom you want to share the folder. You can choose between *Everyone (public)*, *My friends and their friends*, *Friends*, *Some friends*, or *Just me*. You can also specify specific people. If you select *Add specific people* you can enter e-mail addresses, or select contacts.

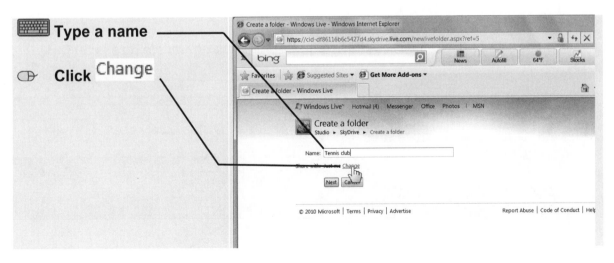

⮌ **Drag the slider to one of the options** ⸻

In this example we have selected Friends.

You can also determine whether your friends are only allowed to view the files, or if they can also add, edit, and delete files:

⮌ **By** Can view files**, click** ▼

In this example we have selected Can view files.

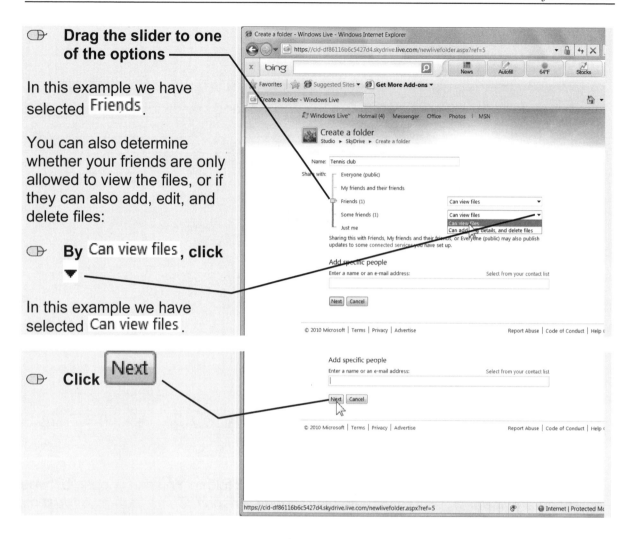

⮌ **Click** Next

12.2 Adding Files

You can use up to 25 GB of storage space. The maximum file size is 50 MB.

⮌ **Click** select documents from y

☞ **Open one or more files** 🦶16

To select multiple files at once, use **Ctrl** or **⇧ Shift**.

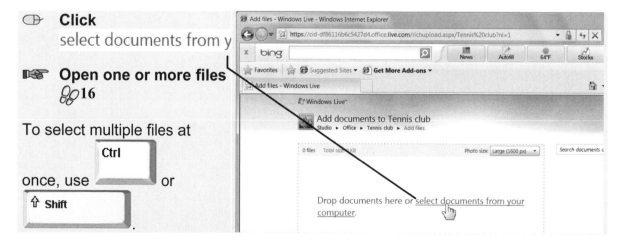

The file has been uploaded:

Click Continue

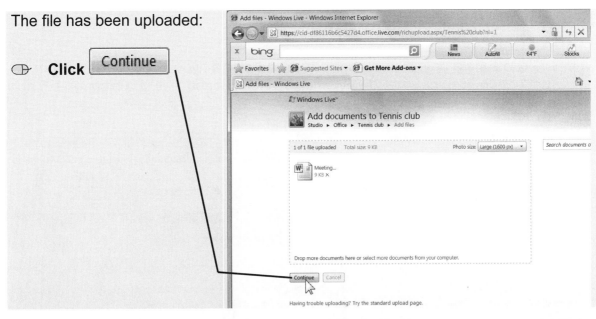

Now you have created a folder and added one or more files to this folder:

To return to *SkyDrive*:

Click Windows Live™

Click SkyDrive

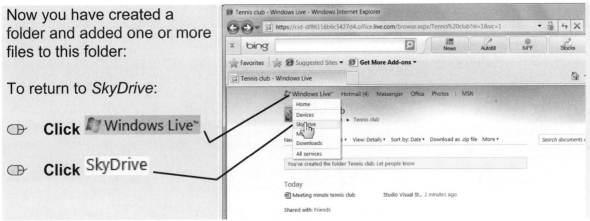

You will see the new folder: ——

Here you can see how much storage space is still available: ——

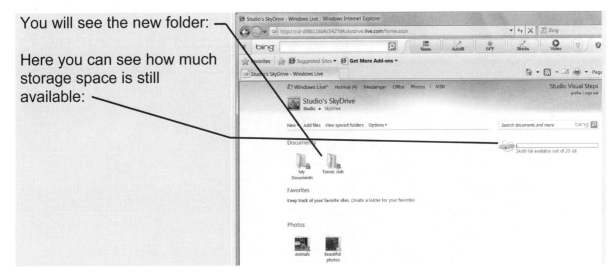

12.3 Sending a Hyperlink

You can send an e-mail message which contains a hyperlink to a main folder. Furthermore, you can include hyperlinks to folders and files in a blog, or a chat message, for example.

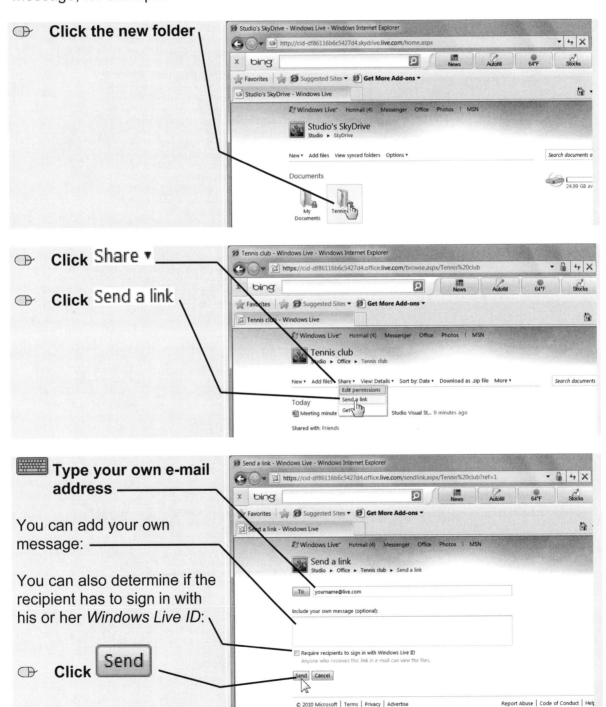

Now you are going to take a look at your e-mail message:

Click Hotmail

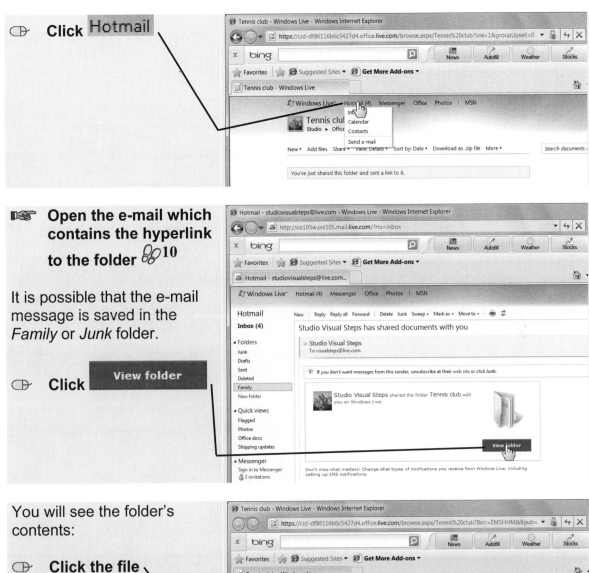

☞ **Open the e-mail which contains the hyperlink to the folder** 👣10

It is possible that the e-mail message is saved in the *Family* or *Junk* folder.

☞ **Click** View folder

You will see the folder's contents:

☞ **Click the file**

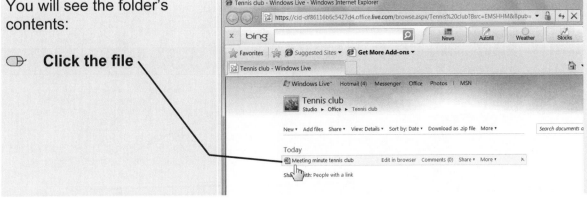

The file will be opened in *Microsoft Word Web App*. With *Word Web App* you can edit documents directly in your web browser, by the website where they are stored:

You can open the file in Word:

You can edit the file in your web browser:

☞ **Click** ✖

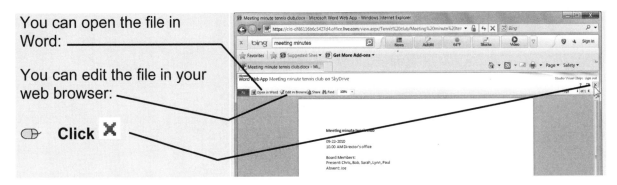

Now you are going to copy a file's web address, and include this address as a link in a blog, or a chat message, for example.

☞ **Click** More ▾

☞ **Click** Properties

To select the web address:

☞ **Click the web address**

☞ **Right-click the web address**

☞ **Click** Copy

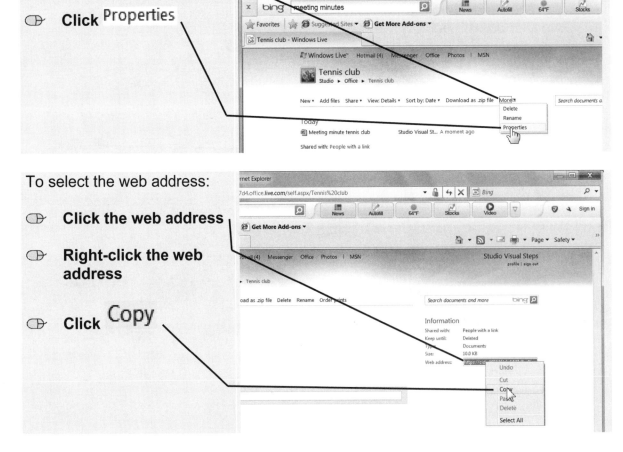

You can paste the link in a blog, or a chat message. You do not need to do this right now.

12.4 Modifying Options

Once you have added a main folder and files in *SkyDrive*, you can still change many different things. For instance, you can add, delete, move, and copy folders and files. You can change the names of folders and files, and you can add descriptions.

You can also modify the permissions of the main folder and you can change the folder type of the main folder. For example, you can change the *Photo* type into the *Document* type, which means that the photos in the folder will not be displayed in *Windows Live Photos*.

☞ **Open the *Tennis club* folder**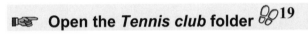

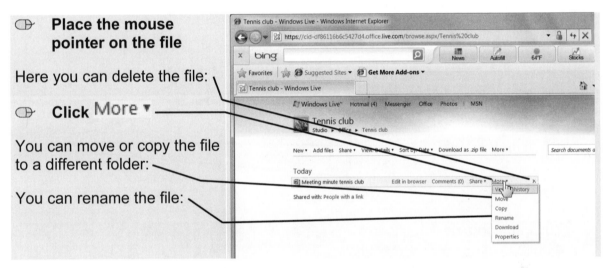

Here you can delete the file:

Place the mouse pointer on the file

Click More ▼

You can move or copy the file to a different folder:

You can rename the file:

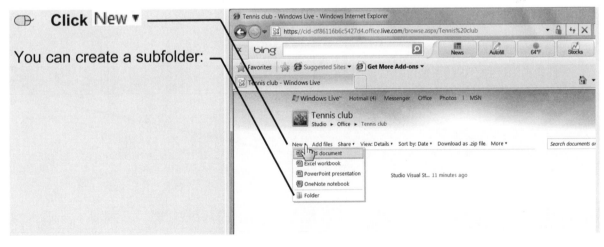

Click New ▼

You can create a subfolder:

You can add new files to the folder: ——————

You can change the view of the files: ——————

You can sort the files differently: ——————

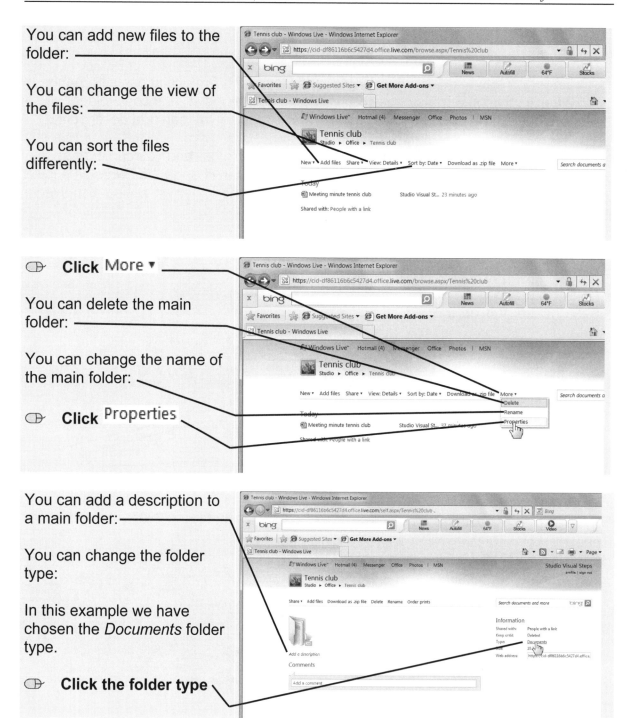

⊕ **Click** More ▾ ——————

You can delete the main folder: ——————

You can change the name of the main folder: ——————

⊕ **Click** Properties

You can add a description to a main folder: ——————

You can change the folder type:

In this example we have chosen the *Documents* folder type.

⊕ **Click the folder type**

If you wish, click the radio button ⊙ next to a different folder type

 Click Save

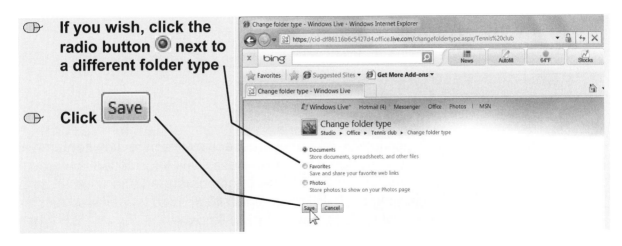

☞ **Sign out with** *Windows Live* 👣²

☞ **Close** *Internet Explorer* 👣⁶

In this chapter you have learned how to create a main folder, and how to add files. Next, we have explained how to send links to folders and files and how to copy links to blogs and chat messages. Finally, we have shown you how to change various options in *SkyDrive*.

💡 **Tip**

Additional information
In this chapter you have learned about the basic features in *Windows Live SkyDrive*. In the help pages you will find additional information. You can access these help pages by clicking Help Center .

12.5 Background Information

Dictionary	
Contact	A collection of data about a specific person, which contains at least the person's e-mail address. This information is stored in the *Contacts* folder. Contacts can be added and used in various programs, such as *Messenger*, *Mail*, and *Hotmail*; you can also allow contacts to view your profile page.
Download	Copying a file to your own computer, from another computer or from the Internet.
File	A collective name for everything that is stored on a computer. A file may consist of a program, a text, or a photo.
Folder type	The folder type determines the position of the folder in the main window of *SkyDrive*. Also, folders of the *Photos* type are displayed in *Windows Live Photos*. To synchronize web addresses with *Internet Explorer*, the folder should have the *Favorites* type.
Link	Also called hyperlink. This is a navigational tool that automatically leads the user to the relevant information when the link is clicked.
Online	Connected to the Internet.
Permission	A setting which you can use to determine who is allowed to view your profile page, your files, your calendar, or a photo album. You can decide for yourself who is allowed to view your *Windows Live Essentials* data.
Upload	Copying a file from your own computer to another computer or to the Internet.
Web address	A website's address, also known as the URL.
Windows Live SkyDrive	*Windows Live SkyDrive* allows you to store, view, and share files online. You can determine who has access to the files and you can open your files from any computer connected to the Internet.

Source: Help for Windows Live Essentials, Windows Help and Support, Wikipedia

13. The Bing Toolbar

The *Bing Toolbar* is an extra toolbar for your Internet browser. On this toolbar you will find a search box for entering keywords to *Bing*, the *Microsoft* search engine. The buttons on the *Bing Toolbar* provide access to various online products from *Windows Live Essentials* and additional *Microsoft* websites. You can sign in with *Windows Live Essentials* from the *Bing Toolbar*. It is also possible to add more buttons to the *Bing Toolbar* by selecting them from the *Windows Live Gallery*.

The *Bing Toolbar* communicates with other *Windows Live Essentials* products in various ways. For example, you can access *Hotmail* from the *Bing Toolbar*.

In this chapter we will first explain how to use the *Bing Toolbar*. Next you will learn how to modify the *Bing Toolbar* to your own liking.

In this chapter you will learn how to:

- use the *Bing Toolbar*;
- modify the *Bing Toolbar*.

 Please note:

To work through this chapter effectively you will need to have a *Windows Live ID*. If you do not yet have a *Windows Live ID,* go to *section 1.2 Create a Windows Live ID* and you can read how to get one.

13.1 Using the Bing Toolbar

Once you have downloaded and installed the *Bing Toolbar*, which you learned about in *section 1.4 Download Windows Live Essentials Products*, it will be visible in *Internet Explorer*.

☞ **Open** *Internet Explorer* ☙¹

☞ **Open the home.live.com website** ☙³

You will see the *Bing Toolbar* at the top of the window:

On the right-hand side of the *Bing Toolbar*:

⊕ **Click** Sign in

☞ **Sign in with your** **Windows Live ID** ☙⁴

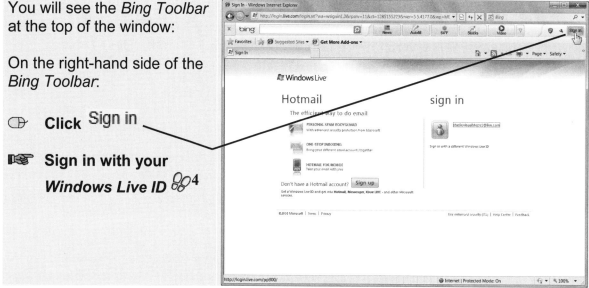

HELP! I do not see the Bing Toolbar

If the *Bing Toolbar* is not displayed in *Internet Explorer* after you have downloaded and installed it, then it has probably been disabled. This is how you enable the *Bing Toolbar*:

⊕ **Right-click the toolbar** **of** *Internet Explorer*

⊕ **Click** Bing Bar

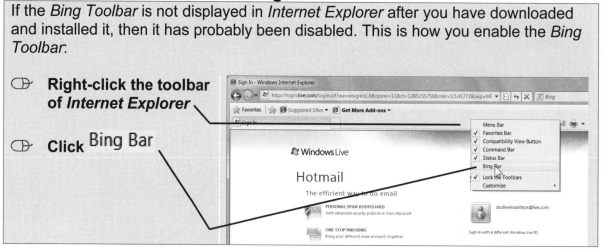

Please note:

When you sign in to *Bing Toolbar* you are also signed in to the *Windows Live Essentials* services, such as *Windows Live Calendar* and *Windows Live Hotmail*.

Here you can enter search terms for *Bing*, the *Microsoft* search engine:

☞ **Click the search box**

You can also search for images or videos:

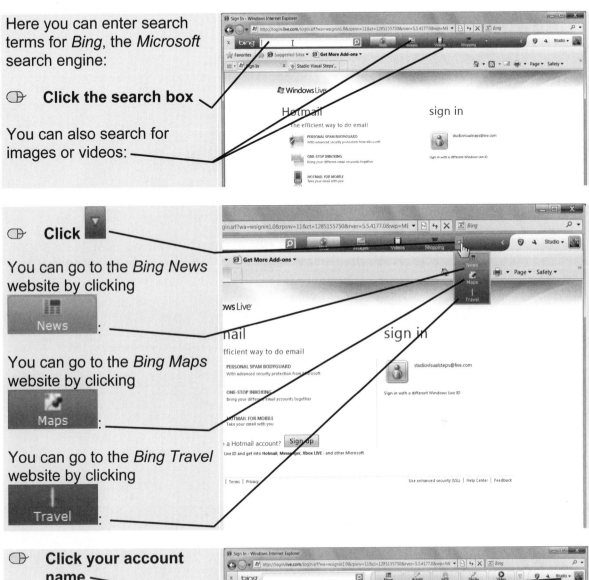

☞ **Click**

You can go to the *Bing News* website by clicking

News :

You can go to the *Bing Maps* website by clicking

Maps :

You can go to the *Bing Travel* website by clicking

Travel :

☞ **Click your account name**

☞ **Click** View your profile

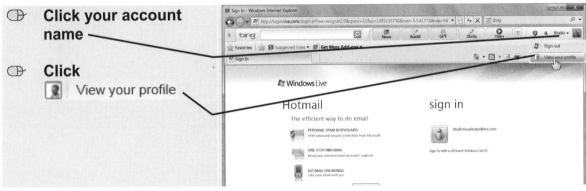

Now your profile page will be opened in a new tab:

By default, the buttons for *Windows Live Hotmail* and *Windows Live Messenger* are not included in the *Bing Toolbar*. If you want to include these buttons on the toolbar, you will need to enable them first:

☞ **Click** 🔧

☞ **Check the box ✔ next to**
   ✉ **Hotmail - Preview yo**

⬚ **Drag the scroll bar downwards**

⬚ **Check the box** ✔ **next to**

   👥 Messenger - View your W

⬚ **Click** OK

You can learn more about this topic in *section 13.2 Modifying the Bing Toolbar*.

Here you see the Hotmail button:

The Messenger button is not displayed in this window. If you want to display this button:

⬚ **Click** ▽

⬚ **Click** Hotmail

Now you will see your *Hotmail* e-mail messages:

You can go to *Hotmail* by clicking Go to my inbox (4).

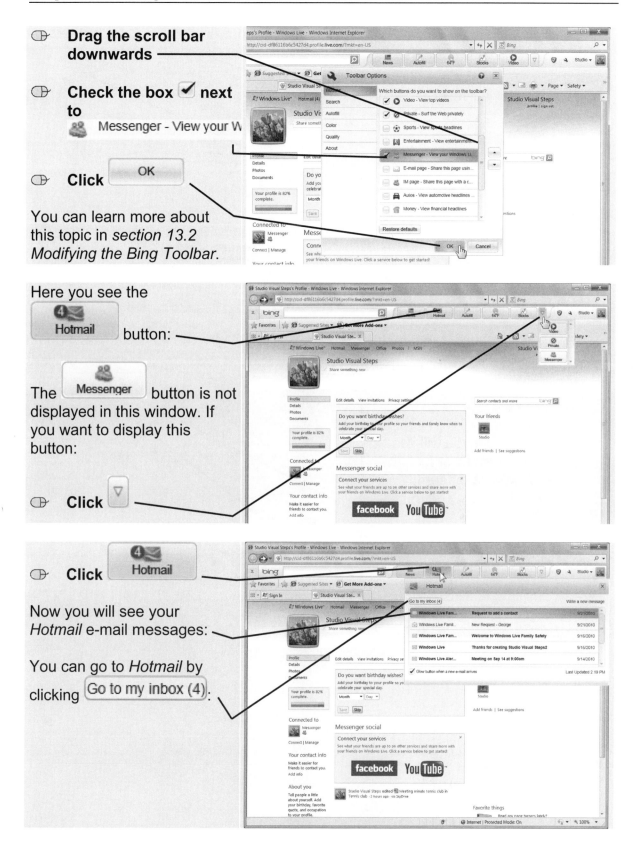

To view recent news items:

⊕   **Click**   News

To close the window:

⊕   **Click** ✕

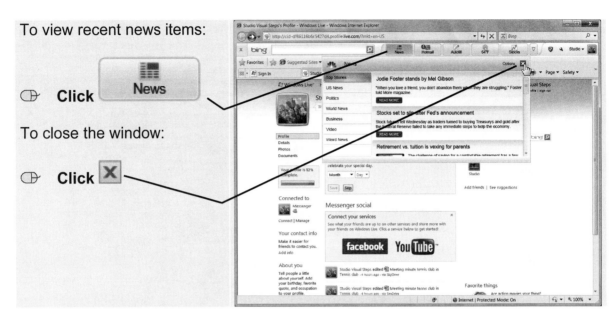

To view the weather forecast:

⊕   **Click** 64°F

In this example you will see
the weather forecast for New
York. To click a different
location, just click Options .

To close the window:

⊕   **Click** ✕

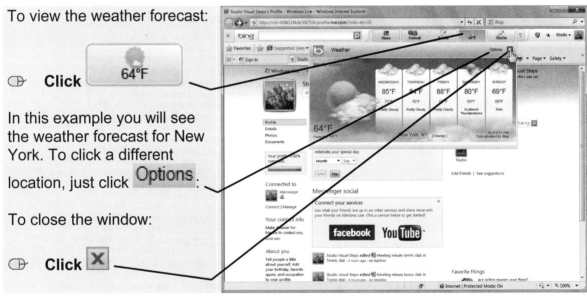

13.2 Modifying the Bing Toolbar

You can modify the *Bing Toolbar* by adding or enabling buttons and changing a number of the settings.

Click 🔧

You can select the buttons you want to add to the Toolbar:

Click Search

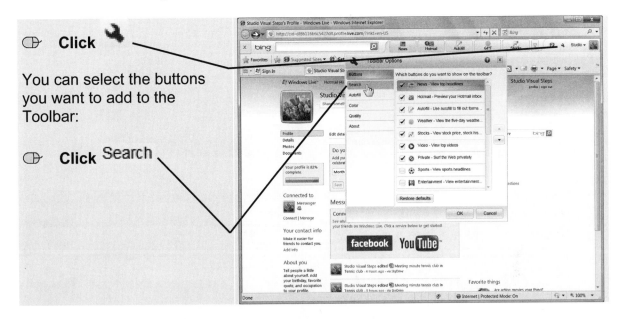

You can change the search options for the *Bing Toolbar*:

You can disable the *Show instant answers* option:

To delete the search history:

Click Clear history

Click OK

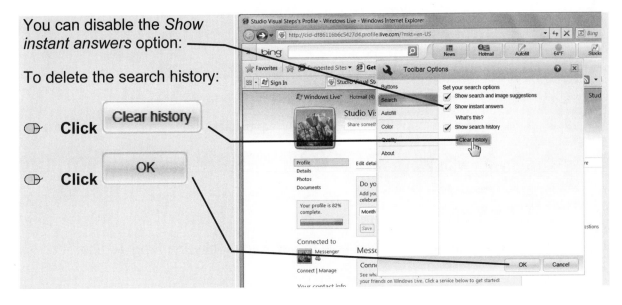

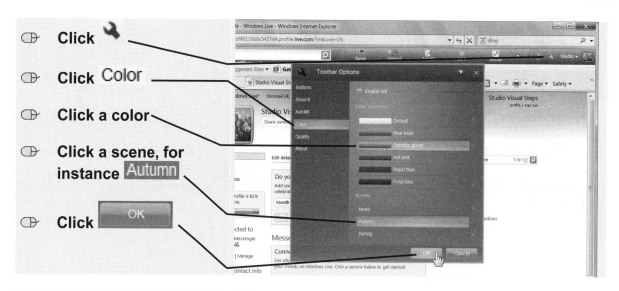

⊕ **Click** ✎

⊕ **Click** Color

⊕ **Click a color**

⊕ **Click a scene, for instance** Autumn

⊕ **Click** OK

Now you will see that the *Bing Toolbar* has changed colors, and that a scene has been added in the upper left corner:

☞ **Sign out with** *Windows Live* 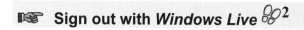2

☞ **Close** *Internet Explorer* 6

In this chapter you have learned how to use and modify the *Bing Toolbar*.

13.3 Background Information

Dictionary	
Bing	*Microsoft* search engine.
Bing Toolbar	An extra toolbar in your Internet browser. Among other things, this toolbar contains the *Bing* search function.
Contact	A collection of data about a specific person, which contains at least the person's e-mail address. This information is stored in the *Contacts* folder.
Internet browser	A program that is used to render web pages, and to surf the Internet. *Internet Explorer* is a browser. To browse, or surf means that you are leaving through pages on the Internet.
Online	Connected to the Internet. By online products we mean products that can be found on the Internet.
Search engine	A web service which you can use to search entire texts on the world wide web, by typing one or more keywords.
Search hints	Hints you get while you are typing keywords in a search engine field. These suggestions are derived from your own search history and from popular previous searches.
Windows Live Gallery	A *Microsoft* website where you can download various applications. These will allow you to modify *Windows Live Essentials* according to your own taste.

Source: Help for Windows Live Essentials, Windows Help and support, Wikipedia

Notes

Write your notes down here.

14. Windows Live Mobile

With *Windows Live Mobile* you can use your cell phone to access *Windows Live Essentials*. This means you can read and send messages in both *Hotmail* and *Messenger*. You can also store the photos you have made with your cell phone directly in *Windows Live Photos*.

If your cell phone does not provide access to the Internet, you can use *SMS Alerts*. After you have signed in with this program, you will receive an e-mail or a chat message, each time a message has been received. You will be able to read this message, as well as send new messages. Furthermore, you can receive an e-mail message to remind you of your calendar appointments. However, some mobile service providers do not support this service.

In this chapter we will explain how *Windows Live Essentials* works via mobile Internet.

In this chapter you will learn how to:

- use *Windows Live Essentials* via the Internet.

 Please note:

To work through this chapter effectively you will need to have a *Windows Live ID*. If you do not yet have a *Windows Live ID,* go to *section 1.2 Create a Windows Live ID* and you can read how to get one.

14.1 Windows Live Essentials Via the Mobile Internet

 Please note:

To use *Windows Live Essentials* via mobile Internet, you will need to have access to the Internet from your cell phone.

 Please note:

Your mobile provider may charge you for using the Internet with your cell phone.

☞ **Establish contact with mobile internet via your cell phone**

If necessary, take a look at your cell phone's manual for additional information.

On your cell phone:

☞ **Open the mobile.live.com website**

☞ **If, necessary, sign in with your *Windows Live ID***

Now you will see the *Windows Live* Home page on your cell phone:

You can access the *Windows Live Essentials* products from the Home page:

You can access your e-mails in *Hotmail*:

Or you can go directly to m.mail.live.com.

On your cell phone:

☞ **Open the m.mail.live.com website**

You can go to *Messenger* from the *Home page*:

Or you can go directly to mim.live.com.

On your cell phone:

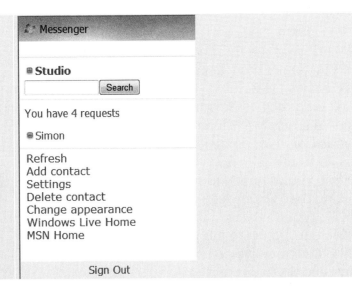

☞ **Open the mim.live.com website**

You can use *Bing* on your mobile:

You can also go directly to m.bing.com.

On your cell phone:

☞ **Open the m.bing.com website**

You can post the photos you have made with your cell phone directly to *Photos*.

To access *Photos*:

On your cell phone:

☞ **Open the mphotos.live.com website**

Tip

Windows Live Essentials via sms
If you do not have access to the Internet on your cell phone, you can still use *Windows Live Mobile*. In order to do this you need to register with *SMS Alerts*. You will then receive an sms whenever you receive a new e-mail or chat message. You can also reply to these messages by sms. You can also receive sms reminders for your *Calendar* appointments.

First, you will need to register with *SMS Alerts*. You can do this from your computer, using the *Windows Live Essentials* website.

You can sign in to the website: http://explore.live.com/windows-live-mobile

You can find additional information about *Windows Live Mobile* in the help pages. You can access the help pages by clicking Help Center, in the bottom right of the page.

 Please note:
Not all *Windows Live Essentials* sms services may be supported by your mobile service provider.

 Please note:
Your mobile provider may charge you for using *SMS Alerts*.

In this chapter you have learned how to use *Windows Live Essentials* via a mobile Internet connection.

14.2 Visual Steps Website and Newsletter

So you have noticed that the Visual Steps-method is a great method to gather knowledge quickly and efficiently. All the books published by Visual Steps have been written according to this method. There are quite a lot of books available, on different subjects. For instance about *Windows*, photo editing, and about free programs, such as *Google Earth* and *Skype*.

Book + software
One of the Visual Steps books includes a CD with the program that is discussed. The full version of this high quality, easy-to-use software is included. You can recognize this Visual Steps book with enclosed CD by this logo on the book cover:

Website
Use the blue *Catalog* button on the **www.visualsteps.com** website to read an extensive description of all available Visual Steps titles, including the full table of contents and part of a chapter (as a PDF file). In this way you can find out if the book is what you expected.

This instructive website also contains:
• free computer booklets and informative guides (PDF files) on a range of subjects;
• free computer tips, described according to the Visual Steps method;
• a large number of frequently asked questions and their answers;
• information on the free *Computer certificate* you can obtain on the online test website **www.ccforseniors.com**;
• free 'Notify me' e-mail service: receive an e-mail when book of interest are published.

Visual Steps Newsletter
Do you want to keep yourself informed of all Visual Steps publications? Then subscribe (no strings attached) to the free Visual Steps Newsletter, which is sent by e-mail.

This Newsletter is issued once a month and provides you with information on:
• the latest titles, as well as older books;
• special offers and discounts;
• new, free computer booklets and guides.

As a subscriber to the Visual Steps Newsletter you have direct access to the free booklets and guides, at **www.visualsteps.com/info_downloads**

14.3 Background Information

Dictionary	
Chat message	A message made in *Messenger*.
SMS	SMS stands for *Short Message Service*. A service that allows you to send or receive short messages with your cell phone.
Verification code	A code that you receive after you have registered your phone number with *Windows Live Mobile*; this code is used to verify your phone number.
Window Live Mobile	An application with which you can access *Windows Live Essentials* from your cell phone.

Source: Help for Windows Live Essentials, Windows Help and Support, Wikipedia

14.4 Tips

💡 Tip

Stop using Windows Live Essentials via sms
If you want to stop *Windows Live Essentials* via an sms message:

In *Windows Live Essentials*:

- Click **Windows Live™**

- Click **Mobile**

- Click **Studio's phone**

Please note: you will see your own account name.

- Click **Stop using SMS s**

- Click **Stop using SMS**

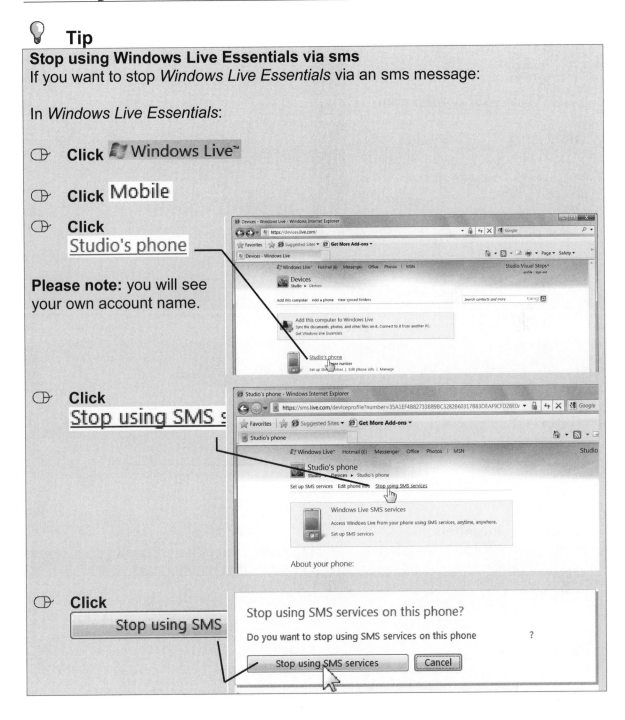

Tip

Disable Messenger messages
You can also disable *Messenger* messages. Here is how you do that:

In *Windows Live Messenger*:

⊕ **Click your screen name**

⊕ **Click** More options

⊕ **Click** Mobile phone

⊕ **Uncheck the box** ☑
    next to
    Allow friends to send m

⊕ **Click** [OK   ]

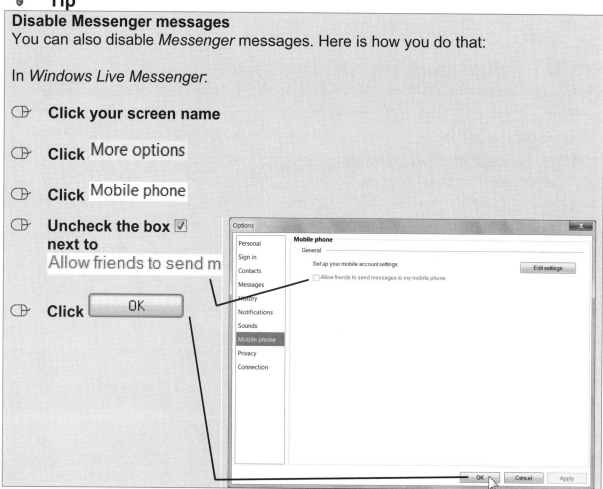

 Tip

Additional Information
In this chapter you have learned about the basic features of *Windows Live Mobile*.
More information about this program can be found in the help pages of *Mobile*. You
can access the help pages by clicking Help Center.

Appendix A. Downloading Practice Files

As you work through this book, you will need to use practice files to execute certain operations. It is a good idea to download these practice files before you begin. Here is how to do that:

☞ **Open *Internet Exporer*** 🐾¹

☞ **Open the www.visualsteps.com/windowslive web page** 🐾³

Now you will see the relevant website for this book. On the *Practice files* page you can download the practice files:

⊕ **Click**
Practice files

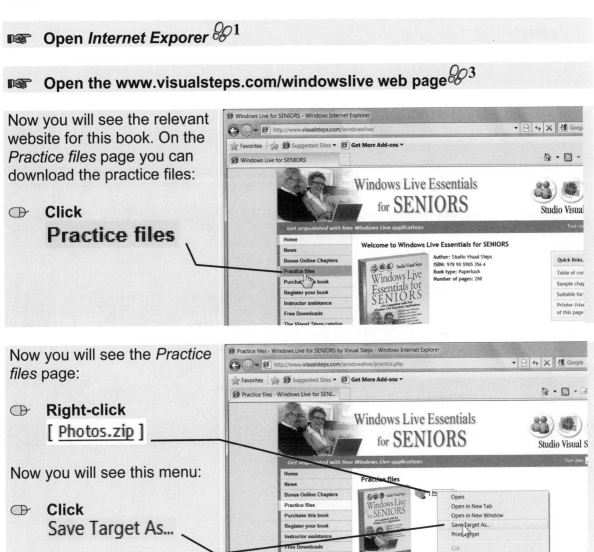

Now you will see the *Practice files* page:

⊕ **Right-click**
[Photos.zip]

Now you will see this menu:

⊕ **Click**
Save Target As...

The folder *Photos* is a compressed folder. First, you need to save this folder to the *Documents* folder.

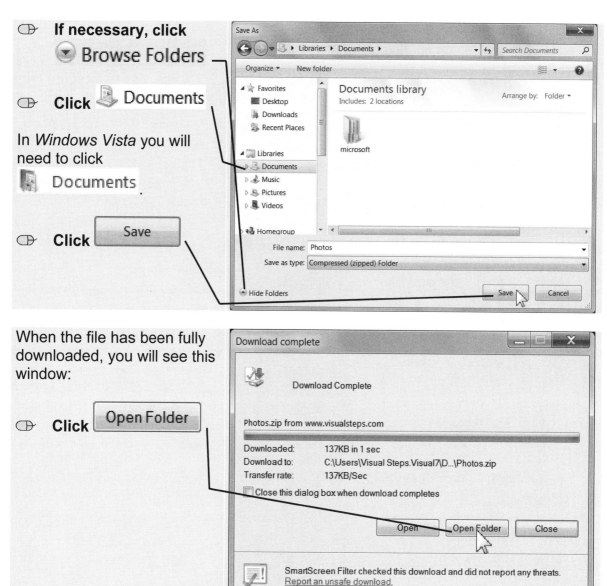

☞ **If necessary, click**

⊙ **Browse Folders**

☞ **Click** 🖳 **Documents**

In *Windows Vista* you will need to click

🖳 **Documents**.

☞ **Click** [Save]

When the file has been fully downloaded, you will see this window:

☞ **Click** [Open Folder]

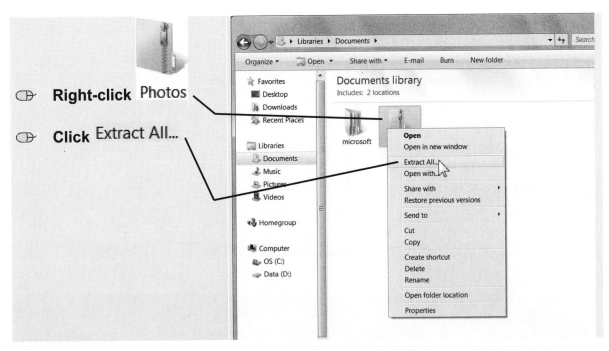

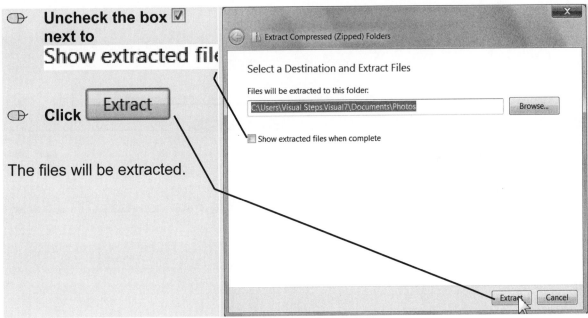

Now the *Photos* folder has been stored inside the *Documents* folder.

You can delete the compressed folder:

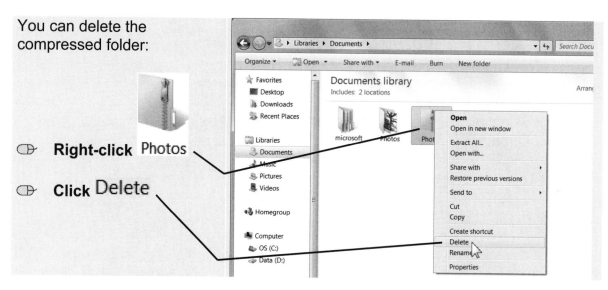

⊕ **Right-click** Photos

⊕ **Click** Delete

Now you will see the *Delete Folder* window:

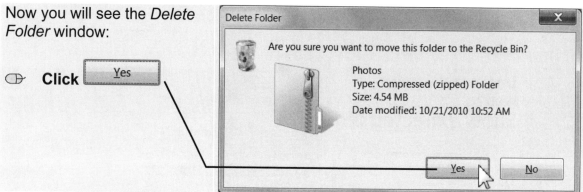

⊕ **Click** | Yes |

The compressed folder has been deleted:

☞ **Close the *Documents* window** &&6

Appendix B. How Do I Do That Again?

In this book actions are marked with footsteps: 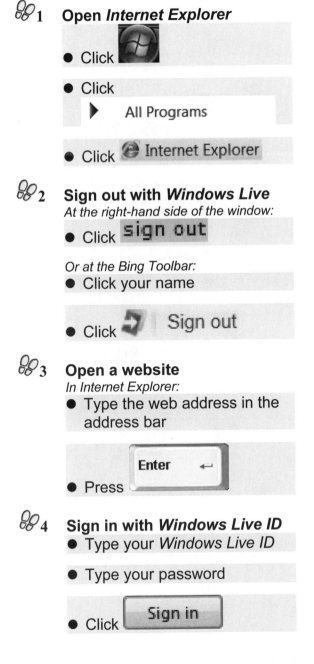1
Find the corresponding number in the appendix below to see how to execute a specific operation.

1 Open *Internet Explorer*

- Click [icon]

- Click
  - ▶ All Programs

- Click 🌐 Internet Explorer

2 Sign out with *Windows Live*
At the right-hand side of the window:
- Click **sign out**

Or at the Bing Toolbar:
- Click your name

- Click 🔁 Sign out

3 Open a website
In Internet Explorer:
- Type the web address in the address bar

- Press **Enter** ↵

4 Sign in with *Windows Live ID*
- Type your *Windows Live ID*

- Type your password

- Click **Sign in**

Or:
- Click your e-mail address

- Type your password

- Click **Sign in**

Or at the top right-hand side of the Bing Toolbar:
- Click **Sign in**

- Type your *Windows Live ID*

- Type your password

- Click **Sign in**

In the program:

- Click **Sign in** [person icon]

- Type your *Windows Live ID*

- Type your password

- Click **Sign in**

5 Select one or more file(s)
- Click a file

Or:
- Click Ctrl or ⇧ Shift
- Click multiple files

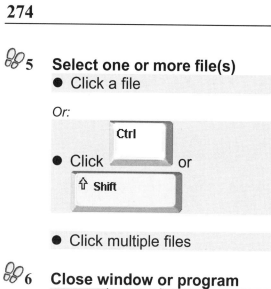

6 Close window or program
- Click X

7 Open *Inbox*
- Click Inbox

Or:
- Click Return to inbox

8 Open a *Windows Live* program
- Click 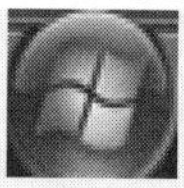
- Click ▶ All Programs
- Click the program

Or:
- Click Windows Live
- Click the program

9 Open the *Options* window
In Windows Live Mail:
- Click 
- Click Options

10 Open e-mail in *Hotmail*
- Click Hotmail
- Click the message

11 Reopen the group
- Click Windows Live™
- Click All services
- Click Groups
- Click the name of the group

12 Sign out to *Windows Live Mail*
- Click 
- Click Options
- Click Mail...
- Click the Connection tab
- Click Stop signing in
- Click Stop signing in
- Click OK

13 Make a new e-mail message
In Windows Live Mail:
- Click Email message

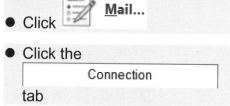

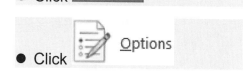

 **14 Save file**

- Click [Save]

- Type a name for the file

- Click [Save]

- Click [Open] or
  [Close]

 **15 Select a folder**
- Click a folder

- Click [OK]

 **16 Open one or more file(s)**
- Click a file

Or:

- Click [**Ctrl**] or
  [⇧ **Shift**] and keep it
  pressed

- Click multiple files

- Release the mouse button

- Click [Open]

 **17 Select a web address**
In Internet Explorer:
- Place the mouse pointer at the beginning of the web address

- Press the left mouse button

- Drag the mouse pointer to the right until the address is selected

 **18 Open a relevant account in *Family Safety***
- Click the image of the relevant account

 **19 Open the *Tennis club* folder**
In Windows Live SkyDrive:
- Click **Windows Live™**

- Click **SkyDrive**

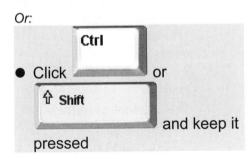

- Click **Tennis club**

 **20 Create password for account**
In Manage accounts window:
- Click the account

- Click **Create a password**

- Type a password

- Retype the password

- Type a password hint

- Click [Create password]

 **21 Disable Guest account**
- Click your guest account

- Click
  Turn off the guest accour

Appendix C. Index